Student Protest

The Sixties and After

GERARD J. DEGROOT

Longman
London and New York

Addison Wesley Longman Limited
Edinburgh Gate,
Harlow, Essex CM20 2JE, United Kingdom
and Associated Companies throughout the world.

Published in the United States of America by Addison Wesley Longman, New York.

© Addison Wesley Longman Limited 1998

First published 1998

ISBN 0–582–35619–9 CSD
ISBN 0–582–35618–0 PPR

Visit Addison Wesley Longman on the world wide web at http://www.awl-he.com

British Library Cataloguing in Publication Data

A catalogue entry for this title is available from the British Library

Library of Congress Cataloging-in-Publication Data

Student protest : the sixties and after / edited by Gerard J. DeGroot.
p. cm.
Includes bibliographical references and index.
ISBN 0–582–35619–9 (CSD). — ISBN 0–582–35618–0 (PPR)
1. Student movements—History—20th century. 2. College students—
Political activity—History—20th century. I. De Groot, Gerard
J., 1955– .
LB3610.S84 1998
378.1′98′1—dc21
98–7586
CIP

Set by 35 in 10/12pt Baskerville
Produced by Addison Wesley Longman Singapore (Pte) Ltd.,
Printed in Singapore

In Memory of
Norman Klockman
(1954–1979),
who knew the joys of being a student

and

In Celebration of
Joshua Charles DeGroot,
born 28 October 1997,
for whom those joys await

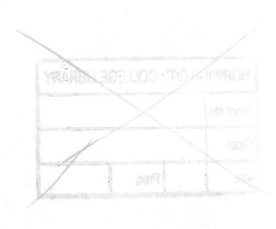

Contents

Preface

Few subjects provoke as much obfuscating nostalgia as the 1960s student movement. Those who lived through the period like to believe that they changed the world. Those born too late play Bob Dylan records and pretend that the world did change. The subject does not, therefore, lend itself to critical analysis. Too often romantic myths and hagiography have been peddled as serious scholarship. This book attempts to break through the mists of nostalgia. It does so partly by placing the 1960s movements within the wider context of post-World War II student protest, thus countering the decade's claim to uniqueness. But it does so mainly because the contributors have all equipped themselves with a hard-edged realism, the better to resist the subject's stupefying romance.

I must credit Professor John Green of the Ray C. Bliss Institute of Applied Politics at the University of Akron for the original idea which inspired this book. He thought that the time had come to produce a book which examined important examples of student protest in various countries from different disciplinary perspectives. I trust that this book is close to his original conception. I must also thank Andrew MacLennan at Addison Wesley Longman for stepping in and agreeing to publish the book on the basis of a short synopsis. Andrew is one of a kind: I challenge any writer to find an editor more gracious, kind and supportive.

The miracle of electronic mail has made producing a collection of this sort infinitely easier. It was enormously reassuring to know that I could get a message to my contributors so quickly, and receive a reply usually on the same day. But the system would have broken down long ago if not for the help of Julian Crowe, a computer wizard at my university who displayed enormous patience with my ineptitude.

I would also like to thank my colleagues Corinna Peniston-Bird, Steve Spackman, Bruce Gordon and Hamish Scott for their timely advice along the way. But, most of all, I have to thank the seventeen other contributors to this book. To a one, they submitted gracefully to my editing, and never once complained about the punishing deadlines which I set. Getting to know them, if only by electronic correspondence, has been the most enjoyable part of producing this book. I am deeply grateful for the chance to work with them.

Gerard DeGroot
University of St Andrews
February 1998

Acknowledgements

The publishers would like to thank University of California Press for permission to reproduce material from Eric Zolov, *Containing the Rock Gesture: The Rise of the Mexican Counterculture*, © 1999 The Regents of the University of California and Gerard J. DeGroot, 'Left!, Left!, Left!': The Vietnam Day Committee, 1965–66', originally published as 'The limits of moral protest and participatory democracy: The Vietnam Day Committee' in *Pacific Historical Review* 64: 1 (February 1995), pp. 95–119, © 1995 American Historical Association, Pacific Coast Branch.

PART ONE

Introduction

CHAPTER ONE

The Culture of Protest:
An Introductory Essay

GERARD J. DEGROOT

On 25 August 1992, Rosebud Abigail Denovo broke into the campus home of Chang-Lin Tien, Chancellor of the University of California. Denovo, aged 19, a some-time student and member of the People's Will Direct Action Committee, was the self-appointed judge, jury and executioner of Tien – enemy of the people. An Oakland police officer, called to the scene, intervened before she could carry out her mission. She lunged at him, and he shot her dead.

On Denovo's body was a note which read: 'We are willing to die for this land. Are you?' By 'land', she meant specifically People's Park in Berkeley, first 'seized' by students from the University in 1969, and the scene of sporadic protest ever since. Denovo's revolutionary career began in the summer of 1991, in response to the decision by the University to build volleyball courts on the park. At the time of her death she was awaiting trial for possession of explosives, which were found with a hit list of campus officials responsible for the decision to build the volleyball courts. On news of her death, 150 supporters rioted in the park. It is fair to say that Denovo, born in 1973, died in the 1960s.[1]

On my first trip to Berkeley during the summer of 1991, I shared a seat on the train with a woman burdened with leaflets rallying comrades to 'the defence of People's Park'. One had to be impressed by her dedication. Not more than 20 years old, she shared the ideals, if not the psychotic self-destructiveness, of Denovo. Memories of the 1969 struggle would have come to both young women as secondhand myth, perhaps handed down by activist parents. Though my acquaintance has probably since graduated and perhaps even

1. The People's Park phenomenon is discussed in G. DeGroot, 'Points of entry: People's Park, Berkeley', *History Today* 43 (1993), pp. 62–3.

joined the 'establishment', a new generation of students now defend the park. Each year, recruits are drawn from the pimply-faced first-year students who listen to 'Maggie's Farm' on CD. In the words of Bob Dylan, 'they keep on keepin' on', clinging to the tawdry symbols of an era which exists only in their imagination. They still march and sit-in, but have added to their armoury some decidedly modern weapons: a website and writs filed in California law courts. When history repeats itself, it does so in stereo and living colour.

The People's Park saga illustrates a central theme of this book. Student protest is not an isolated phenomenon which occurs in diverse locations at distinct times. It is instead a culture, with all the attendant accoutrements: myths, martyrs, ritual, language, costume and formalized behaviour. In her article examining the location of protest, Nella Van Dyke demonstrates that activism which occurred during the 1960s usually took place at institutions which had a tradition of protest sometimes dating back to the nineteenth century. Experience is passed from generation to generation; protesters of the present imitate heroes of the past. This inheritance is passed spatially (across cultures) as well as temporally. As this anthology reveals, students in Mexico, Iran, Korea, China, France, Britain, Germany and the United States borrowed tactics freely from each other. Chinese students in Tian'anmen Square wore headbands copied from earlier Korean and Japanese protests. When protest modes are borrowed, they are grafted onto existing cultural patterns, producing a sometimes strange hybrid. Thus, British students copied American anti-war protests in the 1960s, but did so in a peculiarly British (i.e. moderate) fashion. Students who copy each other often also duplicate each other's failures and disappointments. Though issues might differ, what is most striking about the panoply of student protest is the resonances between movements.

'For as long as there have been colleges there have been students who resisted institutional authority, and times when that resistance has flared into protest', writes Angus Johnston in his chapter. The 1960s are by no means a unique period of activism. Instead, what was unique was the period of quiescence on campus in the two decades before 1960. Students are often at the cutting edge of social radicalism, since they alone possess the sometimes volatile combination of youthful dynamism, naive utopianism, disrespect for authority, buoyant optimism and attraction to adventure, not to mention a surplus of spare time. They perceive themselves as the leaders of a future generation and are often over-eager to thrust themselves into the task of reshaping their society. As Günter

Minnerup contends, student protest sometimes signals a 'vast tectonic shift' in the structure of society or politics, even if, when the dust settles, the changes which result are not what they intended.

In the West, a sense of responsibility to society appears to be widely felt among students, but seldom overtly manifested. In contrast, in Asian societies, as Frank Pieke and Alan R. Kluver discuss, the student's duty to act as a moral guardian for society is deeply enshrined in Confucian tradition. Students are, in other words, *expected* to protest. They see themselves to an extent as actors, fulfilling their role on a cosmic, historical stage. The passion which fuels their activism even leads to a willingness to sacrifice their lives for the cause. Suicide, often by self-immolation, constitutes the ultimate act of remonstration against the state or leader, and at the same time demonstrates the moral legitimacy of the student activist. While some students in the West have been willing to sacrifice their lives for their cause (Denovo being a prime example), they have been rare. This unwillingness to make the ultimate sacrifice has necessarily constrained the impact of protests in the West. Thus, when members of the Vietnam Day Committee (VDC) vowed to block troop trains by lying across the tracks they brought scorn upon themselves because they were quick to remove themselves as soon as a train appeared. On the other hand, those students in the West who have made the ultimate sacrifice have often been judged mentally unbalanced by an intolerant public. When American students set fire to themselves in protest against the Vietnam War, they were not able to lay claim to the same philosophical justification for their act of sacrifice as a Korean student might have.[2]

But the great weakness of student protest is that it is conducted by students. They are, almost by definition, young, reckless and prone to immaturity. They often espouse a naive vision of the world and employ tactics which, due to their lack of experience, fail to take account of the cruel realities of institutional power. As Bertram Gordon discovered through his interviews with some of the Paris marchers of 1968, hindsight is a unflattering mirror. Though many of the participants in the May demonstrations looked back fondly on their experience, they still admitted to naivety and youthful self-indulgence. Ideals which seemed sublime back then, and tactics which seemed brilliant, now appear embarrassingly immature. Gordon's findings have resonance for the participants in almost any student

2. Eight Americans burned themselves to death in protest against the Vietnam War. See David Steigerwald, *The Sixties and the End of Modern America* (London, 1995), pp. 106–7.

movement. Those able to see through the mist of nostalgia often ask: 'How could we have been so silly?'

Much as students would like to believe otherwise, they are very seldom treated with reverence or respect by wider society. Even in countries with a very high rate of participation in higher education, the university-educated are an elite minority often treated with contempt by those denied the university experience. If education is publicly funded, contempt is all the greater. Thus, as nearly every article in the collection demonstrates, it is extremely difficult for students to gain the support and sympathy of the wider public. They have, admittedly, tried. During the Iranian Revolution, student militants worked assiduously to take their movement to the masses, by going into factories to help oppressed workers – often at enormous personal risk. Similar attempts were made by students in France, Germany and Mexico in the 1960s, but with little success. No matter how determined their effort, the students could not shed their elitist image.

But students have done much to widen the gulf between themselves and the rest of the society and, in so doing, have rendered themselves even more deserving of contempt. Few movements have exhibited the mature self-control necessary to resist childish pranks. Granted, these pranks have sometimes had a serious political message, such as when VDC activists mischievously drew attention to trucks carrying napalm shipments to Bay Area docks, or when Mexican students offered government soldiers free literacy tuition. But all it takes is one protester to claim in jest, before the eyes of the world, that he is more interested in an orgasm than peace in Vietnam, and the credibility of the entire movement is jeopardized. Chants of 'DISEMBOWEL ENOCH POWELL!', heard at the University of St Andrews in 1969, must have left bystanders in some doubt about the virtue of the student protesters' anti-racist cause.[3] Too often the pranks are intentionally designed to divide; as if the students feel that the best way to change their world is to emphasize their detachment from it. But, as the VDC experience demonstrates, it is impossible to build a mass movement by thumbing one's nose at the masses.

Pranks and assorted misbehaviour have left student protesters open to manipulation by their arch-enemies, the establishment. As Clare White demonstrates in her comparison of Robert Kennedy's and Ronald Reagan's approaches to 1960s student protest, there is

---

3. My thanks to Julian Crowe for this gem of reminiscence.

a great deal more advantage to be gained from attacking students than in presenting oneself as their friend. They *are* an easy group to attack. By playing upon the Berkeley bogey, Reagan built himself a populist constituency which remained loyal to him in every subsequent political contest he entered. Kennedy, on the other hand, tried to attach himself to the student movement, the political equivalent of trying to mount a bucking horse. Had he lived, he would undoubtedly have discovered that the great problem with students is that they do not remain students forever. After graduation, the transformation from dynamic idealist to selfish cynic is, in many cases, rapid. Political affiliations forged on campus are discarded along with flared trousers and love beads.

Students have also learned that the power of the state can be formidable. In Kwangju, Tlatelolco, Tian'anmen Square and on the campus of Tehran University, student activists learned that there are strict limits to the state's tolerance of their militancy. The massacres of students which occurred in South Korea, China, Iran and Mexico make the actions of the Ohio National Guard at Kent State, or Reagan's little war in Berkeley, pale into insignificance. Those massacres suggest that while students talking of revolution might be tolerated, threatening real revolution always provokes a massive response by established authority. All four incidents occurred under conditions which defied the usual pattern of protest: in other words, students had begun forming alliances with the wider community. The crucial revolutionary mass was coalescing. But all four examples also demonstrate another cruel truth: guns and blood do put a stop to demonstrations. Around the world, leaders have discovered that the best way to kill a protest is to kill protesters. And, as White, Donald Mabry and A.D. Moses have discovered, the public is strikingly tolerant of retribution meted out against students – rather in the way spanking a spoiled child seems to make sense.

A striking feature of student protest is the apparent inevitability of failure. Most movements do not extend their influence beyond the confines of the campus. If miscreant students are safely quarantined within the university precinct, they can be labelled aberrant, naive, misguided or elitist. When protesters succeed in breaking out of the campus, they are brutally crushed. The lesson which Behrooz Ghamari-Tabrizi derives from his study of Iranian student militants is that it is a mistake for students to engage in the politics of the wider world, that they should confine their attention to their own subculture. Yet there is a paradox in this prescription: if students retreat to their ivory tower they merely exacerbate their separation from wider society and run the risk of being held in even greater contempt. Students who agitate only for the improvement of the campus environment, which the public already views as excessively comfortable and exclusive, are not likely to garner respect outside their community. In all societies, young people are sent to university to prepare for positions of leadership and responsibility which they will assume after graduation. It would seem excessively self-centred for students to confine their agitation to issues relating to campus life – the quality of teaching, the range of courses, or the inadequacies of residence hall provision. Thus, in Korean and Chinese tradition, students who try, through protest, to improve their own lives are scorned for their selfishness. And, as Mabry argues with regard to student protest in Mexico, protests which are confined to campus issues are more easily controlled by the government.

Nor have students been conspicuously successful in agitating for change within the university. On campus, they encounter another form of authority which, though usually more tolerant of their excesses, is just as capable of cynical manipulation. This is ably demonstrated by Julie Reuben, who studied the long-term effects of the 1960s agitation for curriculum reform. The demand for a 'relevant' curriculum led students to demand not only new degree programmes (ethnic and women's studies, for instance) but also new methods of teaching. The success of this protest seems profound. New degree programmes were established and remain a prominent part of the curriculum at many universities to this day. But changes in the methods of assessment, recruitment, teaching, and staff selection were short-lived. American university authorities proved remarkably adept at containing, manipulating and re-directing the tide of change, so much so that, when the shouting ceased and the sit-ins ended, status returned resolutely to quo.

The protest experience, in other words, provides hard lessons. In the 1960s, the times were a'changing, but not quite in the way Dylan predicted. In France, Britain, Mexico, Germany and the United States, it was the students' opponents who were most successful at shaping subsequent decades. The political right, dominant in the late 1970s and 1980s, made much of the threat of militancy and the dangerous hedonism of 1960s counterculture. This conservative counter-revolution certainly taught students lessons about the character and strength of authority, not to mention the power of tradition. But students also learned some hard lessons about the flaws in their own revolutionary idiom. Contradiction and hypocrisy were not the exclusive preserve of the right-wing establishment.

The German SDS preached about an anti-authoritarian culture, but could not survive the departure of its leader Rudi Dutschke. The disenchanted of the Vietnam Day Committee learned that participatory democracy is often a glorified term for anarchy. Women in almost every movement learned that a man can be both a revolutionary and a pig. 'Guess Who Does the Dishes in the Red Brigade?' a feature in *The Guardian* asked in 1983. Noble causes do not make people pure.

A fervent desire to change the world does not automatically mean an ability to do so. Some student activists learned this lesson through experience, some at the barrel of a gun. Others learned the lesson over time, when the ideals of student life refused to take hold in the rocky soil of adult life. A die-hard few continue to live the dream by blocking out reality with incense and cannabis. It is easy to be cynical about the student movements of the 1960s, but easier still to be romantic. Play a few bars of 'Blowin' in the Wind', and nostalgia takes hold. Suddenly the most apathetic baby boomer imagines that he, too, manned the barricades.

But cynicism, as any student activist will argue, is a debility which comes with advancing age. In truth, student movements have not been unqualified failures. The student civil rights movement of the early 1960s was instrumental in drawing attention to the racism at the heart of American society. The experiences of white students in that movement inspired them to apply the tactics learned to other causes. But the finest hour of 1960s student radicalism occurred before most people were aware that a student movement existed. The cooperative spirit, dedication and self-sacrifice of the civil rights movement were never again duplicated in subsequent struggles. That movement is perhaps the exception which proves the rule of student protest: because a wide constituency existed outside the campus, the students never had to struggle to establish their legitimacy. And, once they left their safe campuses and descended upon the perilous South, they did not have to prove their courage.

In other movements, successes have been more subtle. Their impact has been most profound in areas least intended. It is, in other words, better to speak of the legacy of student protest, rather than of its achievements. Mexican students did not achieve their goals in 1968, but the way in which they were brutally repressed has changed attitudes within Mexican society, and seems to have made the government more circumspect in its use of force. The same could be said for the reverberations of Tian'anmen Square. As Barbara Tischler demonstrates, women who participated in the student movements of the 1960s learned about the dynamics of agitation and about how deeply imbedded patriarchal tendencies actually are. These lessons proved of enormous value when they formed liberation movements of their own. In Germany, the Green Party, one of the most successful grass-roots protest movements of the twentieth century, learned much from the tactics and frustrations of German students in the 1960s.

It seems that Dutschke's 'long march through the institutions' has indeed occurred, though perhaps nowhere as profoundly as he once hoped. Students who participated in protests have taken with them into the 'real world' some of the ideals and practices they espoused as campus activists. (Granted, one-time agitators still struggle against their arch-enemies, who march at a similar pace through the same institutions.) Some former protesters have inevitably been swallowed by the system and have jettisoned their brave new world in favour of a well-paying job, a house in the suburbs and a Volvo in the garage. Jerry Rubin discovered that organizing a student protest requires skills easily transferable to a capitalist public relations business. But others have carried out their own tiny revolution in their daily lives, thus contributing in their small way to the tide of change. Over time, their idealism has perhaps been tempered, and their goals have been narrowed by experience. But apathy remains for them a sin. Perhaps the most enduring legacy of student protest is personal: a habit of activism carried into later life. The radicalism of Daniel Cohn-Bendit and Gordon Brown might have dissipated, but their belief in the necessity of involvement has not.

The People's Park example is again germane. The great irony of the park lies in the questions it raises about the legacy of the original protesters. The decision to build volleyball courts was taken after a lengthy democratic planning process which arose out of the 1960s campaign for greater political participation and open government. The decade also popularized ideas about beautifying one's living space and creating public leisure sites for everyone to enjoy. It also saw the beginning of the health consciousness movement – natural food, relaxation, exercise. Perhaps, then, it is not entirely sacrilege that the people should play volleyball in People's Park. If that is true, the students who protest today are the conservative counter-revolutionaries, who have not kept pace with progress. They protest because of a need to protest, rather like the shark who must keep swimming in order to survive.

Perhaps the best example of Dutschke's prophecy is the experience of students at San Diego State University who, when budget cuts threatened their education, resorted to traditional forms of protest. As Jim Wood observed, they deliberately copied tactics he had witnessed as a student at Berkeley in the 1960s. But the great difference lay in the ability of the SDSU activists to build bridges to the community. Those bridges were formed in part because of the effects of Dutschke's long march. There were too many people in the San Diego community who realized the value of education and of the university in particular to permit its dismemberment. It is doubtful that SDSU students would have had the same success if they had protested against the Gulf War or some other aspect of government policy. Thus, the San Diego experience reveals the limitations of student protest but also, in the long term, its potential.

CHAPTER TWO

Student Activism in the United States Before 1960: An Overview

J. ANGUS JOHNSTON

> ... it too manifestly appears that a spirit of opposition to govern-
> ment and order has prevailed among the undergraduates ...
>
> Edward Holyoke, President of Harvard College, 1768.

Student activism didn't begin with the sixties. For as long as there
have been colleges there have been students who resisted institutional
authority, and times when that resistance has flared into protest. American students agitated against the Crown in the 1760s and slavery
in the 1830s – a few even fought the draft in the 1860s, a century
before the Vietnam War. When no national causes stirred student
passions there were riots over restrictive regulations, harsh punishment, and other manifestations of *in loco parentis*, the principle under
which college officials wielded parental power to discipline and control.

But the early American higher education system had little in
common with its present-day counterpart. Colleges were small, exclusive, and – by the mid-nineteenth century – peripheral to society.
It was not until after the Civil War that the American academy
began to take on its modern character, as reform spurred increased
enrolment and a newly prominent role in national life. The first
national student groups were founded in the wake of the First
World War, and the depression of the thirties saw an unprecedented
wave of activism at institutions across the nation. The return of
veterans to the campus after the Second World War brought a
surge in college attendance that is only just cresting today, a surge
which created the conditions for the student protests that con-
vulsed the United States in the 1960s.

The author would like to thank Megan Elias, Christine Fecko, Joan Johnston, and
Rebecca Rosenfeld for the valuable insight and assistance which each of them provided during the preparation of this chapter.

The American colleges of the seventeenth and eighteenth centuries were small but influential. Organized along the model of Britain's universities, they emphasized classical education and served an elite population of young white men. Training for the ministry was a core collegiate mission, and that purpose was reflected in every aspect of the institutions' administration. Regulations were strict and comprehensive, and discipline was harsh – corporal punishment was widespread until the early eighteenth century.

Tensions over the restrictions of college life grew as the nation's campuses began to draw an older, more experienced student body. Protest was scattered and largely individual until the mid-1700s, but that changed as colonial dissatisfaction with British rule grew – Harvard, Princeton, and Yale all hosted denunciations of the Stamp Act at their 1765 commencement ceremonies. The words and deeds of patriots gave citizens new ideologies of opposition and strategies of protest, and the collegians of the era were quick to apply the lessons of colonial resistance to their own domestic situation.

Harvard, the oldest American college, was the first to erupt into rebellion. In the autumn of 1766, incensed by the serving of rancid butter in the dining hall, the students staged a walkout, setting the stage for a decade of confrontations and rioting that spread throughout the colonies. Protests ranged from the personal (as when gangs of Harvard students broke the windows of overly strict tutors) to the political (as when Princetonians staged their own version of the Boston Tea Party), but all were cloaked in the rhetoric of liberty and revolution.

British America supported fewer than ten colleges on the eve of revolution, and the early republic saw a flood of new school creations. In 1860 there were more than two hundred institutions of higher education in the United States. But despite this institutional growth, the academy was actually losing ground. Most colleges were tiny and underfunded, and the population as a whole was growing faster than enrolment. The nation's academic leaders had reacted to the intellectual and political ferment of the French Revolution by withdrawing from engagement with society, and the increasingly elastic social and economic structures of a modernizing America rendered a college education less and less relevant to personal advancement. A succession of reform efforts failed to make much impact, and at mid-century a degree provided neither useful instruction nor entrée into a profession. By 1860, only 1 per cent of white American men would attend college.

Those students who did attend often found both the curriculum and the governance system archaic. As religious suasion lost force and the quality of students dropped, serious disciplinary problems became more common. Brawls – between students and faculty, students and locals, students and police – were frequent and sometimes fatal, and colleges were ill-equipped to keep order. In 1807, Princeton students relieved their boredom by neglecting their studies, drinking, and setting fires. The administration suspended a few of the worst offenders, and the students responded with open rebellion – rioting and occupying a campus building, forcing the administration to close the college. Half the student body was suspended, but Princeton erupted in violence again and again in the years to follow.

Several colleges experimented with more liberal discipline in the antebellum era, hoping to reduce student insurrection by moderating the chafing authority it rose up against. Some even introduced student self-government in one form or another, though such experiments were usually short-lived. The University of Virginia's founder, Thomas Jefferson, envisaged a university governed by its constituencies working together, with disciplinary infractions adjudicated by a student court empowered with legal authority and a jail of its own. But Virginia's state government resisted this appropriation of its prerogatives, students refused to give evidence against each other, and internal democracy did not keep the campus from erupting in some of the worst student riots in the nation's history. By the mid-1830s the students of Virginia, once the nation's most progressively administered college, had gone so far as to organize and arm a militia to resist the school's 'tyrannical' faculty.

Compounding the consternation of university administrations in the antebellum era was the rise of fraternal organizations. Fraternities' secret rituals struck a nerve in a Mason-obsessed society, their independence represented a direct challenge to institutional order, and their intercollegiate character – fraternities were the first truly national student organizations – raised the spectre of a shadowy new power in the land.

American higher education hit bottom sometime around the Civil War, and in the closing decades of the nineteenth century the nation's small, poor, intellectually vague colleges began to give way to modern universities – large centres of advanced research and specialized professional education. State colleges received a huge boost from federal 'land grant' legislation, which provided support for a new class of public colleges. Land grant institutions provided training for work alongside a liberal arts curriculum – practical education for working people. Colleges for women and blacks burgeoned and coeducation grew dramatically after the war, with racial integration lagging behind. The boom gave a growing number of non-elite youths access to higher education, and freed the older private schools of the north-east to focus more exclusively on the children of the wealthy. Blacks, women, and the poor were still underrepresented, but the college population grew steadily, becoming more diverse with each passing year.

The explosion in higher education brought with it a new kind of student life. Extracurricular activities flourished as fraternities came out into the open, joined by intercollegiate athletics, student clubs, literary societies, and sororities. Undergraduate society matured from the defiance of the early nineteenth century into an independent, self-possessed culture outside of, rather than opposed to, the control of the university. In reaction to this transformation, new, more formal relationships grew up between students and their schools. Sports teams evolved from ad hoc agglomerations of undergraduates to formal representatives of the campus, organized, administered, and coached by school employees. Student self-government caught hold, as colleges and universities empowered elected councils to adjudicate violations of institutional rules, channelling students' hunger for power and relevance into the service of the status quo. Where there were tensions between the demands of *in loco parentis* and the implications of the new approach, they were by and large worked through within the system, and insurrection went into steep decline. By the turn of the century, observers of universities which had just a few decades earlier faced open and general rebellion were fretting over the 'fastidious', 'overrefined' character of the new crop of undergraduates.[1]

Attempts to channel students' extracurricular impulses further strengthened them. As fraternities and sororities were given more of a role in housing and feeding the student population, they came to see themselves as independent partners in administration with prerogatives of their own. Student newspapers flourished, and came to expect, if not always receive, the respect and latitude that accompanied American traditions of press freedom. In 1902 the University of Nevada responded to a smallpox scare with a 'semi-quarantine' which confined only those students living on campus. Where their

1. Joan D. Hedrick, 'Harvard indifference', *The New England Quarterly* 49 no. 3 (Sept. 1976), p. 356.

grandparents would have erupted into riot, the Nevada collegians met, voted on a course of action, then held an organized protest, voting to defy the quarantine by marching into town. The student paper took up the cause, acting as the impassioned advocate of an outraged citizenry.[2] Student protest was becoming more thought-ful, more considered, and less violent, but the repercussions for those who dared to defy collegiate authority had changed little – Nevada's administration suspended a third of the student body and expelled the editor of the paper.

The settlement house movement, founded in London in 1884 and imported to the United States shortly thereafter, was one of the first socially aware manifestations of college students' new pro-pensity for concerted action. Settlement houses, located in slums and staffed primarily by college women, provided practical assist-ance, education, and cultural opportunities to the poor. Some in the at times paternalistic movement shied away from political solu-tions to the problems they confronted, but others lent support to a variety of progressive reforms. By providing leadership to the nascent discipline of social work, settlement workers also helped to spur the continuing transformation of the college curriculum.

Radicalism flourished on the American campus in the decades before the First World War, with the establishment of a variety of campus-based political clubs and the founding of the Intercollegiate Socialist Society (ISS), the country's first national political organ-ization for students. ISS had more than fifty college chapters at its peak in 1915, and though it went into decline during the war, it survived to emerge more than four decades later as one of the most influential radical organizations of the 1960s.

During the first two years of the Great War many American collegians took staunchly isolationist stands, stands which put them at odds with public opinion and the vast majority of faculty and administrators. It was in this climate that the federal government created the Reserve Officers Training Corps (ROTC), a new national programme of on-campus military training. Although land grant legislation had included provision for military education, ROTC – directly supervised by the War Department and made mandatory at many schools – brought an unprecedented military presence to the American campus. One national poll found that nearly four students in five opposed it. Protests against ROTC and the prospect

2. Sally Springmeyer Zanjani, 'George Springmeyer and the quarantine rebellion of 1902: student revolt reaches the University of Nevada', *Nevada Historical Society Quarterly* 23 no. 4 (Winter 1980), pp. 287–9.

of American entry into the war were at first widespread, but dissent virtually evaporated in early 1917, when Germany began sinking American ships bound for Britain. What little opposition remained was stifled when the United States went to war.

The anti-communist Red Scares of 1918–19 muffled radicalism even further. Students were unable to get anti-war views aired in the campus press, and some were subjected to disciplinary action just for endorsing pacifism. A few leftist student groups survived the twenties, but the primary centres of organizing in that decade lay elsewhere. The National Student Federation of America (NSFA), founded in 1925, gave the country its first large-scale association of student governments, emphasizing student rights and international cooperation and working to strengthen student government. Christian student organizations flourished, with the Young Men's and Young Women's Christian Associations (YMCAs and YWCAs) in the forefront. The YM-YWCA movement reached its apex in the twenties, and though most members were apolitical, a minority did use the organization as a vehicle for social and political activism.

Although the percentage of young Americans attending institutions of higher education trebled in the first three decades of the twentieth century, and working-class youths were beginning to find their way to college in substantial numbers, the American academy was still in the main an elite one. Student leaders of the twenties tended to be well-off, with fraternities the arbiters of campus power. When collegians did act up, it was most often due to either apolitical exuberance or frustration with Victorian social restrictions. Pockets of activism existed – leftist students in the north-east protested against the treatment of the anarchists Sacco and Vanzetti, while the nation's black colleges saw unprecedented student strikes – but in general social comment took the form of bohemian free thought or Menckenesque critique more often than leftist analysis.

The depression came slowly to the American campus. Just one in eight young people were enrolled when the depression hit, and that minority was skewed to favour the children of the wealthy. In 1929 just one in five college men – and one in ten women – fully supported themselves in college, and most students' families paid all their bills. Many students were insulated from the worst of the economic devastation for the first few years after the crash, as their parents spent their way through their savings. College enrolment actually rose in the early years of the depression – the students forced to drop out were offset by others with the wherewithal to take their places. But enrolment fell in 1931, and again in 1932. Tuition revenue dropped, state funding was slashed, and alumni giving plummeted. Schools raised fees, cut expenses, and fired faculty. The depression had arrived, and students took notice. Anxiety grew as more and more graduates failed to find jobs, the campus press began to discuss the plight of unemployed and underemployed students, and students began to organize.

The first mass organizing of the depression decade came out of New York City's three public campuses – Hunter, City, and Brooklyn. Tuition-free and predominantly working class, these schools served a disproportionately Eastern European and Jewish immigrant community that had strong roots in radical activism and little cushion from the depredations of economic reversal. When the president of City College blocked distribution of a leftist campus newspaper in 1931, suspending its publisher and ten supporters, his action sparked citywide protests. Afterward the students involved formalized their ties, declaring themselves the National Student League (NSL) in time for a spring 1932 convention.

In the beginning, NSL was national in name only, but its timing was fortuitous and its leadership showed a real knack for emphasizing issues of broad concern. The group's platform combined an endorsement of students' rights and economic palliatives with opposition to discrimination and war – an agenda with strong appeal to a range of left and liberal collegians. Though never particularly large itself, NSL was able to mobilize huge numbers of non-member students in its campaigns. From the start it attracted the attention of the Young Communist League (YCL), the youth auxiliary of the Communist Party, and these well-organized students quickly took a dominant role in the group. Before long, NSL became an asset to, and at times an instrument of, the YCL.

The spectre of war hung over the college scene in the early thirties. That era's students had been raised in the shadow of the Great War, and many saw it as an instrument of capitalist imperialism, a war sold to the nation with platitudes about democracy and used as the pretext for an assault on civil liberties. Male students feared being called to serve in the next war, and many resolved not to go.

In England in February 1933, students of the Oxford Union declared that they would 'in no circumstances fight for ... King and country'. The declaration was taken up at universities across Britain, and the spring saw campaigns for home-grown versions of the Oxford Pledge at nearly a hundred American campuses. One poll found 39 per cent of American students unwilling to go to war under any circumstances, with another third intending to refuse unless the United States itself was invaded. When NSL held a one-hour National Student Strike Against War in 1934, on the April anniversary of the US entry into the First World War, 25,000 students participated, making it the largest student protest in America to date.

NSL's partner in the 1934 strike was its forebear in leftist organizing, the Intercollegiate Socialist Society. Renamed the League for Industrial Democracy (LID) in 1921, the group had spent the 1920s as a network of study groups, discussing politics but rarely entering the fray. NSL's success spurred LID to action, and in 1932 it refashioned its campus chapters into the Student League for Industrial Democracy (SLID), and began to organize. Congressional investigations into munitions profiteering and bankers' roles in America's entry into the First World War confirmed the suspicions of an already jaded student body, and the 1935 anti-war strike drew co-sponsorship from NSFA, YM-YWCA chapters, and student governments across the country. In all, 175,000 students took part in the protests, a sevenfold increase from the previous year's strike.

NSL and SLID merged in late 1935, creating the American Student Union (ASU). Although SLID officials had doubts about so close an alliance with the communists, the membership of the two groups, less doctrinaire than their leaders, overwhelmingly supported consolidation. Unaffiliated students, mostly liberals, accounted for nearly half of ASU's membership and were well represented on its Board of Directors, but NSL and SLID divided staff positions amongst themselves, reserving real power for the initiated. Neither subsumed their identity into that of the new group; each remained an undigested element, bound to its ideological line and – in the case of NSL – beholden to the adult wing of the Communist Party.

The two factions shared common ground on domestic issues – both saw education as a right rather than a privilege, both took strong stands in support of civil liberties and racial and gender equality, and both endorsed the protection of the poor from the ravages of the depression economy. On international issues, however, a split was developing. As fascism emerged as a potential threat to the Soviet Union, the American Communist Party began to look to the United States as a potential ally in the impending struggle. SLID's socialists were still committed to anti-interventionism, but NSL's communists were no longer so sure.

The 1936 anti-war strike was a tremendous success. As many as 500,000 students, nearly half of the college population of the United

States, were said to have participated. Some turned their energies to political theatre – taking a cue from the Bonus Army that had marched on Washington to demand early payment of their Great War veterans' benefits, a group of Princeton undergraduates dubbed themselves the Veterans of Future Wars and demanded their hypothetical bonuses in advance. A VFW craze – the name itself a play on the name of the Veterans of *Foreign* Wars, one of the nation's largest veterans' groups – swept the nation's colleges. More than four hundred schools launched chapters in the months that followed, and some even started VFW auxiliaries such as the Future War Profiteers of America. Legitimate veterans' organizations were, predictably, enraged, and the 'movement' petered out by the end of the year. In the meantime, students had found a way to link traditions of collegiate pranksterism with the more sober issues of the day.

But just as anti-interventionism was reaching its high-water mark in the United States, events in Europe were casting its basic precepts into doubt. Italy's invasion of Ethiopia had given an indication of the fascists' expansionist agenda. The Spanish Civil War made the costs of isolation impossible to ignore, particularly once American college students and graduates – totalling some 500 by 1938 – began to travel to Spain to fight fascism. Pacifists and isolationists would continue to oppose American involvement in European conflicts, but the masses of American students were no longer with them. ASU abandoned the Oxford Pledge at its Christmas 1937 conference, in a vote that reflected both the growing communist domination of the group and the general campus disillusionment with isolationism. The 1938 strike was overwhelmingly oriented toward anti-fascist solidarity.

By the time war began in Europe in 1939, something close to a consensus of student opinion was coalescing around the anti-fascist cause. With the British and French declarations of war, off-campus attitudes were beginning to follow. But by the start of the fall semester, ASU was gearing up to abandon its position at the vanguard of American anti-fascism, and in the process squander most of the goodwill the student movement had built up during the previous decade.

The reversal was prompted by the Nazi–Soviet pact of August 1939. With Hitler's regime suddenly an ally of the Soviet Union, the communist 'Popular Front' against fascism was rendered obsolete, and YCL found themselves saddled with allegiances directly opposite to those of the anti-fascist majority they had worked so hard to build. Though only a minority of ASU's members, YCLers dominated the group's leadership and out-organized their opponents, and ASU began to move back toward neutrality. When the final confrontation came at the end of 1939, the result was decisive. The group's delegates rejected a resolution condemning the Soviet invasion of Finland by a vote of 322 to 49, and went on to endorse an isolationist foreign policy. By mid-1940 two thirds of ASU's membership – the disorganized non-communist constituency – had left the organization.[3] ASU took up the interventionist banner again after Germany's 1941 invasion of the Soviet Union, but it was too late – the organization was by then little more than a shell.

In the absence of national leadership, interventionist students did little large-scale organizing between the collapse of ASU and the American entry into the war. Isolationist students were more active, but more divided – they spanned the political spectrum from the pro-Soviet ASU to the hyper-patriotic 'America First' crowd, with no shortage of mutually hostile factions in between. Impressive local demonstrations were still held – Columbia University drew nearly a thousand students to its 1940 peace strike – but ASU had left a vacuum that could not be filled in the brief time left before the country went to war.

Campus-based activism virtually disappeared after Pearl Harbor. The college population dropped by nearly a third as the nation's male students went off to fight. Wartime rationing severely restricted the travel necessary for regional or national coordination, and home front work occupied time and energy which might otherwise have been devoted to political organizing. Perhaps most important, the national climate was a barren one for dissent. Conscientious objection to military service was negligible in the United States during the Second World War, and opposition to the war's aims was, if anything, even less in evidence.

The campuses were depopulated, quiet, and focused on the task at hand. To the extent that American students were engaged in organizing, it was through groups like the patriotic, pro-Allied Student Defenders of Democracy or in war relief efforts coordinated by campus religious organizations and student war councils. A few efforts were made to begin building a national, even international student movement (as when a 1942 gathering called by SLID alumni and Eleanor Roosevelt brought together student veterans from more

3. Robert Cohen, *When the Old Left Was Young: Student Radicals and America's First Mass Student Movement, 1929–1941* (New York: Oxford University Press, 1993), pp. 296–8.

than fifty countries), but they achieved little. In 1943, students from
several dozen campuses met to form the United States Student
Assembly (USSA), but the founding convention was marred by
infighting, as the new group's leadership barred communists in an
attempt to prevent an ASU-style takeover. With or without the left,
USSA was never able to establish itself as a serious activist force.

The end of the war brought with it a surge in enrolment which
transformed the university forever. Youths who had put their education on hold during the war returned to campus, joined by others
for whom the doors to higher education were opened by military
service. The GI Bill, passed in 1944, granted unprecedented federal
financial support to veterans seeking to pursue post-secondary
education. By 1947, 2.3 million Americans were enrolled in college
– a 50 per cent advance over the last pre-war numbers. One million
of these students, nearly half the student population, were veterans
of the Second World War.

Veterans tended to be older than their classmates, and many had
family responsibilities. Some completed their education as quickly
as possible, devoting only minimal attention to extracurricular
pursuits. Others, though, believing that experience had given them
a perspective which could be of value to their fellow students, became
involved in fraternities, veterans' groups, and student government.
Administrators welcomed veteran participation in student activities
and governance, and ceded new responsibilities to this older, more
mature cohort.

One of the most widespread interests among American veterans
was international student outreach. At the war's end, several international student meetings were held in Europe, culminating in a
1946 world conference in Prague which established the International Union of Students (IUS), a left-leaning, ostensibly independent body. The American delegation to Prague – an ideologically
diverse group representing ten campuses and a similar number of
student and youth organizations – returned convinced of the need
for a new union of American students, and set to work organizing
one. The following summer students from more than 350 colleges
and universities participated in the constitutional convention of the
United States National Student Association (NSA).

The founding meetings of the new group took place in an environment of deep factional division. Alumni and adult advisers cautioned students about their experience with communist infiltration
in the thirties, while anti-communist students engaged in an intense
organizing campaign to ensure their side was strongly represented.

Communist delegates, perhaps 10 per cent of the total, were embattled, but the students of NSA did not ban communist participation, as USSA's founders had four years earlier. Instead they adopted the student-government-based membership structure of the moribund NSFA and, in a closely fought vote, barred all national organizations from membership. They thus left their doors open to students of all political persuasions, but set an ideologically neutral hurdle to participation – election or appointment through student government – that was bound to keep communist membership low.

In the substantive debates that followed, NSA passed a Student Bill of Rights which set down an expansive conception of student civil liberties and academic freedom, and which declared that the rights it enumerated should not be abridged on the basis of race, religion, or political views. Although the delegates made clear that efforts to achieve an end to racial discrimination in higher education should proceed with sensitivity to regional differences, the association's stand – much closer to ASU's than to NSFA's – was strong enough to drive most white Southern schools away.

Many students at NSA's founding convention were hostile to IUS's geopolitical orientation, but a majority was interested in pursuing the possibility of membership. An affiliation resolution with a variety of conditions attached passed overwhelmingly in 1947, but when IUS endorsed the Soviet-backed coup in Czechoslovakia the following year, antipathy between the two groups was confirmed. In the years after the split, NSA moved toward a more binary Cold War posture, helping to create a pro-Western IUS alternative in the early fifties while articulating a steadily more emphatic anti-communist world-view.

At about the same time the association, in severe financial difficulty, entered into a clandestine relationship with the United States government, accepting secret financial support from the Central Intelligence Agency. The CIA relationship, which was unknown to all but the association's top officers, provided more than half of the association's budget and continued for fifteen years. Although the relationship was for more than a decade regarded as symbiotic by those few students in the know, it became increasingly untenable as the country's political climate changed. When the secret funding was exposed in 1967, it sparked bitter criticism from across the political spectrum.

Beyond NSA, there was little national student organizing during the McCarthy era. The communists had a few organizing victories in the late forties, but political repression and uninspiring policies led to a near-total loss of influence in the fifties. Organizations of the non-communist left, including the liberal Students for Democratic Action (SDA) and a variety of socialist student groups, suffered similarly. When national groups did gather a substantial following, it was most frequently as organizers of a popular local campaign, as when Columbia University's SDA chapter fought fraternity discrimination in the early fifties.

NSA's influence is harder to measure. It had no mass base on campus, but its efforts to strengthen local student government made other organizing possible. Student leaders were exposed to a wide spectrum of political and social views at the association's National Student Congresses, which attracted many hundreds of participants each year. And debates over affiliation or disaffiliation with the association frequently served as a context for the airing of important political questions on campus at a time when there was otherwise little dialogue.

In the late fifties, in the wake of the Sputnik humiliation, the United States lavished money and attention on its higher education system. The first Americans to come of age in the youth culture of the rock and roll era headed off to college, and their younger siblings, the baby boom generation, would provide a tremendous influx of new students. College enrolment would nearly treble in the sixties. In this climate of expectancy, new groups and causes began to revitalize the campus scene.

A student peace movement arose in the east and mid-west, giving birth to the Student Peace Union, the Campus Peace Union, and Student SANE (an affiliate of the National Committee for a Sane Nuclear Policy). SPU emerged as the dominant campus peace organization after 1960, but for a while all three were active in campus organizing against nuclear testing and encroaching militarism. At the same time, students at black colleges began experimenting with anti-segregation sit-ins in a wave of actions that, while tentative, suggested a new willingness to act on the part of students who had often been dismissed as conservative and uninvolved. In 1958 NSA, a bellwether of mainstream student liberalism, came out against nuclear testing and launched a project to train Southern students to prepare their campuses and communities for desegregation.

The year 1960 was an extraordinary one for American students. In January the venerable Student League for Industrial Democracy became the Students for a Democratic Society (SDS). In February, students in North Carolina staged a sit-in at a segregated lunch counter that sparked a wave of protests across the South. (NSA helped get the word out through its new Atlanta race relations office, opened just a month earlier.) In April, veterans of the lunch-counter sit-ins met in Raleigh to form the Student Nonviolent Coordinating Committee (SNCC). In May, students from the University of California at Berkeley were beaten by police while demonstrating outside a closed meeting of the House Un-American Activities Committee, and in September students from more than forty colleges gathered at William F. Buckley's Connecticut estate to form Young Americans for Freedom (YAF), an association of conservative students.

'The Age of Complacency is ending,' the sociologist C. Wright Mills wrote that summer. 'We are beginning to move again.'[4] He was right. Within a few years, SDS would be the institutional heart of the New Left. SNCC would be the other pillar of the movement, first as a daring, effective force for civil rights agitation, then as the earliest, strongest voice for Black Power. Berkeley would be the epicentre of the decade's activism, a powerful force and symbol. And YAF would be the most important conservative student group in American history. The decade was only a few months old when Mills wrote his prescient words, but the Sixties had arrived.

It is difficult to generalize productively about the first three centuries of American student agitation. Political currents, economic trends, and – critically – the changing demographics of higher education have impelled dramatic shifts in the means and ends of protest over the course of the nation's history. Freedom of expression has nearly always been an area of concern, as has the more general question of the student's relationship to the university, but once one ventures farther afield, the narrative becomes multiple and contradictory. Before 1960 American students banded together to tear down authority, to open up institutions, to force social change – but also to build up, to close off, even to preserve the status quo. They organized locally around national issues, nationally around global issues, and on every level in between and beyond.

The diversity of student activism before the watershed year of 1960 is relevant to the student of later organizing for at least two reasons. First, the early history shows us that no movement is truly *sui generis*, that each draws on and reacts against a wealth of prior work. Few communities are as lacking in institutional memory as students, among whom a new generation of leaders may rise and

4. C. Wright Mills, 'The New Left', in *Power Politics, and People: The Collected Essays of C. Wright Mills* (New York: Oxford University Press, 1963), p. 259.

disappear every few years. But ignorance does not imply discontinuity – the activism of past generations shapes and prefigures what comes later, whether the participants know it or not.

The sweep of early activism also serves as a reminder of the diversity of what followed, a diversity which has only just begun to find its chroniclers. In the sixties and after, students of all races, religions, sexual orientations, and classes, women and men at private colleges, public universities, and commuter schools, engaged in serious, playful, violent, peaceful, separatist, interracial, conservative, liberal, radical activism around a dizzying array of causes from the most dryly academic to the most painfully personal. This cacophony of voices resonates with the cacophonies that preceded it, and it offers a far richer story than has traditionally been told.

CHAPTER THREE

The Location of Student Protest: Patterns of Activism in American Universities in the 1960s

NELLA VAN DYKE

The 1960s are synonymous with student protest: demonstrations against the Vietnam War, sit-ins, takeovers of university administration buildings, the killings at Kent State. Colleges and universities were central locations for protest during the 1960s, and, as a result, certain institutions have earned enduring reputations as centres of activism, including the University of California at Berkeley, the University of Wisconsin, and the University of Michigan. However, even during the 1960s, the majority of American colleges did not experience significant student protest. This chapter examines the factors that influence the location of protest activity, and attempts to explain why protest occurred on some American campuses and not others.

Student protest in historical perspective

For many, the political turmoil of the 1960s seems an anomaly, a unique period during which chaos erupted on college campuses. But American colleges and universities have long been a location of protest activity. After the political quiescence of the 1940s and 1950s, the 1960s did appear markedly more restive. However, it was the 1940s and 1950s which were unusual, not the 1960s. University students have been one of the most politically active populations throughout history, both in the USA and in other countries.

Throughout history and around the world, students have protested about a variety of topics, sometimes related to the university and at other times involving wider society. Students have been instrumental in most major social upheavals, including the French

27

and Russian Revolutions, the recent protests which influenced the dissolution of the Soviet Union, and others. Most sociologists now agree that students are one of the most active social groups because they are free from many of the constraints which prevent others from acting.[1] Most do not have families or full-time jobs for which they are responsible. They have more free or discretionary time than most people, and less to lose. They will not jeopardize their career or leave children without a caretaker should they be arrested for protest activities.

In the United States, students have been active since before the American revolution. They have been motivated to protest about issues ranging from the seemingly mundane matter of cafeteria food quality, to more profound issues, such as the abolition of slavery. They have consistently fought to improve conditions at their colleges and universities, and to maintain some control over curricular and housing arrangements. During the 1960s, students on many campuses protested over university-related issues, the curriculum (including the provision of African American Studies courses and degrees), cafeteria conditions, and dormitory hours and regulations.[2]

Many of the issues prominent in the 1960s had precedent in earlier decades. Cafeteria conditions, which motivated protests on 25 per cent of American campuses in the 1967–68 academic year, provoked protest as early as 1766, when Harvard students complained: 'Behold our butter stinketh and we cannot eat thereof.'[3] Protests over the presence of detachments of the Reserve Officer Training Corps on campus, which provoked a great deal of unrest in the 1960s, had their precursors in the late nineteenth-century demonstrations at a number of state land grant universities, including Wisconsin and Illinois, over mandatory military training. American students also have a history of protest around larger social issues, including the abolition of slavery and opposition to war. Clearly, many issues which appear unique to the 1960s actually had precedent.

Factors influencing the location of student protest

A comprehensive survey of campus protest was conducted by the American Council on Education (ACE) in 1969–70, the peak years

1. Doug McAdam, *Freedom Summer* (New York, 1988), *passim*.
2. See the previous chapter, by J. Angus Johnston.
3. Seymour M. Lipset, 'Political controversies at Harvard, 1636 to 1974', in S.M. Lipset and David Reisman, *Education and Politics at Harvard* (Berkeley, Calif., 1975), p. 35.

of the 1960s protest wave. The ACE determined that 43 per cent of American higher education institutions had some protest during this academic year.[4] Other studies conducted in the late 1960s and early 1970s found that activism was more likely to occur at institutions which are more selective, and at larger institutions.[5] More selective institutions are those which have tougher admissions standards and therefore are generally of higher academic quality. In this study's sample of colleges, 71 per cent of the most selective institutions experienced activism, while only 23 per cent of the least selective institutions did. For example, Harvard University, one of the premier universities in the USA, saw a great deal of student protest during the 1960s. Less selective institutions, such as Central State College in Oklahoma, saw little.

Two explanations have been proposed for this higher prevalence of student protest activity at more selective institutions. Some have argued that these institutions have more liberal students and faculty, and that these individuals are likely to engage in protest activity.[6] These explanations focus on the individual, arguing that there is nothing about the more selective colleges *per se* that encourages or fosters protest, but that these locations happen to attract more protest-prone individuals. But this explanation seems unsatisfactory, since it underplays the role of the institution in providing an atmosphere which nurtures protest activity and gives little credit to group dynamics at the institutions in question. A collection of scattered individuals, no matter how liberal or prone to protest, will not protest without group connections and interactions. Individuals rarely engage in protest activity alone. It is within groups of individuals that situations are perceived, shaped and framed in such a way as to inspire collective action. Thus, selective colleges may include faculty who are more involved in national political affairs, students from wealthy or prestigious families who have a tradition of political involvement, or a sense of personal power born of a lifetime of witnessing the fruits of assertiveness through family experiences. Together, these individuals may form a campus culture which is political, attuned to political events, and active. It is not the

4. Alexander W. Astin, Helen S. Astin, Alan E. Bayer and Ann S. Bisconti, *The Power of Protest* (San Francisco, 1975), p. 42.
5. Alan E. Bayer and Alexander W. Astin, *Campus Disruption During 1968–1969* (Washington, DC, 1969), p. 341; Garth Buchanan and Joan Brackett, *Summary Results of the Survey for the President's Commission on Campus Unrest* (Washington, DC, 1970), pp. 18–21; Harold Hodgkinson, 'Student protest: an institutional and national profile', *The Record* 71 (1970), p. 537.
6. Lipset, 'Political controversies', pp. 31–2.

individuals alone who will inspire collective protest activity, but the political culture of which they are a part. Such a culture encourages the belief that social problems are the concern of those present on campus, and that those individuals have the power and responsibility to act. Some campuses have a more or less active political culture, which influences the levels of protest.

There is an alternative explanation regarding why more selective institutions see more political protest. It suggests that students at more elite institutions have more resources with which to mobilize.[7] These institutions themselves may be better endowed financially to provide services and material resources to students, and the students themselves may come from wealthy families which provide them with resources. These resources might include money, which can be used to fund organizations, printing costs, and office supplies, but also free time, which wealthier students may have more of, due to the fact that they may not need outside employment while at university.

Research has also discovered that activism is more likely to occur on large campuses, with larger student populations. Thus, Michigan State University, a large public institution of approximately 35,000 students, is more likely to host protest activity than Siena Heights College, also in Michigan, with its student population of 650. Two explanations for this phenomenon have been offered. Some have argued that students at larger universities are more isolated.[8] This may lead them to protest either because it creates feelings of unhappiness with current conditions (that sixties malaise, alienation), or because there is a lack of adult interaction and supervision which might otherwise keep students from engaging in protest activity. While this explanation is plausible, most research suggests that isolated individuals are the least likely to participate in social movements.[9] Those more connected to other people are more likely to engage in protest.

7. This proposal is based on the work of John D. McCarthy and Mayer N. Zald, *The Trend of Social Movements in America: Professionalization and Resource Mobilization* (Morristown, NJ, 1973).

8. Lipset, 'Political controversies', pp. 99–100.

9. Roger V. Gould, 'Collective action and network structure', *American Sociological Review* 58 (1993), pp. 182–96; McAdam, *Freedom Summer*, pp. 50–3; David A. Snow, Louis A. Zurcher, Jr. and Sheldon Ekland-Olson, 'Social networks and social movements: a micro-structural approach to differential recruitment', *American Sociological Review* 45 (1980), pp. 787–801; Verta Taylor, 'Social movement continuity: the women's movement in abeyance', *American Sociological Review* 54 (1989), pp. 761–75; among others.

An alternative explanation is that larger universities are more likely to have a critical mass of protesters. Research suggests that large-scale protests will not happen unless such a critical mass exists.[10] In other words, unless a sizeable number of people are interested in participating in the protest, the protest will not happen. There is more diversity among the student population of larger universities, and the students at larger universities know more people. Since more socially connected individuals are more likely to protest, larger universities are more likely to have a sufficient number of like-minded individuals who will join together and instigate a protest.

Research on the campus unrest of the 1960s has consistently failed to take a long-term approach to examining the phenomenon. As has already been established, protest activity has a long history on college campuses. Some researchers have shown that hold-over organizations of activists may link different protest waves.[11] The women's movement of the 1960s, for example, was the second wave of feminist activism in the United States. Organizations which endured from the 1930s to the 1960s influenced the emergence of the women's movement in the 1960s. Others have demonstrated how cultural organizations, such as folk-song clubs, summer camps or cafés and restaurants may continue an activist culture and play a role in the emergence of protest activity later. In the research presented in this chapter, measures of past activism are examined in order to analyse the influence of history on subsequent protest activity.

Thus, from the factors outlined above, three hypotheses regarding the location of student protest can be proposed and will be tested in this article:

Hypothesis 1: Colleges which are more selective will experience more protest activity. This effect will remain even when controlling for tuition level, which will suggest that economic resources are not the only factor involved in this influence.

Hypothesis 2: Larger institutions will be more likely to experience student protest activity, even when controlling for student isolation.

10. Mark Granovetter, 'Threshold models of collective behavior', *American Journal of Sociology* 83 (1978), pp. 1420–43; Gerald Marwell and Pamela Oliver, *The Critical Mass in Collective Action: A Micro-Social Theory* (New York, 1993).

11. Maurice Isserman, *If I Had a Hammer: The Death of the Old Left and the Birth of the New Left* (New York, 1987); Aldon Morris, *The Origins of the Civil Rights Movement* (New York, 1984); Leila Rupp and Verta Taylor, *Survival in the Doldrums: The American Women's Rights Movement, 1945 to the 1960s* (New York, 1987).

If supported, this will suggest that a critical mass of students rather than isolation leads to student protest activity.

Hypothesis 3: Activism on campus will be influenced by a history of activism at a college. Protest cultures and long-standing activist organizations influence the location of student protest.

Data and methods

In order to examine which factors influence the location of protest activity on college campuses in the USA in the 1960s, a data set containing information on 422 colleges and universities will be used. The occurrence of student activism on campus will be measured by looking at whether or not the college had a chapter of the radical student organization, Students for a Democratic Society (SDS), on campus during the peak of the 1960s protest wave, the spring of 1969. The sample includes 150 activist colleges, and 272 non-active institutions. A random sample of non-activist institutions was selected from a college guide, *American Universities and Colleges*, published in 1964.[12]

In order to test the idea that a history of activism influences later protest activity, past activism was measured by the presence or absence of two student movement organizations in the 1930s: the American Student Union (ASU) and the Student League for Industrial Democracy (SLID). These data were collected from the organizations' newsletters.

Data on the characteristics of the colleges came from *American Universities and Colleges* and the *Comparative Guide to American Colleges* (1963).[13] Because we are interested in how college selectivity influences the emergence of protest activity, measures of selectivity were taken from one of the college guides, as were measures of the tuition fees charged by the institutions, and whether or not the institutions were public or private. These variables should provide some idea of what aspects of selectivity influence the presence of student protest activity.

In order to examine the dynamics of how the size of the institution influences protest activity, measures were also collected from the college guide on the size of the institution, the percentage living in halls of residence, and the faculty/student ratio. The variables

---

12. Alan M. Cartter, *American Universities and Colleges* (Washington, DC, 1964).
13. James Cass and Max Birnbaum, *Comparative Guide to American Colleges* (New York, 1963).

on the percentage of students living in halls of residence and the faculty/student ratio will provide a measure of student isolation. In this way it is possible to determine whether large institutions have more activism because of student isolation, or because of sheer numbers of activists, a critical mass. If the variable for number of students is found to significantly influence the presence of activism, but the variables measuring isolation do not, it will suggest that the latter explanation is correct.

In order to test which variables significantly influence the location of student protest, a multivariate logistic regression model was used. Logistic regression allows us to examine the influence of each variable while controlling for the other variables. In other words, the statistical model includes all of the variables, and is able to identify the unique effect of each variable while simultaneously examining the effects of the others (it does this through techniques of calculus). By testing the effects of all the variables simultaneously, we can be assured that what appears to be the effect of one variable is not caused by one of the other variables: thus, it rules out the possibility of spurious effects appearing to be real effects. Logistic regression is appropriate for this question because it uses a dichotomous dependent variable, in this case, whether or not a college was a centre of student activism.

Findings

Hypothesis 1: Colleges which are more selective will experience more protest activity. The results of the regression analysis (see Table 1) demonstrate support for this hypothesis. Those colleges with more selective admissions standards are more likely to experience student protest activity. This influence occurs even when we control for economic resources, suggesting that these colleges may have cultures which encourage more student political activity. It appears that some colleges maintain political cultures over long periods of time, which may influence student actions. More selective institutions may be more likely to maintain such a political culture due to the presence of a more politically active and aware faculty and student body. The most selective colleges are often the most prestigious, and attract excellent faculty and students. These individuals, because of their personal or familial backgrounds, may be more politically involved than those at less selective institutions. Together, they may create a campus culture which views political activism as a viable means of expressing discontent and working for change.

TABLE 1   *Estimated Effects of Selected Independent Variables on the Presence of Activism on Campus During the 1960s*

Independent Variable	
Past Activism (PASTACT)	2.4835***
	(0.3020)
Selectiveness of School (COMP2)	0.3432*
	(0.1421)
Tuition (TUITION)	0.0013*
	(0.0001)
Public School (PUBLIC)	1.1291*
	(0.5096)
% of Undergrads in Dorm (DORM)	−0.0082
	(0.0058)
% of Students who are Foreign (FORPERC)	0.1454*
	(0.0623)
Faculty/Student Ratio (FSRATIO)	−0.0111
	(0.0218)
Size of School (LARGE)	1.9632***
	(0.3466)
Difference in −2 Log Likelihood	163.846
from model with only intercept	8 d.f.

***p<.001   **p<.01   *p<.05   N=422

Hypothesis 2: Larger institutions will be more likely to experience student protest activity, even when controlling for student isolation. The results of the analysis (see Table 1) demonstrate support for this hypothesis as well. Larger institutions are more likely to be the location of student protest activity. Large institutions are seven times more likely to have hosted 1960s student activism than smaller institutions. This effect occurs even when we control for the student/faculty ratio and the number of students in the dormitory, suggesting that student isolation is not the underlying mechanism at work here. Interestingly, the variable for the percentage of students who are foreign is significant. This suggests that the diversity of large institutions makes them more likely to experience student protest activity.

Hypothesis 3: Activism on campus will be influenced by a history of activism at a college. Table 1 demonstrates support for this hypothesis as well; those institutions which had a history of past activism were three times as likely to experience protest activity during the 1960s. This finding suggests that some colleges may have political cultures and traditions which endure over many years, influencing the emergence of protest activity time and again. This influence may occur through political or cultural organizations on or off campus, through myths and stories which are traded within an institution, or through information, ideologies and tactics which individuals pass on over time.

Discussion

As expected, several factors influenced the location of student protest during the 1960s: those institutions which were more selective, had larger numbers of students, and had a history of activism were more likely to experience student protest activity. However, this is a list of characteristics. What do these colleges or universities look like? An examination of two colleges will reveal how institutions vary in their institutional characteristics, culture, and the prevalence of student protest activity.

Since its founding in the seventeenth century, Harvard University has been a frequent site of student protest activity. Throughout the eighteenth and nineteenth centuries, Harvard hosted activism on a wide range of issues, including cafeteria food conditions, as well as abolitionism, anti-war protests, and the like. As this study has demonstrated, institutions which have a history of protest activity are more likely to experience subsequent student protest. Harvard, with its long history of student protest, is a perfect example of such a school. It seems likely that this effect is in part due to the persistence of a student culture which carries with it a political element. Political action has a history on the campus, and is seen by Harvard students as a response option when they have a grievance with the university administration, the US government or society in general.

Harvard also possesses the other two characteristics found to predict the location of student protest activity. It is one of the most selective colleges in the country. That is, its students must pass very difficult admissions standards to gain entry. As this study demonstrates, highly selective institutions like Harvard are more likely to host student protest, possibly due to a political culture on campus which is sustained by well-trained and politically involved faculty, and students with political interests or a sense of personal efficacy. Harvard is also a relatively large institution, with a student population of over 12,000 in the early 1960s. Larger universities have a

more diverse student population, and because of the large population, a critical mass of activists may be more likely to form and
protest together.

Midland Lutheran College, in Fremont, Nebraska, experienced
only a handful of student protests during the 1960s, fewer in total
than Harvard experienced during any one semester during the same
decade. Although one might suspect that this is due to the different
locations of the two colleges (Harvard is located in the metropolitan
Boston area), previous research has shown that the population of
the city in which the college is located does not influence the prevalence of student protest activity.[14] The results of this study help to
explain why Midland Lutheran did not experience student protest:
it does not possess any of the characteristics found to influence
protest. It does not have a history of protest activity: there were no
protests at Midland Lutheran during the 1930s, a fairly active period
in US history. It is a small college: its student population of only
675 in the early 1960s was insufficient to sustain protest activity.
Midland Lutheran is also a non-selective school: it does not have
difficult admissions standards. Because of these factors, it does not
appear to have a student culture which is political. Historically, the
students at Midland Lutheran have not been inclined to protest
when they have found themselves unhappy with conditions at the
college or in society.

Although this research examined the factors which influenced
the emergence of student protest activity in particular locations
during the 1960s, it can be argued that the same factors influence
the location of student protest activity during other time periods,
including the present. Although we do not necessarily think of the
1990s as a particularly active time, some colleges, such as Harvard
University, or the University of California at Berkeley, still experience a very high incidence of student protest activity. This may be
due to protest cultures which endure over time on these campuses,
not to mention the continued existence of the other significant
factors revealed in this study.

14. Nella Van Dyke, 'Hotbeds of activism: locations of student protest', *Social
Problems* (forthcoming, 1998).

PART TWO

The International Student
Movement of the 1960s

CHAPTER FOUR

The Eyes of the Marcher: Paris, May 1968 – Theory and Its Consequences

BERTRAM GORDON

This chapter is the story of the marchers and other participants in the uprising, sometimes known as the 'events', in France of May 1968. It focuses on how they saw the movement as they were participating and in retrospect nearly thirty years later. Accordingly, interviews of participants in the May events were used to draw up a list of themes basic to understanding what happened in France. To put their comments into historical perspective, however, it is best to begin with a brief chronological overview.

Having emerged from the Algerian war in the early 1960s, under the leadership of General Charles de Gaulle, president of the Fifth Republic, France underwent a period of rapid economic modernization and social change. Workers' wages, however, remained relatively low. A rural exodus sparked an increase in poverty in working-class suburban districts, such as Nanterre in the Paris region. France also witnessed a growth in the salaried urban middle classes, many of whom considered Gaullism outmoded. To Roberto Ballabeni, a participant in the May movement, the Algerian war had put in place an autocratic Gaullist regime, possessing 'a police power incompatible with the state of law, [a] survival of Vichy and the colonial wars'.[1]

Purchasing power stagnated in 1966 and 1967 and unemployment increased, especially among the increased numbers of young people on the job market. A trebling of the university student population in ten years devalued diplomas, degraded working and living conditions, and fed a growing student discontent. Professors raised in a traditional and hierarchical culture offered educational programmes which new students, the products of a more permissive

1. Roberto Ballabeni, personal communication, 24 November 1997. All translations in this article from the French are my own, except where otherwise noted.

consumer society, found increasingly irrelevant. The *UNEF* (*Union Nationale des Étudiants Français*, National Union of French Students) included only about 10 per cent of students, while anarchists, Trotskyist, and Maoist groups, notably the *UJCml* (*Union des Jeunesses Communistes marxistes-léninistes*, Union of Marxist-Leninist Communist Youth) made inroads among students opposed to the American war in Vietnam.[2]

Early 1968 witnessed student protests in Nanterre, where a new university had been built in a neighbourhood of *bidonvilles*, jerrybuilt worker housing. On 8 January, after speaking in Nanterre, Minister of Youth and Sports François Misoffe was challenged by Daniel Cohn-Bendit, protesting against the government ban on men visiting women's university residences. His open challenge to the minister enhanced Cohn-Bendit's prestige in the Nanterre movement and added to growing protests there, leading to student occupation of the 'tower', a main campus building, and the creation of the 22 March movement with Cohn-Bendit as one of its leaders.[3] When the government suspended classes at Nanterre, student sit-ins followed. Opposed to the students at first, the Communist Party (*PCF, Parti Communiste Français*) now reversed its position. On May Day (1 May), workers' organizations marched from the Place de la République to the Bastille. Two days later, a meeting of students in the Sorbonne was broken up by police. Following the refusal of the government to allow a televised programme on the student movement, demonstrators set up barricades and occupied much of the Latin Quarter during the night of 10 May. While negotiations continued intermittently between government and student representatives, workers' unions called a solidarity general strike. On 13 May, the tenth anniversary of the Algerian crisis that had brought de Gaulle to power, a worker–student solidarity march took place. A student occupation of the Sorbonne followed.[4]

Within two days of the mass march, the *CGT* (*Confédération Générale du Travail*, General Confederation of Labour, France's largest trade union), in close affiliation with the *PCF*, jumped on the bandwagon. While interested in organizing strikes and securing their control over the Left, the *PCF* and *CGT* did not seek a revolutionary overthrow

2. Alain Monchablon, 'Mai 1968', in Jean-François Sirinelli (ed.), *Dictionnaire historique de la vie politique française au XXe siècle* (Paris, 1995), p. 603.

3. Laurent Joffrin, *Mai 68: histoire des événements* (Paris, 1988), p. 58. See also Hervé Hamon and Patrick Rotman, *Génération*, vol. 1, *Les Années de rêve* (Paris, 1987), pp. 400–2.

4. Lucien Rioux and René Backmann, *Ce jour-là: 11 mai 1968, l'explosion de mai, histoire complète des 'événements'* (Paris, 1968), pp. 241–2.

of the Gaullist state. Strikes now spread throughout the country, including many public services as well as factories, until France was paralysed with an estimated three to six million on strike by 18 May.[5] At first the government tried to break up the demonstrations and de Gaulle seemed uncertain how to handle the situation. On 27 May, however, Prime Minister Georges Pompidou reached an accord with the *CGT* by offering higher wages and shortened hours. The agreement, however, was rejected by Renault workers. On the 28th a change in government seemed possible and François Mitterrand indicated that he was available to take over as president and head a leftist coalition with Pierre Mendès France as prime minister, in the event of de Gaulle's resignation. Living conditions in Paris were worsening, with the growing work stoppage and food shortages which led to hoarding.[6] At this point, de Gaulle mysteriously disappeared. He turned up in Baden-Baden, Germany, where, after conversations with General Jacques Massu, commander of the French military forces there, he returned to Paris to announce, on the 30th, new parliamentary elections. Later the same day, there was a demonstration along the Champs-Élysées in support of de Gaulle and order. These events took the momentum away from the student movement.[7] On 23 and 30 June, elections gave a landslide victory to the Gaullists.

Nearly thirty years after the 1968 events, their meaning is still debated.[8] Participants expressed their views at the time, and continue to offer them, aware, however, of the importance of protecting reputations. In addition, the many arguments about May 1968 are almost always abstract. Each, however, is representative of the events and ideas of those turbulent days. Goals were not always clearly articulated. Jacques Rémy had fought as a member of the *services d'ordre* for leftist groups from his arrival at the Sorbonne in 1963–64. With the *UNEF* in 1968, he took part in violent struggles against the extreme right-wing Occident group.[9] Rémy recalled that

5. Joffrin, *Mai 68*, pp. 174–5, 364.

6. Ian Dengler, unpublished notebooks (2), 28 May 1968. Dengler's notebooks include many interviews and other written sources, datable to within a month or so of the events of May–June 1968.

7. Edmond Bergheaud and Nicole Duault, 'Cette nuit, le Quartier Latin s'est senti seul face au pouvoir, aux partis, aux syndicats', *France Soir*, 31 May 1968.

8. The *Institut d'Histoire du Temps Présent* (*IHTP*) in Paris is sponsoring a research group that during the academic year 1997–98 is running a seminar, 'Les années 68: événements, cultures politiques et modes de vie', see the *IHTP* web site, ihtp-cnrs.ens-cachan.fr.

9. Jacques Rémy, personal communication, 9 November 1997. For Rémy's activities in the leftist *service d'ordre* see Hamon and Rotman, *Génération*, vol. 1, pp. 417 and 438–40. For *Occident*'s perspective, see also 'Occident pourquoi?' tract, undated, in

many participants had been politically uninvolved prior to May, that they had discovered politics only as events unfolded, and that their goals had often been unclear 'even while we militated very assiduously'.[10] Ian Dengler, who marched in the flag line of the 13 May procession of hundreds of thousands of people from the working-class districts of eastern Paris to the student Latin Quarter, kept detailed notes of the developing events. At the Sorbonne, he 'tried to talk to some history students today about reform but it is clear that they really don't understand what they are after'.[11] On the other hand, goals were sometimes clearly expressed. A *lycéen* in May 1968, Dominique Natanson saw in descending order of import-ance: (1) more liberty for the youth, (2) solidarity with Vietnam, (3) hatred of the police state, (4) the rejection of Gaullism, and (5) the struggle for a human socialism.[12]

In analysing the participants' views of 1968 eleven significant themes emerge. Addressed in the order they emerge from the interviews, they begin with the understanding of the French movement as part of a larger world phenomenon. The second theme is the quest for an egalitarian as opposed to sectarian polit-ical and hierarchical social order. Third is the movement as radical Left or *gauchiste*, 'more red than Mao', as the *Espresso* cover that featured the 13 May march proclaimed.[13] Fourth is the emphasis on socialism and the amelioration of workers' lives; fifth the arguments for cultural revolution and libertarian transformation. Sixth is the vision of May 1968 as a breakthrough in the emancipation of women, and seventh how the events are seen as a failure. The eighth and ninth themes refer directly to the students, with eight the issues of university entrance requirements and examinations and nine the role of the police and reprisals for participation in the demon-strations. The tenth theme is that of spontaneity and the long-term effects on participants, and the last that of the overall importance of May 1968 in twentieth-century France.

The first theme, the international nature of the movement, must be seen in its global context. Jacques Rémy emphasized opposition to the American war in Vietnam, engendered among children of the

Archives Nationales, Paris (cited hereafter as *AN*), 78AJ36, and François Duprat, *Les Journées de Mai 68, les dessous d'une révolution* (Paris, 1968), pp. 157–62.

10. Rémy, personal communication, 9 November 1997.

11. Dengler, unpublished notebooks (3), 9 June 1968.

12. Dominique Natanson, personal communication, 27 October 1997.

13. The *Espresso* cover was entitled 'Più Rossi di Mao', and is in Dengler, unpub-lished notebooks (1), 13 May 1968.

old colonizing power (France), and pictured as a David against Goliath struggle.[14] The legacy of the Algerian war was of intense combat between '*bolchos*' (Bolsheviks or communists) and '*fachos*' (fascists), successors of the *OAS* (Secret Army Organization), which had conducted a terror campaign in the early 1960s to keep Algeria French. In addition, the inspiration of the Resistance from World War II days, despite the anti-Gaullism of many demonstrators, played a role.[15]

To Dengler, the movement was part of the world of 1968 that included the Czech reform, revolutionary activity in Italy, and the Vietnam war. It marked the Maoist high point in the European model, which unfolded in the context of China's 'awesome Maoist Red Guard flare', the popularity of Che Guevara, and a general advance which, despite the 1968 Olympic slaughter and collapse in Mexico, extended to Nicaragua in 1979. The Maoists, among the most active groups in Paris in May 1968, were doomed as they (the *UJCml*) and the Trotskyist *JCR* (*Jeunesse Communiste Révolutionnaire*, Revolutionary Communist Youth) were overwhelmed by democratic praxis and the triumph of the bourgeois model. Maoists and Trotskyists got their general strike and discovered that it was largely without meaningful consequences. Instead they were defeated 'in the public opinion dismemberment machine'.[16]

The second major theme is the quest for an egalitarian and open, as opposed to sectarian, political and social order. Rémy emphasized the hatred of racism, anti-Semitism, and colonialism.[17] Jacques Sauvageot of *UNEF* argued that 'we can think of the present movement as a consequence of the anti-imperialist struggle. Our solidarity with struggles in the third world cannot be overemphasized.'[18] This included, for the 22 March leadership, opposition to 'Zionist imperialism'.[19] Pitched battles, possibly instigated by police provocateurs, broke out between groups of Jews and Muslims in the Paris working-class quarter of Belleville, spurred possibly by the anniversary of the June 1967 Six Day War.[20]

14. Rémy, personal communication, 9 November 1997.

15. Rémy, personal communication, 9 November 1997, also Balabeni, personal communication, 24 November 1997.

16. Dengler, interview, 15 November 1997.

17. Rémy, personal communication, 9 November 1997.

18. Jacques Sauvageot, interviewed by Hervé Bourges, in Hervé Bourges (ed.), *The French Student Revolt: The Leaders Speak*, trans. B.R. Brewster (New York, 1968), p. 28. All interviews cited in this book were done by Bourges, unless otherwise indicated.

19. 22 March movement, interviewed ibid., p. 57.

20. Dengler, unpublished notebooks (2), 3 June 1968; also 'Après les vifs incidents de Belleville', *Le Monde*, clipping, ibid., 4 June 1969.

Dean Savage, at the time an American graduate student studying sociology in Paris, recalled that the protesters inside the 'liberated zones' (the occupied university facilities) replicated the hierarchical order of the old society they had claimed to reject. It was, he said, a striking sociological lesson.[21] Of course, not all the social hierarchies of the old order were reproduced within the 'liberated zones'. The Catholic Church, for one, did not reappear in the occupied universities.[22] Moreover, there were specifically excluded groups, which included those defined as 'moderate' and 'bourgeois'. During the discussion of how to take *ORTF* (*Office de la Radiodiffusion-Télévision Français*, French Radio and Television Broadcasting Office) headquarters, a boy demanded 'that all the moderate students leave the room, you are not true revolutionaries'.[23] An anarchist periodical claimed nothing was forbidden except to be on the Right.[24] At the occupied Odéon theatre, a sign read: 'in the present circumstances, the Odéon is closed to bourgeois spectators'.[25] Anarchist groups also complained of exclusion from decision-making in the occupation of the Sorbonne.[26] Influenced by their older friends, the students generally favoured Left-wing positions against the American involvement in the Vietnam War. From the Left they also borrowed a critique of capitalism and some of France's large corporations, but they did not take stands in favour of the abolition of money or bank accounts.[27]

Alain Geismar, a leader of *SNE Sup* (*Syndicat National de l'Enseignement Supérieure*, National Union for Higher Education, representing a third of the university teaching body), opposed parliaments since they represented only the bourgeoisie and were therefore inadequate for the purpose of overturning bourgeois society.[28] Sauvageot opposed the possible accession of Mitterrand, and opposed even the existence of parliamentary debates, which, he argued, were boring.[29] The *Comités d'Action* occupying the Sorbonne opposed elections as 'a counter-revolutionary manœuvre seeking to draw the workers into the legality of their oppressors'; the slogan '*Élections – trahison*'

21. Dean Savage, interview, 3 December 1997.
22. Dengler, interview, 11 December 1997.
23. Quoted in Dengler, unpublished notebooks (1), 15 May 1968.
24. *L'Enragé*, no. 1 (1968), p. 2; in *AN*, 78AJ53.
25. 'L'Odéon occupé', press clipping in Dengler, unpublished notebooks (1), 16 May 1968.
26. *ORA* (*Organisation Révolutionnaire Anarchiste*), tract, undated; in *AN*, 78AJ53.
27. 'Anti-capitalism' was the key word of the entire movement according to Hamon and Rotman, *Génération*, vol. 2, *Les Années de poudre* (Paris, 1988), p. 668.
28. Alain Geismar, interviewed in Bourges (ed.), *French Student Revolt*, p. 39.
29. Sauvageot, interviewed ibid., p. 18.

(Elections – treason) appeared in the literature of the *JCR's Avant-garde Jeunesse.*[30] To Dengler, May 1968, with its assumption that elections could solve nothing and marching everything, seemed the last anti-democratic mass movement in European history.[31]

The third significant theme is the 1968 movement as radical Left or *gauchiste.* O. Castro of the 22 March movement declared: 'We are to the left of the *PCF.*'[32] Geismar of the *SNE Sup* asked for the installation of 'direct democracy', specifically challenging the delegation of powers to executives, deputies, and council members. What was new in 1968, he said, was that all those 'commissioned' to serve as spokespeople for the movement at any level were permanently revocable by meetings of the base at any time.[33] A tract, however, argued that students were in fact a privileged group, with the time and affluence to take stock of the state and society.[34] Referring to the students occupying Censier, a branch of the University of Paris, Dengler wrote:

> Censier treats workers exactly as the Trotskyists, only with less ideological palabre[sic: palaver] . . . like miraculous baby puppies that need milk and lots of love (which the evil *CGT* never gives). How often I have seen workers leave because no one cared to talk to them. The workers who are accepted are those who come from the *Comité d'Action,* but that is a very specific group, already open or imbued with parallel ideas. The worker who just drifts in for a look is treated with all the intellectual disdain and scientific detachment a technician would have for his children: surprise to find that they have anything to say to him, after he has arranged things so well for them.[35]

Nadja Tesich, a writer whose opposition to the American war in Vietnam brought her to Paris, recalled later that 1968 was 'almost a bourgeois revolution' but was really more an uprising of kids of the wealthy classes who went out and wrecked their parents' cars.[36]

The fourth issue of import was that of worker power and socialism, which many groups proclaimed. Cohn-Bendit and Jacques

30. Coordination des Comités d'Action, 'Élections, cadeau empoisonné', tract, in Dengler, unpublished notebooks (3), 9 June 1968; and 'Élections – trahison', supplement to the *Avant-garde Jeunesse,* 24 June 1968 and 'Mobilisation', tract, Censier, 25 June 1968; both in Dengler, unpublished notebooks, appendix.

31. Dengler, interview, 15 November 1997.

32. O. Castro, in 'Round Table on Radio Luxembourg', 17 May 1968, in Bourges (ed.), *French Student Revolt,* p. 70.

33. Geismar, interviewed ibid., p. 37.

34. 'Amnistie des yeux crevés, nous sommes en marche', tract, Censier, in Dengler, unpublished notebooks (1), 16 May 1968.

35. Dengler, unpublished notebooks (3), 13 June 1968.

36. Nadja Tesich, interview, 3 December 1997.

Duteuil, another leader of the 22 March movement, saw workers' control as the first step in the creation of a classless society. 'Workers' control', they argued, 'must be installed to destroy capitalism.'[37] Geismar wished to 'scrap the boss and the wage earner', along with the notion of profit. This was to be replaced with what he called 'workers' control', and decentralization.[38] Students protested against the maintenance of elites and demanded an increase in the percentage of working-class students in the universities.[39]

The Trotskyist *JCR* wanted large businesses nationalized and run by workers' committees and a workers' government to replace de Gaulle's.[40] The Maoist *UJCml* called for revolution against unemployment, low wages, the 'revisionist' leadership of the *PCF*, and the 'bureaucratic' leadership of the *CGT*. Workers, according to the *UJCml*, should be satisfied with nothing less than a dictatorship over the 'exploiters'.[41] Communist and *CGT* supporters, in contrast, argued that the barricades were unproductive and that they alone represented the workers' true interests, that the students were running out of steam and could never bring about real amelioration for workers.[42] Some students, however, expressed concern that they were not sufficiently close to the workers. Two students at the elite *École Normale Supérieure* recognized that this distanced them from the workers but insisted that they had rejected all bourgeois values. Given a choice – as they saw it – either to become hippies or make revolution, they had opted for the latter. Now, their task as intellectuals was to 'de-mystify' established beliefs such as the value of speaking well. It was more important, they said, to speak the language of the workers.[43]

The spirit of the coordinators of the revolutionary groups at Censier, Dengler wrote:

> is a particularly moralistic bourgeois one, even if they are quite willing to do an enormous amount of work. They are in the movement, and that is often enough. Ideological coloring is essentially that of

37. 22 March movement, interviewed in Bourges (ed.), *French Student Revolt*, p. 51.
38. Geismar, interviewed ibid., pp. 42–3.
39. Rémy, personal communication, 9 November 1997.
40. Jeunesse Communiste Révolutionnaire, 'Travailleurs, étudiants', tract, 21 May 1968.
41. UJCml, Cercles 'Servir le peuple', tract, 'Et maintenant aux usines!', 7 May 1968; in Dengler, unpublished notebooks (1), 8 May 1968.
42. Dengler, unpublished notebooks (3), 11 June 1968.
43. Jean-Claude Kerbourc'h, 'Les promenades d'un rêveur éveillé, les Normaliens: "princes du sang?" ou "éveilleurs de conscience?"', *Combat*; in Dengler, unpublished notebooks (2), 28 May 1968.

the *nous sommes en marche* (we are marching), which in the name of libertarian culturalism proclaims the cultural revolution of human decency and *anti-bureaucratie*... If the revolution succeeds, she [a specific activist] will be one of the first to help it into a new elitist phase, even if it is in spite of all her self proclaimed desires to end *bureaucratie*. She is a sympathist [*sic*], socially and economically so secure, that nothing will seriously change her position in the social order, and 'profoundly' moved by the 'injustices' of the present system. Socialism, to her as to a large number of 'revolutionaries' is essentially the legalistic harmonization of the political structure to correspond to contemporary socio-moral standards.[44]

When Dengler found the bathrooms in the Sorbonne under water (after plumbing was blocked) and floors desperately in need of cleaning, he commented that 'when the revolution comes there still is going to have to be some division of labor'.[45] The revolutionaries of 1968, he later argued, ignored economics and made errors trying to impose peace, unity, and featherbedding without more productivity in an anti-capital argument. 'I looked upon much of the left [he added] as just instituting a Perónist style social reactionary *putsch*, a Stalinist model, in the name of handout and privilege.'[46]

A socialist revolution, according to *SNE Sup*, would lay the basis for a cultural revolution, the fifth major theme.[47] Participants called for freedom of expression, including the playing of 'The Battle of Algiers' and scatological movies, and a destruction of the monopoly censorship of *ORTF* and the French state. Referring to Cohn-Bendit's January 1968 challenge regarding the 'sexual misery' of students, Rémy wanted to change a France 'governed by Tante Yvonne' (Aunt Yvonne, the wife of de Gaulle), portrayed as a repressive force governing the sexual lives of students.[48] Jacques Libert, then a second-year mathematics student at the Halle aux Vins section of the University of Paris, said that '*On avait besoin de liberté* [more liberty was needed] ... a little like the hippie type movements in the USA'.[49] Posters on the walls of the Sorbonne proclaimed: 'Suppress all alienation', 'De-Christianize the Sorbonne', and 'the more I make revolution, the more I want to make love'.[50] 'Imagination has taken

44. Dengler, unpublished notebooks (2), 4 June 1968.
45. Ibid., 6 June 1968.   46. Dengler, interview, 15 November 1997.
47. 'The SNE Sup explains', in Bourges (ed.), *French Student Revolt*, p. 94.
48. Rémy, personal communication, 9 November 1997.
49. Jacques Libert, personal communication, 24 October 1997.
50. 'Sorbonne: troisième nuit révolutionnaire', *Le Monde*, 17 May 1968.

power' also appeared frequently on posters.[51] During debates at the occupied Sorbonne, someone, identified as an anarchist, demanded the 'right to urinate where I like'.[52]

Among the more extreme advocates of libertarian cultural change were the Situationists – their name taken from their desire to find or create 'situations' in which 'repressive cadres will act as such'.[53] The Strasbourg-based Situationists, whose best-known spokesmen were Guy Debord and Raoul Vaneigem, denounced all pretence of privilege. They argued that proletarian revolt was to be a festival or it was nothing at all and that the rules were simple: 'to live instead of devising a lingering death, and to indulge untrammeled desire'.[54] Anticipating subsequent cultural criticism, they held that language itself needed to be made new. 'Compared to the Strasbourg absolutists,' wrote *The Times* of London, 'Monsieur Cohn-Bendit is a weather-beaten conservative.'[55]

To Dengler, the Situationists held narrowly sectarian views, expressing an anti-democratic self-indulgent sex-driven sophistry in the name of special privilege for themselves. He saw them as having an enormous appeal with their slogans and arguments which evoked 'untrammeled desire', a kind of violence that reminded him of that urged against the bourgeoisie in George Sorel's *Reflections on Violence*. The hidden message of violence in 1968, however, he saw as directed against women. Dengler remembered that women occasionally commented on this message of sex and exploitation. Where, he asked, were the women in this discussion of rights and privileges? Where were the *rentiers*, the people upon whom the tax burden usually falls, the bourgeois classes? 'They were enjoying this, so I assumed that the direction of criticism favored their point of view.'[56]

'Everyone was in a state of celebration or euphoria,' recalled Nadja Tesich. 'I went to the Sorbonne and listened to all of it. I never believed from day one that they would take power – because they were too chaotic and disorganized.'[57] The Sorbonne, wrote Dengler at the time, was

---

51. F. Gaussen and G. Herzlich, 'Naissance d'une "Université Critique" au Quartier Latin', *Le Monde*, 15 May 1968. For some of the poetry written in May 1968, see 'L'heure des poètes', *Le Monde*, 1 June 1968.
52. Jean-Claude Kerbourc'h, 'La nuit des ANARS', *Combat*; in Dengler, unpublished notebooks (1), 23 May 1968.
53. 'Les jeunes dans la société', *Analyses et Documents*, no. 322 (7 June 1968), p. 25; in Dengler, unpublished notebooks (2), 5 June 1968.
54. Situationist International, *Ten Days that Shook the University* (London, n.d.), p. 23.
55. 'Books behind the barricades', *The Times*, 21 July 1968.
56. Dengler, interview, 15 November 1997.
57. Tesich, interview, 3 December 1997.

an incredible *bordel* [shambles]: 24 hours a day, group discussions, parades, booksales, folksingers, CIA agents, rightest commando groups, northvietnamese dancing, tourists, student action groups, anarchist gas mask demonstrations, puddles of mud, thousands of leaflets, posters and graffiti, hula girls, women's rights demonstrators, african liberation committees, sunday orators, radishes, potatoes, 25,000 apples (a gift of some breton peasant cooperative, and so on . . .

One of his friends went out with a black flag and a bludgeon to be photographed by tourists, brought into the Latin Quarter in tour buses, at one franc per picture.[58] Despite the many claims both in 1968 and thereafter that freedom of expression was a major issue, Dengler recalled that free expression was often denied to those perceived as 'bourgeois', 'moderates', or 'fascist'. The insurgents wanted to see the films that the government and *ORTF* had refused to show but curtailed their own adversaries' freedom of expression. The issue, Dengler argued, was not really freedom of expression but the insurgents' wish to have the same access to information – films in this case – as did the elites who controlled the state.[59]

The sixth significant characteristic of May 1968 is the perception of a breakthrough to a new, more open society. Some participants later took the optimistic view that even if the revolution failed, it opened the way to subsequent reforms in favour of democracy, educational reform, women's equality, and ecological awareness in France. This opening was believed to have occurred because of a heightened concern for educational and social reform and the fact that many of the participants were subsequently successful in French political and cultural life.[60] To Bernard Jeanne, a geography student in Rouen, the goal of the uprising was 'to move society'. France was locked into '*bien-pensant*' (right-minded moralist orthodox) traditions regarding the places of women and youth. 'The youth were awaiting a breath of fresh air.'[61] Serge July, a veteran of the May events, later said that without his Maoist experience among the workers in 1968, he could not have created the newspaper *Libération*.[62] Annette Lévy-Willard, now a journalist with *Libération*,

58. Dengler, letter in unpublished notebooks (2), 6 June 1968. For the Breton regionalists, see Yann Fouéré, 'L'Europe aux cent drapeaux', tract, 20 June 1968; in *AN*, 78AJ56.

59. Dengler, interview, 13 June 1997.

60. See the list of participants' subsequent careers in Hamon and Rotman, *Génération*, vol. 2, pp. 652–4.

61. Bernard Jeanne, personal communication, 24 October 1997.

62. Serge July, cited in Hamon and Rotman, *Génération*, vol. 2, p. 631. For background to *Libération*, see pp. 582–6.

saw the events as a revolt against social injustice and specifically an advance for women in terms of enhanced sexual freedom, more fun, and an end to oppression.[63]

In contrast to the optimistic argument that the 1968 movement opened the door to desired social change is the seventh theme, the view that it was a failure. In their account of the 1968 revolt, Hervé Hamon and Patrick Rotman found many participants believing that the dream of social change had ended with the failure of the May revolt. Having 'abandoned the chimera of changing society from above, by decree, by the sole will of a partisan group', few 1968 veterans were especially hopeful when the Left was elected to power in 1981. The Left's shift from millenarian idealism in 1968 to more pragmatic policies during the Mitterrand years, especially after the turn away from economic nationalization in 1983, left some radicals deeply disillusioned – the dream was over.[64] Ballabeni recalled that students and especially workers had acted in an old-fashioned way, with revolutionary myths of the 1871 Commune and World War II Resistance. The results in many ways had been different from those anticipated in 1968. 'We helped in the delivery of a France more modern, more democratic . . . more neo-liberal', he argued.[65]

The eighth major issue was university entrance requirements and examinations. Geismar of *SNE Sup* opposed the 'academic mandarinate', a university structure that he argued was an integral part of 'modern capitalist society'.[66] Sauvageot wanted students to be allowed to determine the methods by which degrees would be awarded, with tests no longer based on essays but instead on group discussion, and students participating in the final decisions.[67] To Sauvageot, the creation of 'student power' meant students holding permanent veto power over their administration rather than actually running the universities.[68] An international group of English-speaking and French students occupied the British Institute in Paris and demanded the creation of a new General Assembly of students and staff to run it. Dengler described this occupation as being organized 'in typically British fashion: they only open from

63. Annette Lévy-Willard, personal communication, 9 October 1997.
64. Hamon and Rotman, *Génération*, vol. 2, pp. 627–8.
65. Ballabeni, personal communication, 24 November 1997.
66. Geismar, interviewed in Bourges (ed.), *French Student Revolt*, p. 33.
67. Sauvageot, in 'Round Table on Radio Luxembourg', 17 May 1968, ibid., pp. 67–8.
68. Sauvageot, interviewed ibid., pp. 15 and 23. See also 'The UNEF proposes', ibid., p. 85.

11 to seven in the evening, and never admit more than 25 people
"as that is all the fire regulations permit".'[69]

For Dengler, the problem of the university lay in the contrast
between ideological egalitarian demands and a necessarily selective
system:

> Ideally I suppose it would be necessary to create a selective mechan-
> ism that in itself does not reinforce class differences, but, realistic-
> ally, it is difficult to propose a successful model. Perhaps the truly
> possible solution would be the acceleration of the proletariat to bour-
> geois privileges, since it somehow seems to be the bourgeoisie that
> makes itself the new avant-garde. The Situationists present this as the
> greatest single danger, but as they themselves are the best example
> of *arrivistes* in this sense, I don't think their model is particularly
> valid. All the Trots [Trotskyists] and *UJCml* seem determined to pre-
> serve their ideological control of the 'masses' by denying their egali-
> tarian political rights. Tactically, this is perhaps the only solution (via
> Lenin) but it is not the most refreshing of intellectual utopias.[70]

Point nine was the 'free our comrades' and 'no reprisals' issue.
One of the difficulties of the French education system is that students really are a class and, accordingly, usually behave as a class,
protecting their interests. Education is not a high priority. Dengler
pointed out that no one in 1968 called for tighter standards, more
books, longer class hours, or more rigorous assessment. They were
not planning to quit being students.[71] Students were nearly unanim-
ous in condemning anyone disturbing the procedure of examinations as they did not want to lose their year of studies.[72] Allowing
the university to be a privileged political entity led to large numbers of non-students taking advantage by posing as students. This
was hard for those interested in general reform who did not want
to elevate a new student elite.[73] Cohn-Bendit argued that low-cost
university restaurants and housing should be opened to 'all young
people, whether students or not' but his argument only broadened
the category of youthful privilege.[74] The slogan '*CRS* = *SS*' also

69. 'The Institute Britannique Populaire, Paris', tracts in Dengler, unpublished
notebooks (2), 5 June 1968; also Dengler, letter in unpublished notebooks (2),
6 June 1968.

70. Dengler, unpublished notebooks (3), 9 June 1968.

71. Dengler, interview, 13 June 1997.

72. 'Près de six cents interpellations au cours des violents incidents du quartier
Latin', *Le Monde*, 5–6 May 1968; in Dengler, unpublished notebooks (1), 4 May 1968.

73. Dengler, interview, 13 June 1997.

74. Daniel Cohn-Bendit, in 'Round Table on Radio Luxembourg', 17 May 1968,
in Bourges (ed.), *French Student Revolt*, p. 80.

reflected a student concern with authority but was directed not
against the Paris police but against the *CRS* (*Compagnies Républicaines
de Sécurité*, National Security Guards) as anti-community hired mer-
cenaries.[75] The students did not reject force as such.

The tenth theme is that of spontaneity during May 1968 and the
lasting effects of the events on the participants. Cohn-Bendit claimed
a 'spontaneity' for the movement that was its strength because its
'anarchy', 'disorder', or 'uncontrollable effervescence' prevented
Gaullist authorities from co-opting it. What mattered most, he said,
was not to work out a reform of capitalist society but to launch an
experiment that would break completely with that society. Thus the
1968 movement, he argued, would be an experiment that might
not last but 'which is revealed for a moment and then vanishes. But
that is enough to prove that something could exist.'[76] Nearly thirty
years later, Rémy recalled that in 1968 there had been 'no goals, no
plans, only sensations and good feelings and a desire to see to a
conclusion what had been begun'. The memory of his activism was
'at the same time very far [removed in time] and very strong, [leav-
ing] an indelible trace for us [the participants]' which is not easy
to pass on to others.[77] Tesich used Milan Kundera's metaphor to
remember it as a time of lightness, when everyone, including old
and middle-aged people seemed young. She recalled a romantic
period when one could be a worker and a poet, when people were
more important than machines.[78]

The last theme is that 1968 was the greatest movement in twentieth-
century France. Some twenty-five years after the events, a French
historical dictionary called it the 'most important French social
movement of this century', adding that its characteristics and significance remained uncertain.[79] Observers have, indeed, frequently
seen May 1968 as a watershed, either in the minds of participants
or in real political or social change. However, de Gaulle was likely
to retire soon anyway and was likely to be succeeded by Pompidou.
Educational reforms were modest and they continue to be. As feminism and ecology were gaining ground in the United States and
elsewhere, the linkage of changes in France is better made to historical forces larger than the May 1968 movement. Cohn-Bendit,

75. 'The March 22nd Movement states its case', ibid., p. 102. For *CRS* excesses,
in opposition to the Paris police, see Gerald Suberville, 'Le désordre . . . c'est la
police', tract, 26 May 1968.
76. Cohn-Bendit, in 'Round Table on Radio Luxembourg', 17 May 1968, in Bourges
(ed.), *French Student Revolt*, pp. 78 and 81.
77. Rémy, personal communication, 9 November 1997.
78. Tesich, interview, 3 December 1997.   79. Monchablon, 'Mai 1968', p. 603.

for example, who in 1989 became Adjunct to the Mayor of Frank-furt, was elected in 1994 to the European Parliament on the German Green Party ticket.[80] The consumer society continues to provoke debate in France, as elsewhere.

The weakness of the linkage of 1968 to shifts in political and social history or even to changes in the ideas of its participants does not mean that the movement was unimportant. Those who glorify France and 1968, however, underestimate the problematic realities of workers' social conditions, access to information, and women's rights. As Dengler observed, May 1968 was part of a larger Maoist wave – even if not all the activists were Maoist – that captured much of the Left worldwide, cresting with the Chinese Red Guard movement and subsiding perhaps only with the Sandinistas after 1979. Studying the minds of the participants in France from the documents of the period and in retrospect shows that they made it into an 'event' retrospectively even as it progressed. Middle-class student participants even at the time often considered the May events as a big festival; many subsequent views appear nostalgic for a youthful exuberance when social problems seemed less intractable than thirty years later and when 'all seemed possible'. Tesich's recollection of 'a time of lightness, when everyone . . . seemed young' and Rémy's of 'only sensations and good feelings' seemed representative of many activists thirty years after. Many were conscious of having made a mark in history, of having achieved a certain immortality by their association with the 1968 events. Romanticization of the uprising and the failure to examine its real causes and consequences on a world scale, however, is probably why the French continue to repeat the debates of 1968, as they continue to discuss the same issues. In this case it appears that, in the words of George Santayana, 'those who cannot remember the past are condemned to repeat it'.

80. Vanessa Schneider, 'Daniel Cohn-Bendit, 52 ans, mascotte de Mai 68, rêve d'un retour politique en France. En écolo pour les européens de 1998', *Libération*, 8 December 1997.

CHAPTER FIVE

'A Demonstration of British Good Sense?' British Student Protest during the Vietnam War

SYLVIA ELLIS

Introduction

The British student movement during the 1960s was undoubtedly less violent, less radical and more easily controlled than those in continental Europe and the United States of America. There were no barricades, no petrol bombs, no fire hoses, no tear gas, no heavy rioting, no national university strikes or general strikes, no mass destruction of property and no shootings. Yet the protest that did occur – however muted – was part of the international phenomenon of student radicalism that reached its climax in 1968. And, as elsewhere, Vietnam played a crucial part in politicizing British youth. Even though there was no causal link between events in South-East Asia and student protest in Great Britain, as one commentator observed, the Vietnam war 'fanned the flames of student revolt'.[1]

Nationally the effects of student empowerment were felt at higher education institutions as different as Oxbridge and Enfield's College of Technology. There were sizeable sit-ins – some of them disruptive – at the universities of Hull, Essex, Leicester, Aston, Bristol, Keele, Leeds, Manchester and Birmingham and the colleges of Guildford and Hornsey. Meetings headed by controversial speakers were also routinely disrupted, most notably those of Patrick Gordon Walker, Secretary of State for Education and Science, at Manchester in 1967; Denis Healey, Secretary of Defence, at Cambridge in 1967; Patrick Wall MP at Leeds and York in 1968; Duncan Sandys MP at Bradford in 1968; and a lecture on germ warfare at Essex by an

1. George Robertson, 'The generation gap and the defence of Britain', *Contemporary Review* 240 (1983), p. 73.

eminent scientist from Porton Down in 1968. This chapter will focus, however, on events at the London School of Economics and Grosvenor Square, and the previously unstudied activities of students in the North-East of England, in order to show that, despite many universal concerns, the moderate nature of British politics had a stabilizing effect upon British student protest. The North-East has been chosen because in the 1960s it was a locality which contrasted markedly with London. It was an area particularly insular, introspective and conservative. Nevertheless, the scale and nature of North-Eastern student protest more accurately reflects the whole British picture; a picture that the more militant events in the nation's capital have long overshadowed.

Along with the Civil Rights movement, the growing opposition to the war in Vietnam was the dominant force influencing American student radicalism and particularly the New Left. Many students in the USA openly questioned their country's foreign policy, seeing it as imperialist and in clear contradiction to espoused American values of justice and democracy. Europe also experienced a wave of student revolt, characterized by a renewed anti-Americanism that was itself prompted by US action in Vietnam. Around the world the Vietnam war was crucial in 'energizing' students for a number of reasons. First, the war appeared immoral to the younger generation. Television pictures and press reports brought the nature of the war home to people in graphic detail. To radical students, it was an undeclared, secretive and barbaric war, and represented an abuse of American power. Secondly, the fact that a Third World, peasant people were managing to defend themselves against the world's leading superpower led many to believe that oppressive authority could, and should, be challenged. As Tariq Ali, a British student leader, commented on reaction after the Tet Offensive of early 1968: 'The Vietnamese were demonstrating in the most concrete fashion imaginable that it was possible to fight and win. This fact was critical in shaping the consciousness of our generation. We believed that change was not only necessary, but possible.'[2]

Thirdly, students began to connect oppression abroad to oppression at home. As Ronald Fraser, an oral historian wrote: 'From the actual involvement of American universities in the war effort to the symbolic comparison of an authoritarian university regime to US domination of a small country, the response was one of outrage, of drawing analogies between their own situation and the revolutionary

2. Tariq Ali, *Street Fighting Years: An Autobiography of the Sixties* (London, 1987), p. 169.

Vietnamese struggle.'[3] In Britain, the Radical Student Alliance outlined the complexity of this thinking in one of their official publications:

> The path from the examination-room to the paddy-fields of Vietnam may appear to be a rather long and devious trek; this is because of our neat habit of separating issues into their 'well-defined' compartments – defined of course by academics who function in the main, as the intellectual servants of the 'status quo'. . . . But the path of Student Power rejects this segmentation of our thought-processes, this narrow channelling of the mind. . . . There is a social pattern to these events which can be traced back to the social and economic organisation of societies – in other words examinations and support for the American policy in Vietnam – both emanate from a certain type of society, from the same social set-up known as monopoly capitalism in Britain today.[4]

In the United States, Vietnam had additional personal significance to students who faced the possibility of being drafted. In contrast, since British students were extremely unlikely to become directly involved in the war, Vietnam was mainly of humanitarian and symbolic importance.[5] In domestic terms, the Labour Government's diplomatic support of US involvement in Vietnam was seen by the British New Left as yet another act of betrayal by a government with few ethical principles.

Provincial Protest

Vietnam did not, however, inspire most British activism; internal university issues did. Although mobilizing later than the Students for a Democratic Society (founded in 1962) and the Free Speech Movement at Berkeley in 1964, in universities and colleges across Britain students demanded increased participation in university policy-making, especially from 1967 onwards. Students complained about and took action on their role – or lack of it – in university decision-making and management. They wanted involvement and input into the content and presentation of courses, freedom of expression, increased access to academic staff, and greater involvement in the governing bodies of their universities and colleges. They

3. Ronald Fraser, *1968: A Student Generation in Revolt* (London, 1988), p. 5.
4. T. Fawthrop, ' "Education or examination", Radical Students' Alliance 1968', in Colin Crouch, *The Student Revolt* (London, 1970), pp. 72–3.
5. Anthony O. Edmonds, 'The Vietnam War and the British student left: a study in political symbolism', *Vietnam Generation* 5 (1994).

debated the usefulness and fairness of the examination system. British students were also politicized over a whole range of local, national and international issues. However, it was the messy combination of university-based concerns with wider societal ones which character-ized much British student protest. When one examines an area like the North-East of England – geographically distant from Westminster and 'conservative' in terms of student politics – one can see this range and combination of issues prompting student action.

As elsewhere, much of the student protest was parochial in nature and the trend towards participatory democracy is apparent. For instance, in 1967, students at Durham protested against in-creases in canteen food prices. Nearly 100 students held an 'eat-in' in which they took their own food into the university's recreational centre and boycotted all university meals. Placing pickets at the entrance to the dining-room, student activists succeeded in per-suading all but ten students to boycott the meals.[6] North-Eastern students also actively protested over 'bad landlords' who charged high rents for poorly maintained dwellings and over fees, especially increases in overseas students' fees.[7] Many of these local protests combined with regional or national ones to the extent that, at the beginning of February 1967, 4,000 students from around the country lobbied Parliament in protest at increased fees for overseas students.[8] Later in the month, as part of a national day of protest on this issue in which an estimated 100,000 took part, 350 students attended a march and rally in Newcastle city centre.[9] Newcastle University students also lobbied for, and eventually succeeded in getting, mixed halls of residence (a victory student leaders hailed as 'a great step forward'), as well as paid sabbaticals for Student Union officials.[10]

Despite the predominance of local and university concerns, a number of domestic and international issues also attracted student attention. Apart from the war in Vietnam, the other main issue that provoked unease was apartheid in South Africa. Protest on this subject led to many acts of civil disobedience and even, on occa-sion, illegality. Prior to Newcastle University's rugby match in

---

6. Newcastle *Evening Chronicle*, 13 October 1967, p. 1 (hereafter *Chronicle*).
7. *Chronicle*, 7 November 1967, p. 6; 1 December 1965, p. 15; 1 February 1967, p. 1.
8. Philip G. Altbach (ed.), *The Student Revolution: A Global Analysis* (Bombay, 1970), p. 368.
9. *The Courier: The Newspaper of the Students of Newcastle*, 22 February 1967, p. 1; *Palatinate: Durham University Newspaper*, 9 March 1967, p. 1.
10. *Chronicle*, 12 October 1967, p. 13.

January 1968 against the all-white University of Pretoria and the Orange Free State team, anti-apartheid slogans three feet high were painted on stands and other buildings at Gosforth rugby ground. Although the perpetrators were not caught, students were the chief suspects due to the vehement opposition heard from left-wing students prior to the planned games.[11] When the fixtures were announced, some fifteen activist students tried, via a number of official routes, to get the matches scrapped or officially condemned. Similar action took place at Durham, Bristol and Exeter where the two South African teams also played. At St Andrews the pitch was invaded by students once the match began.[12]

Race was also a potent issue. Enoch Powell's anti-immigration speeches meant that his lecture tours of Britain's higher education institutions during 1969 and 1971 were highly controversial. Powell's visit to the North-East in 1969 provoked a confrontation that was repeated throughout the country. The lecture theatre of Rutherford College (later part of Newcastle Polytechnic) was occupied by students – largely members of the Left Wing Society and the University's Socialist society – hoping to prevent Powell from speaking. The police, perhaps hoping to avoid a clash between the gathering right-wing students and those inside the building, told those sitting-in that Powell would not speak and had left Newcastle. Once the students had left the building, it emerged that Powell was still going to speak. Scuffles between the various student groups and members of the public had to be controlled by the seventeen police assigned to the event.[13]

What is perhaps most noticeable about student activism in the North-East is the delay between events there and events in the United States and elsewhere in Great Britain. In this region student militancy lagged behind the rest of the country, with students obviously getting much of their inspiration and motivation from the perceived success of student protests elsewhere. Certainly student newspapers reveal lengthy discussions of incidents in the USA and at the London School of Economics (LSE), and the mood of student militancy around the world. This period undoubtedly saw increased radicalism in the North-East, even if at Durham that mainly meant that the Labour Club became the most popular and most active university club. What characterized much of North-Eastern student protest – and in this it was a microcosm of the wider British student

11. *Chronicle*, 6 January 1968, p. 1.   12. *Chronicle*, 9 November 1967, p. 11.
13. *Courier*, 22 January 1969, p. 1.

movement – was that the numbers involved were always relatively small, usually between 10 and 100, and that most of the protest was organized and/or supported by members of far-left student groups, including communists, socialists, Trotskyists and anarchists. Furthermore, whatever the cause behind student demonstrations and rallies, banners and charts proclaiming 'Long Live Ho Chi Minh', 'Victory to the NLF' and the like could be seen and heard.

Events at the LSE

Protest at the London School of Economics is usually cited as the first major evidence of a new student radicalism in Great Britain. The first stirrings of student unease at the LSE occurred in November 1965 and were prompted by a classic mixture of purely university matters and concerns over international events. The Rhodesian unilateral declaration of independence (UDI) in November 1965 had provoked a demonstration by LSE students to Rhodesia House. Shortly afterwards, in February 1966, David Adelstein, a 'firm believer in mass participative democracy', became president of the students' union.[14] In June of the same year it was announced that Dr Walter Adams would become the new Director at LSE. Adams, Principal of University College in Rhodesia, was criticized by many students on the left for his decision to stay in post after UDI, but given that it was the summer vacation it was not until the autumn term that student reaction to this news fully emerged. The realities of Adams's activities in Rhodesia soon became irrelevant as the issue of student participation and representation in university affairs came to the fore. The LSE authorities overreacted to student criticism of the new Director and to their demands to question him, by taking disciplinary action against Adelstein, who had written to *The Times* on the issue (in response to a letter by one of the Court of Governors, Lord Bridges). Anti-authoritarianism and freedom of expression were now high on the students' agenda. Over a thousand students signed a petition denouncing Adelstein's persecution and the union council soon voted to boycott lectures. Colin Crouch, a student activist, felt at the time that this was 'quite a radical step'. Although he later admitted that 'in retrospect it was really very little', and even though the majority of LSE students remained apathetic, this was the genesis of LSE's national reputation as the centre of British student militancy.[15]

14. Colin Crouch, *The Student Revolt* (London, 1970), pp. 33–5.   15. Ibid., p. 44.

The next major confrontation between LSE students and the university's administration came during the 1967 Lent term, when the appointment of Adams was still being debated. At the beginning of February, during a demonstration outside a lecture theatre, whose use by the students had been banned, a scuffle developed. A school porter had a heart attack and died. Again, the school authorities took action. This time the president of the students' union and the president of the graduate students' association, having been found guilty of disobeying the Director's orders not to hold a meeting on the subject of his replacement, were rusticated until the following academic year. Another boycott of lectures was organized, along with a sit-in in support of students' demands that the sentences be quashed. The LSE was duly occupied for eight days and nights.[16] Approximations of the numbers sitting-in range from the Director's estimate of 50 students to *The Times*'s estimate of 500.[17] The level of support for the lecture boycott is also difficult to ascertain as estimates range from 10 to 75 per cent.[18] According to a survey of 2,800 of LSE's full-time students carried out by one of the School's social scientists, Tessa Blackstone, 'in most cases it was not just an extremist minority, but a majority of students who wanted to be involved in the administration of the schools'.[19] When the students threatened to continue their action into the summer term, the governors backed down and suspended the sentences against the presidents. A further concession was that students were also allowed to be consulted on academic matters via a new staff/student committee.[20]

Things quietened considerably during the next year, despite minor activities related to the Conservative Society's invitation to Powell to speak at the School.[21] The next time the LSE hit the headlines was in connection with the October 1968 Grosvenor Square demonstration. After a student union debate, between 800 and 1,000 LSE students occupied the school buildings during the weekend of 25–27 October to show support for the anti-Vietnam war demonstration and to provide sanctuary and medical assistance to demonstrators, if necessary.[22] They also argued that some of the School's governors were 'accomplices' in the war, in that they sat

16. Tessa Blackstone *et al.*, *Students in Conflict: LSE in 1967* (London, 1970), pp. 1–2.
17. *The Times*, 15 March 1967, 16 March 1967, in Blackstone *et al.*, *Students in Conflict*, p. 2.
18. Ibid., pp. 2–3.
19. Tessa Blackstone, *New Society*, 4 July 1968, p. 20 (80% response rate).
20. Crouch, *Student Revolt*, p. 60.   21. Ibid., pp. 69–70.
22. *The Times*, 25 October 1968; Roger Hadley and Tessa Blackstone, 'Who occupied LSE?', *New Society*, 5 December 1968, p. 845.

on the boards of companies which supplied materials for the war.[23] Adams inflamed the situation by using his emergency powers to order the closure of the School, although he admitted this was only done 'formally' as it was in reality impossible to physically close buildings which were already occupied.

A survey of 110 of the occupants found that a majority, 68 per cent, strongly opposed US involvement in Vietnam, with another 19 per cent opposing it, and a mere 7 per cent supporting the Americans. Still, 31 per cent of the students were 'out of sympathy' with the initial cause of the occupation: the decision to take over the School for the Vietnam demonstration. In addition, 'contrary to many assumptions . . . "non-militant" or at least non-political students *were* significantly involved in the occupation'. It seems that Adams's decision to close the School was even more important as all but two of those surveyed opposed this action. Blackstone concludes that the protest was in response to the actions of the School's administration.[24] Although Vietnam was originally the mobilizing force behind the occupation, the event was inflamed by the actions of the governing authorities, which in turn escalated the crisis into a question of student oppression.

While events at LSE proved recurrent, radical and dramatic by British standards, one must remember that in many ways the School and its students were atypical. The LSE, founded in 1898 by Fabian Socialists, was unique in that it was basically a one-faculty social sciences institution, and its students were traditionally more radical in disposition.[25] It was also widely believed (with justification) that the School's authorities were particularly reactionary and prone to overreaction. The small-scale student activity in the North-East was probably more typical of the majority of universities and colleges across Britain.

Grosvenor Square

Television pictures of students attempting to 'storm' the US Embassy during the Grosvenor Square demonstrations of 1967 and 1968 are the most potent symbol of British youth protest and the country's

23. *The Times*, 26 October 1968, p. 1.
24. Hadley and Blackstone, 'Who occupied LSE?', p. 845.
25. This was confirmed by Blackstone's findings during the March 1967 sit-in (although no data from other universities were available for comparative purposes). Blackstone *et al.*, *Students in Conflict*, pp. 45–6.

anti-war movement. Yet politically aware students in Britain had participated in protests against the Vietnam war from as early as 1962, usually through the Campaign for Nuclear Disarmament and other pacifist movements. When, in February 1965, the United States began bombing North Vietnam in response to an attack on the US barracks at Pleiku, demonstrations were immediately held at a number of universities across Britain. As many as 250 students attended a protest meeting at Edinburgh and the Vietnam Committee at Oxford organized a demonstration outside the US Embassy.[26] Emulating the Harvard teach-in, the first British teach-in on Vietnam came in June 1965 at Oxford.[27] British students also engaged in a variety of alternative methods of protesting on Vietnam. For example, eggs, snowballs and red paint were thrown at American officials and student 'spy rings' were set up in universities to find links between American-sponsored research schemes and the war in Vietnam.[28] Students also engaged in research related to events in Vietnam. Two students at Newcastle University spent eighteen months compiling secondary material for a report entitled 'War – A New Perspective'. The study reported on chemical and biological warfare in Vietnam, and although the authors claimed it was not an anti-Vietnam war pamphlet, the findings condemned the American government's decision to put research and development on chemical warfare into practice.[29]

Mass demonstrations against the war were a direct product of student activism. To students from around the country – divided by physical distance, ideology and disagreements over methods – Vietnam proved to be 'common ground'.[30] The Grosvenor Square demonstrations were organized by the Vietnam Solidarity Campaign (VSC). Founded in January 1966 by the Trotskyists Tariq Ali and Pat Jordan, with the help of Bertrand Russell and the Peace Foundation, VSC proved to be the largest and most radical British anti-war group. Although not exclusively a student group, most of VSC's supporters were youthful. In their view, the oppressed side in

26. *Daily Worker*, 11 February 1965, p. 1; and Ali, *Street Fighting Years*, pp. 38–9.
27. 'The first British teach-in on Vietnam', leaflet produced by University College London Union and London School of Economics Union, Modern Records Centre, Warwick University; *The Times*, 17 June 1965, p. 8.
28. Demonstrators carrying anti-Vietnam War banners threw about 20 eggs and snowballs at American delegates (including Ambassador Philip Prezise) outside the Ministry of Finance, and red paint was thrown at a US Embassy official during a visit to Sussex University to talk about Vietnam. *Evening Chronicle*, 4 January 1968, p. 1; 26 February 1968, p. 7.
29. *Chronicle*, 7 December 1967, p. 5; *Courier*, 21 February 1968, p. 1.
30. Fraser, *1968*, p. 111.

the Vietnam conflict was the National Liberation Front and consequently their slogans and objectives were 'Victory to the NLF' and an 'End to Labour Complicity in the War' – in direct contrast to the more pacific slogans of the other major anti-war group, the communist-run British Council for Peace in Vietnam (BCPV). The BCPV criticized the VSC for slogans which made 'not a call for unity but a call for disruption'. But the VSC believed that, far from narrowing their scope by insisting people take sides, 'by adopting a decisive and clear-cut position it is much easier to mobilize effective support. By watering down one's aims, one merely becomes so diffuse that one is totally ineffective.'[31]

Whether due to its strident views on the war, or because of its organizational abilities, the VSC was able to gain the interest of students and young people across Britain, establishing local chapters at most large universities. A variety of peace groups had been demonstrating at the American Embassy in Grosvenor Square since 1965. However, their scale, and the organizers' more radical profile (including talk of violent revolution), ensured that the VSC marches attracted much more publicity. The first mass march (planned to coincide with calls from Berkeley for worldwide demonstrations) on 22 October 1967 attracted around 10,000 people and resulted in 44 arrests.[32] Interestingly, assaults on policemen were usually confined to vicious biting. The marchers reached the doors of the US Embassy before police turned them back.[33] The next march, on 17 March 1968, shortly after the Tet Offensive, had even larger numbers, with estimates ranging from between 10,000 and 25,000.[34] However, the size of the demonstration and its purpose were overshadowed by a violent confrontation between some of the marchers and the police, who failed to prevent the demonstrators reaching Grosvenor Square and the Embassy building itself. Accounts of the violence vary considerably. Tariq Ali, in a piece that revealed the interweaving of New Left politics with counterculture symbolism, argued that the violence reported in the media was exaggerated:

> Arms were linked across the square as the mounted police charged through us to try and break our formation. A hippy who tried to offer a mounted policeman a bunch of flowers was truncheoned to the ground. Marbles were thrown at the horses and a few policeman

31. 'Why solidarity?', *Vietnam Solidarity Bulletin* 1 (November 1966), in J. Askins Papers, Modern Records Centre, Warwick University.
32. Ali, *Street Fighting Years*, p. 129; *Chronicle*, 23 October, 1967, p. 1.
33. Ali, *Street Fighting Years*, p. 160.
34. *The Times*, 19 March 1968, p. 8; Ali, *Street Fighting Years*, p. 179.

[*sic*] fell to the ground, but none were surrounded and beaten up. The fighting continued for almost two hours.[35]

Clearly the violence, though protracted, remained fairly limited. VSC membership and the notoriety of its leadership grew as a result of the coverage the March demonstration received.

The final large-scale VSC protest came on Sunday, 27 October 1968. Partly due to events in France in May 1968, but also due to increased public awareness, this demonstration received a great deal of attention while still in its planning stage. The press devoted many column inches to predicting who would march, why they would march, and whether some marchers would attempt to foment violent revolution. In the event, there was a massive turnout, with perhaps as many as 100,000 taking part.[36] But, despite the fears of many within the 'fourth estate' and the secret services, the march passed off relatively peacefully, except for a few skirmishes between the police and a breakaway Maoist group who insisted, against the advice of the organizers, on entering Grosvenor Square.

The Grosvenor Square demonstrations not only provide the most visible connection between student activism and Vietnam, they also provide the clearest indication of the potency of Vietnam as a force for mobilization of the student body. Students from around the country arrived in London via rail, coach and car, including a small contingent from the North-East. Nevertheless, the majority of marchers were based locally. According to Paul Barker's survey conducted during the October 1968 demonstration, more than half the marchers were students and about 75 per cent were categorized as either students or young people.[37] Vietnam was undoubtedly the main reason for marching. Some 97 per cent of students said they were protesting against US policy in Vietnam, while 87 per cent said they were protesting against British policy on Vietnam.[38] However, many of the same students also said that they were protesting against 'the general structure of British society' and 'capitalism in general', indicating a greater degree of radicalism.

The continued heavy losses in Vietnam, the activities of the VSC and the Grosvenor Square demonstrations all sparked greater interest in the subject of Vietnam amongst students. This is evidenced

35. Ali, *Street Fighting Years*, p. 180.
36. Fraser, *1968*, p. 251. *The Times'* figures were 25,000. *The Times*, 28 October, 1968, p. 1.
37. Under 25 years of age. Survey of 270 protesters (about 1% of the total), Paul Barker, *New Society*, 31 October 1968, p. 631.
38. Ibid., p. 632.

by the number of speakers invited to universities and colleges to talk on Vietnam. Tariq Ali notes in his memoirs that he 'was deluged with invitations to speak from all over the country'.[39] A number of accounts from students themselves testify to the strength of feeling on this issue and the impact the war had on their politics. For example, David Triesman, a Maoist student activist at Essex University recalled:

> The Vietnam war was probably the decisive [event], for it jarred people into taking their socialism more seriously. For many the war produced a whole series of knock-on effects in their political consciousness which took them right to the heart of their own society and its economic character. And that produced a seed bed . . .[40]

Outside St Nicholas Cathedral, Newcastle, priests, nuns, housewives and businessmen joined students in an all-faith silent vigil for peace in Vietnam. One of the students expressed a common view on the issue: 'I think the Americans are legally and morally wrong. I don't think they have any right to be in Vietnam.'[41]

NUS

Vietnam was also a factor in the increasing disillusionment students felt toward the National Union of Students (NUS), and which ultimately contributed to student unrest. The NUS was already seen by many students to be too pedestrian and too compliant with university authorities and the government. Some universities, including Keele and Hull, went as far as disaffiliating or passing motions of no confidence in the NUS, due to the philosophy of, and voting system employed by, the executive.[42] The NUS appeared to be failing to keep up with the wave of new student demands. Vietnam further tarnished the Union's image in the eyes of student activists as it failed to take any sort of leadership role on the subject, largely because of constitutional restrictions on the discussion of political issues. Clause 3 of the Constitution stated that the Union should pursue its objectives:

> in entire independence of all political and religious groups or propaganda. Matters which are essential to the full consideration of educational issues may be included in discussion, but it shall not be the

39. Ali, *Street Fighting Years*, p. 115.   40. Fraser, *1968*, p. 110.
41. *Chronicle*, 11 November 1967, p. 3.
42. *Courier*, 1 February 1967, p. 1; *Palatinate*, 9 February 1969, p. 10.

role of the National Union of Students to provide a general political forum.[43]

The Union was also led during the mid to late sixties by rather conservative, apolitical men, Geoff Martin and Trevor Fisk. This led to the formation of alternative, more proactive organizations such as the Radical Student Alliance (RSA), a coalition of the student democratic left which was formed in 1966 by students who felt the NUS leadership had lost touch with the feelings and concerns of its membership. Later in 1968 the revolutionary left formed a similar coalition, the Revolutionary Socialist Students Federation (RSSF). Both these groups helped organize anti-Vietnam war activities.

The fact that the NUS Conference was unable to discuss, or vote, on the issue of Vietnam led to a great deal of frustration amongst delegates. Frustration turned to anger when Martin, in a statement to *The Times* prior to the October 1968 Grosvenor Square demonstration, advised the 400,000 NUS members: 'The trend to violence must be halted. Ignore the demonstration, it won't help the Vietnamese people.' Further playing on establishment fears, Martin argued:

> NUS defends the right to peaceful demonstrations. But we see student political involvement as a matter of brain, not brawn. Many groups planning violence on Sunday are conning the students and the general public into believing their main concern is Vietnam. It is not, their purpose is confrontation with the police. . . . These political hooligans, many of whom are not students, admit they want a 'weekend revolution'.[44]

Although the subsequent conference in Margate censured the leadership for 'blatant abuse of their position', the damage was already done.[45] By 1971 the Executive was forced to admit that the 'first time they were likely to debate Vietnam was when the war was over' and urged the Conference to amend the Constitution to allow potential debate on international issues. A delegate from Aston University stressed the importance of Vietnam to the student body and also reminded the leadership that the NUS was 'regarded, even now, as a reactionary Union', which was not surprising considering 'how many times . . . unions like Keele had brought motions

43. Constitution of the National Union of Students, in M.J. Thorn, 'Revolutionaries and reformers: a history of the National Union of Students (UK) 1968–1988', Warwick University 1991, M. Phil. thesis, p. 19.

44. *The Times*, 24 October 1968, p. 1.

45. NUS Conference, Margate, 22–25 November 1968, NUS Year Book 1968, p. 149.

on Vietnam which NUS Conference had not discussed. The issue had mobilized a large section of the youth movement and added emphasis to the Leftward movement inside NUS.'[46] The following year, the April 1972 Conference at Birmingham University debated the first NUS motion on Vietnam.[47] By that stage, however, the war in Vietnam was nearly over and the issue had long since lost its resonance with students.

Conclusion

In Britain, Vietnam played the same part as it did in the rest of Europe – it was the ultimate irritant to a student generation beginning to challenge authority and to question the excesses of Western capitalism. However, student protest in Great Britain was not as intense as in other countries for a number of reasons. Not least of these was the fact that Great Britain was an established participatory democracy. The majority of students and the working classes still had faith in the parliamentary system. Moreover, as David Caute has remarked: 'It all depends on the reaction of the authorities.'[48] Although Britain did experience a degree of overreaction on the part of university authorities, particularly at the LSE, and the media undoubtedly exaggerated the violence surrounding Vietnam demonstrations, in general, British authorities, particularly central government and the police, kept student protest in perspective and soon learned how to keep control and maintain the support of the majority of the student body.[49] This contrasted dramatically with more incendiary events in Italy and France where university rectors called in the police to evict students from campuses. This heavy-handedness acted as a trigger for further student support as more moderate students reacted not to the initial reason for student action but to repression by authorities.[50] In West Berlin police officers openly photographed students attending peaceful protests. While no one doubts the presence of intelligence officers and plain-clothed

46. NUS Conference, Lancaster University, 29 March–2 April 1971, NUS Year Book 1971, p. 41.

47. NUS Conference, Birmingham University, 10–14 April 1972, NUS Year Book 1972, p. 39.

48. David Caute, *Sixty-Eight: The Year of the Barricades* (London, 1988), p. 320.

49. According to Halloran *et al.*, the British media defined the 27 October demonstration as violent before, during and after the event. J.C. Halloran *et al.*, *Demonstrations and Communications: A Case Study* (Harmondsworth, 1970).

50. *New Society*, 4 April 1968, p. 487.

police at Grosvenor Square and other demonstrations, overt acts of surveillance such as this did not occur.[51] In Britain, the only overt police violence of any note was that which occurred at the Grosvenor Square demonstrations, particularly the riding of police horses into largely peaceful crowds. In general, the police avoided the use of such measures as water cannon to control the large crowds in London and responded more subtly with smaller groups of demonstrators, as Powell's visit to Newcastle illustrates.

Politicians also, with some notable exceptions, took a moderate, sensible line on student protest; even though the surge of student radicalism did prompt considerable alarm. In October 1968, prior to the Grosvenor Square demonstration, the House of Commons voted on a bill providing for the identification, imprisonment and deportation of people other than British subjects who took part in or helped to organize public demonstrations. Although the bill was defeated, the fact that 62 MPs voted for it is a testament to the nervousness of a sector of the British establishment. Also the Attorney-General, Sir Elwyn Jones, considered prosecuting the leaders of VSC under the 1936 Public Order Act which prohibited the formation of paramilitary bodies.[52] This tells us how close those in the home of social democracy came to panic. In this sense the student movement was significant. James Callaghan, the Home Secretary, was probably relieved to say after the October 1968 Grosvenor Square demonstration that the rally had passed off relatively peacefully and that it was 'a demonstration of British good sense'. According to Callaghan:

> Self-control was shown by the mass of the demonstrators. Discipline and restraint were displayed by the police, who remained completely calm even under the provocation of the disorderly charging and shoving in Grosvenor Square. I doubt if this kind of demonstration could have taken place so peacefully in any other part of the world.[53]

So, while Vietnam did 'fan the flames of student revolt', to continue the analogy, in Britain very little oil was poured onto the fire of discontent by those in authority, and the fire was ultimately contained.

Still, the British movement of the 1960s clearly mobilized more students than ever before and although, by and large, events in Great Britain lacked the drama and the passion of protest in the

51. *New Society*, 18 May 1967, p. 739.   52. *The Times*, 24 October 1968, p. 1.
53. *The Times*, 28 October 1968, p. 1.

USA and in parts of continental Europe, its importance in pricking society's conscience on such issues as Vietnam should not be underestimated. The anti-Vietnam war movement in Britain had its biggest impact – on the public and the politicians – due to the commitment and sheer weight of numbers provided by students and young people.

CHAPTER SIX

Protest and Counterculture in the 1968 Student Movement in Mexico

ERIC ZOLOV

As Mexico prepared to host the XIX Olympiad, scheduled for autumn 1968, the nation welcomed the opportunity to parade its financial and political stability before the eyes of the world. This was the first time a developing nation had been selected for the honour of hosting the Olympics, and for many observers – both domestic and foreign – it portended Mexico's entry into the First World club. By the end of the year, however, the illusion of social harmony undergirding a stable political system had been shattered. From late July to early October 1968, as final preparations for the games were underway, massive student protests rocked the nation's capital. Hoping to take advantage of world attention, the students openly called into question Mexico's authoritarian government and the conservative social values which helped sustain it. Unlike earlier student or worker protests which focused on specific causes, the 1968 student movement embodied a larger symbolic challenge to presidential, if not parental, authority. This placed the students in a contradictory position in terms of public support. On the one hand, the students succeeded in claiming a moral authority by challenging the closed political system led by the ruling Partido Revolucionario Institucional (PRI). On the other hand, by flaunting traditional patriarchal values, many protesters undermined support from the very social forces they meant to represent. Faced with the prospect of continued disturbances throughout the Olympics, the government put a decisive end to all protest when army troops orchestrated a brutal massacre of unarmed demonstrators, including innocent bystanders and children. The games opened as scheduled, but the protests and massacre transformed the political and social consciousness of future generations of youth.

In assessing the Mexican student movement, one must not isolate it from a larger global context. Not only were students conscious of revolts elsewhere in the world – from Third World liberation struggles to the Paris uprising – but the influence of those movements was also present in the images, language, clothing styles, music, and protest strategies employed by Mexican students. As a result, the Mexican movement reflected a unique fusion of protest discourses. Local concerns combined with an awareness of global trends. Around the world similar movements were challenging antiquated political and social structures, forging new styles of opposition which broke free of doctrinaire models. Of particular note was that political protest had merged with countercultural dissent: not only were political institutions under attack, but social and cultural sensibilities were also. It was, as one Mexican critic noted on the eve of the protests, a historical moment indebted to the impact of 'Che Guevara, Malcolm X, Allen Ginsberg, Fidel Castro and Mick Jagger'.[1] Still, unlike protests in the United States, the Mexican movement was no 'love-in'; in an authoritarian society, sporting long hair alone made one a target for repression. But an air of countercultural dissent nonetheless underlay the students' revolt. Called La Onda ('the wave'), this incipient countercultural movement manifested itself especially in the aftermath of the massacre when, with avenues to political dissent closed, mass countercultural protest filled the vacuum.

As Charles de Gaulle had famously discounted the possibility of student unrest in France, so too Díaz Ordaz, Mexico's President from 1964 to 1970, rejected the likelihood of protest, even as capital cities around the world felt the reverberations of the Paris uprising and the 'Prague Spring'. Mexican elites boasted of the social harmony achieved under the PRI's forty-year reign, while other Latin American countries succumbed to military dictatorship or were threatened by guerrilla insurgency. Founded upon the ashes of revolutionary upheaval, the PRI – the *Institutionalized* Revolutionary Party – provided a stable climate for investment through its monopoly of domestic politics and corporativist control over labour and the peasantry. In the official discourse of the PRI, all disputes were resolved within the rubric of the 'Revolutionary Family', a euphemism for authoritarian rule. The benefits of such stability were clear. By the mid-1960s foreign observers were hailing the so-called Mexican Miracle: 6 per cent annual growth, a stable exchange rate, and a growing middle class. Indeed, the approaching

1. Carlos Monsiváis, 'Mexico 1967', *La Cultura en México*, 17 January 1968, p. 8.

Olympics were heralded by the PRI-dominated mass media as evidence of the nation's transformation from a bandit-ridden, agrarian economy into a modern, industrialized nation. Yet economic growth was contradicted by mounting social inequalities (despite revolutionary platitudes to the contrary) and a one-party system which made a mockery of constitutional liberties. Thus, for critics of the regime, hosting the Olympics served to highlight the dictatorial nature of decision-making and the distorted economic priorities of the ruling party.

Student clashes with the feared *granaderos* (riot police) were certainly nothing new. From solidarity protests with striking dissident union workers at the end of the 1950s, to clashes over transportation rate hikes and the closing of rock'n'roll clubs in the mid-1960s, a mounting cynicism toward government authority characterized youth opinion. But in sheer size and level of organization, nothing prepared the government or society at large for the protest which erupted during the summer of 1968. The immediate circumstances marking the start of the protests were at one level unrelated, and relatively inconsequential. For this reason, there is an aura of 'spontaneity' surrounding the student movement itself, though this belies the high degree of internal organization and planning which in reality characterized the students' later actions. In late July *granaderos* responded in a brutal manner to three separate incidents in the capital: a rumble between rival university gangs, a march celebrating the Cuban Revolution, and a protest against earlier police incursion of a vocational school.[2] Perhaps at an earlier time, these events would have simply added to the litany of student conflicts. But with the example of student uprisings in Europe and the United States, the opportunity for a collective response now fell within the realm of the possible. More importantly, with the approaching Olympics student organizers recognized an opportunity to lever public opinion, if not world attention, in their favour. What they did not count on, however, were the extremes to which the regime would go to prevent disruption of the scheduled games.

Rather than intimidating, police repression tied to the above incidents catalysed an immediate response by student activists from the National University (UNAM) and the vocational Politechnical Institute, the largest university systems in the capital. This initial

2. The description which follows is based upon the chronologies in Evelyn Stevens, *Protest and Response in Mexico* (Cambridge, Mass., 1974) and Elena Poniatowska, *Massacre in Mexico*, trans. Helen Lane, (New York, 1975).

group drew up a preliminary list of demands and discussed the notion of organizing a general student strike to protest against police brutality more generally. As word of the meeting spread, students at university-affiliated high schools and vocational schools around the capital spontaneously declared their solidarity and captured several city buses (a familiar tactic of student activists), which were used to blockade streets. Police and army infantry pursued the protesters, firing tear gas and clubbing heads with rifle butts. Just after midnight on 30 July, the government responded with a disproportionate use of force: bazooka blasts forced open the baroque wooden doors of the San Ildefonso High School located in the downtown district where numerous students and teachers had been holed up. The invasion of the UNAM-affiliated high school not only violated the constitutional protection of school autonomy, but led to dozens of wounded and arrests, including of neighbourhood residents, some of whom had poured boiling water onto soldiers in an attempt to prevent them entering the school. On 1 August, the President appealed for reasoned submission in his famous 'extended hand' speech:

> Public peace and tranquility must be restored. A hand is stretched out; Mexicans will say whether that hand will find a response. I have been deeply grieved by these deplorable and shameful events. Let us not further accentuate our differences.[3]

At the same moment, however, Javier Barros Sierra, the widely respected rector of UNAM, led a march of some 80,000 students down a principal avenue of the city. Signs reading 'The outstretched hand has a pistol in it' signalled the students' cynicism toward dialogue; a coffin marked 'Dead Government' was paraded about. Within a week, a formal strike committee was formed representing over 150 public and private high schools, colleges, vocational schools, and universities throughout the capital, and in the provinces. If the strike had begun as a movement of solidarity by students fed up with arbitrary repression, with the formation of a National Strike Committee (CNH) the movement now looked to broaden its constituency around the country. Significantly, the CNH had an organizational structure which made it difficult if not impossible for a single leadership figure to emerge. A rotating committee of student representatives composed the leadership council, which itself was beholden to the decisions of a larger conference of student

3. Quoted in Stevens, *Protest and Response*, p. 203.

delegates. The purpose was twofold: it both limited the potential for *caudillo*-like personalities to emerge, while shielding the movement from disintegration once government forces began arresting student activists. This highly democratic structure was not always organizationally efficient, but its impact was profound. To the students and their public supporters, it revealed the capacity of Mexicans to shun authoritarian practices through grass-roots organizing. For this reason, the 1968 student movement became celebrated by future generations as the birthplace of Mexico's civil society.

Formalized in the CNH, the student movement actually pushed for reformist goals. Unlike student movements in the United States or France, the Mexican movement did not advocate a distinctive radical social or political agenda. In fact, the CNH made a point of distancing itself not only from leftist opposition parties (including the communists), but from other student groups, some of whom advocated a more radical approach grounded in the model of the Cuban Revolution. Rather, student demands and discourse were carefully structured in terms of respect for the revolutionary Constitution of 1917, which already contained guarantees of free speech, democratic process, and economic redistribution. Yet the sheer audacity of students in invoking these rights implied that the regime had shortchanged the population in fulfilling the goals of revolutionary upheaval set forth some fifty years earlier. As one student leader remarked:

> Our arms were the Constitution; our ideas; our peaceful, legal demonstrations; our handbills and our newspapers. Were these the arms of hard-liners? Of course they were. Here in our country anything that represents a spontaneous movement on the part of the people and of students, an independent popular organization that forthrightly criticizes the despotic regime that unfortunately rules our lives, is considered dangerously militant.[4]

Six demands formed the actual framework of the students' official petition:

1. Freedom for political prisoners
2. Elimination of Article 145 of the Penal Code
3. Abolition of the Riot Police (*granaderos*)
4. Dismissal of the Mexico City Chiefs of Police
5. Indemnization for victims of repression
6. Justice against those responsible for repression.

---

4. Poniatowska, *Massacre in Mexico*, p. 128.

Though the demands were at one level decidedly narrow in their focus, the issues they raised struck at the heart of the ruling regime's authoritarian practices. For instance, Article 145 referred to the so-called 'social dissolution' clause of the Federal Penal Code which dated to World War II efforts to fight internal subversion. Since then, however, the clause had been used as a quasi-legal basis for government repression. Article 145 provided harsh penalties against those who 'in word, writing, or by whatever other means propagate ideas, programs, or conduct that tend to produce rebellion, sedition, riots, disorders, and the obstruction of the functioning of legal institutions'.[5] Taken together, these demands amounted to an implicit critique of a political and judicial system which, monopolized by the PRI, negated the possibility of democratic representation and legal oversight. Yet nowhere did the students call for the resignation of the President, much less cancellation of the Olympics.

What the students did insist upon, however, was that all political negotiation on these demands be made 'public', that is, within full view of the mass media. At one level this was a tactical decision meant to avoid the mistakes of other groups in the past which, in settling for closed-door negotiations, had discovered the government's agility at dividing and conquering. But if the demand was tactical in that it aimed at avoiding cooptation, it also had strategic implications. For, by settling on nothing less than a public dialogue with the President, the students meant to underscore the utter absence of legislative recourse, despite the formal trappings of a competitive party system. Furthermore, such implicit attacks on the centralization of power called into question the moral authority not only of the ruling party but of the President himself, a position which directly violated the 'unwritten rules' of protest politics in post-revolutionary Mexico. As a recent work on the subject argues, what gave the student movement its historical significance was the protesters' irreverence for a political system which negated the existence of a civil polity.[6] In their directness and simplicity, they thus challenged the very legitimacy of the PRI to govern justly and democratically.

5. Cited in Marco Bellingeri, 'La imposibilidad del odio: la guerrilla y el movimiento estudiantil en México, 1960–1974', in Ilán Semo (ed.), *La Transición Interrumpida: México, 1968–1988* (Mexico City, 1993), p. 53. Article 145 was not abolished until 1970.

6. César Gilabert, *El Hábito de la Utopía: análisis del imaginario sociopolítico en el movimiento estudiantil de México, 1968* (Mexico City, 1993), pp. 153–219; Soledad Loaeza, 'México 1968: los orígenes de la transición', in Semo (ed.), *La Transición*, pp. 15–47.

The student movement had no 'be-ins' or 'love-ins', no massive rock concerts which blended psychedelic music and drugs with political discourse. Though growing numbers of urban middle-class youth took a passionate interest in foreign rock bands and the countercultural styles being introduced from abroad, as well as a renewed interest in Latin American folk-protest song, Mexican students were not yet looking to 'drop out' from the system so much as stand up to it. In actuality, the tone of the movement resembled a cross between the early civil rights marches in the United States and the more contemporaneous marches in Paris, Prague, Berkeley and elsewhere, where solemnity mixed with festivity and a shared protest culture was evident. Men marching in short hair and suits were accompanied by those in long hair and jeans; women in dresses accompanied those in trousers and mini-skirts. In part, this diversity reflected generational differences and thus was a measure of the students' growing base of support. But it also reflected the eclectic cultural sensibilities of the student population itself, influenced on one hand by seasoned student organizing and, on the other, by a mounting countercultural attitude and style (La Onda) which had begun to transform Mexico's middle-class population.

The origins of La Onda date back to the mid to late 1950s with the introduction of rock'n'roll along with such screen icons as James Dean, Marlon Brando, and Elvis Presley. Alarmed by rising delinquency, the media adopted the phrase *rebeldismo sin causa* ('rebellion without a cause') as a way of underscoring the purported links between imported mass culture and the new insolence of youth. But despite initial public outcry, by the mid-1960s a culture industry composed of local as well as transnational forces was actively marketing the rock revolution to a generation of Mexican middle-class teenagers. Grounded in a fusion of local and foreign rock styles, La Onda (as the movement was being called by 1967) offered middle-class youth, especially, a means to feel a part of a global countercultural phenomenon. Indeed, La Onda had already generated conflicts within the family over changing youth sensibilities: skirmishes over hair length, language, dress, and choice of music reflected the shifting parameters of parental authority. But it was in the context of political protest that the fashion of rebellion acquired a more menacing valence for the public at large. Gestures of defiance once associated with teenage mass media trends were now explicitly linked with a broader assault on authority itself. The student movement, therefore, not only raised confrontations in the streets, it entrenched brewing conflicts in the home, as many students were forced to choose between obeying their conscience or the directives of their parents.

This was especially true for women.[7] Female participants in the student movement found themselves confronted not only by the obstacle of overcoming the privileged male terrain of political organizing, but by the much stricter parental demands limiting their involvement. If La Onda had begun to open up a new realm of personal freedom for women, experienced in the shortening of skirts and the wearing of trousers, the student movement radicalized that experience by placing women on an equal footing with men. While more traditional divisions of labour occurred – for instance, women were generally responsible for organizing meals for re-turning student brigades – women also found themselves on the frontlines of protest, having their voices heard and sharing the dangers of repression with their male cohorts. For these women, participating in the movement was nothing short of a totally transformative experience, which instilled self-respect and led to the questioning of traditional gendered values. The notion that women were to be 'protected' by men was cast aside, not only by the realities of social protest, but by the ideology of a democratic movement as well:

> We fought shoulder to shoulder [with the men] and we couldn't see any difference between what were our roles and battles and what were theirs' ... In this period we were all androgynous. We were brave fighters, the same as any man ... We didn't see any difference in what we needed as women and what men needed ...[8]

If women were successful at carving out a respected role as parti-cipants and even leaders in the movement, the conflicts at home were often more traumatic. Numerous parents could not come to terms with the fact that their daughters were involved in public protest; that they returned home after dark and even spent the night in strangers' homes; that they had found a voice which would not be readily silenced. Thus, in certain cases, women found them-selves thrown out of the house by parents who 'refused to permit their homes to be considered "like a hotel"'.[9]

The organizational strategy of the movement took on various forms, which reflected both the centrality of student energies and

7. The following discussion is based on Deborah Cohen and Lessie Jo Frazier, '"No Sólo Cocinábamos..." Historia Inédita de la Otra Mitad del '68', in Semo (ed.), *La Transición*, pp. 75–105.

8. Ibid., p. 103.   9. Ibid., p. 99.

the need to overcome the preponderance of government propaganda disseminated by the mass media. For one, student activists worked hard to cast the movement as fundamentally democratic in its goals, in order to counter government claims of 'subversive elements' underwriting the unrest. As institutional channels for reform – elective office, state bureaucracies, large sectors of the press – were monopolized by the direct influence of the ruling party, protest politics necessarily shifted onto the terrain of the everyday and a battle for the hearts and minds of the citizenry. This was done, for instance, by forming numerous 'people-to-people brigades' which took their message directly to the bureaucrats, workers, housewives and others they met on the streets, in marketplaces, at the entrances to factories, on public transportation, wherever they might be heard. Through these brigades, the students handed out leaflets listing their demands while appealing to a language of constitutionality. They also collected donations; these helped to fund the cause and counter accusations of foreign support. With the participation of students trained in drama, street theatre modelled on the 'happenings' staged at Berkeley also became part of the tactical repertoire. Such groups role-modelled different sectors of the population in staged street confrontations designed to draw an unsuspecting public into a debate over student protest.[10] When the government utilized a discourse of *rebeldismo* (i.e. juvenile delinquency) in an attempt to identify student actions – such as painting graffiti and commandeering buses – with wanton violence, the students defended their actions in terms which challenged this representation. This was revealed in especially dramatic fashion during the so-called Silent March on 13 September, when tens of thousands of people paraded in silence down a principal avenue of the capital, many with adhesive tape over their mouths. As one placard stated: 'To the People of Mexico: You can see that we're not vandals or rebels without a cause – the label that's constantly been pinned on us. Our silence proves it.'[11]

A second strategy employed by the students was to 'poach' on government-ritualized domains in an effort to reappropriate their meanings.[12] Such spaces included, for instance, the Angel of Independence statue and, most importantly, the Zócalo (central

10. For examples see Poniatowska, *Massacre in Mexico*, pp. 20–2 and Stevens, *Protest and Response*, p. 207.
11. Poniatowska, *Massacre in Mexico*, p. 55.
12. The term 'poach' comes from Michel de Certeau, *The Practice of Everyday Life* (Berkeley, Calif., 1988), p. 37.

plaza), 'the neurological point of monopolized ritual space'.[13] The temporal transformation of the Zócalo from a regimented parade arena reserved for ceremonial design into a festive, declamatory public meeting ground was profoundly symbolic in its implications. 'We had to take over the Zócalo; we had to deconsecrate the Zócalo – and we did, three times', explained one student protester.[14] At the same time that 'taking command of the streets' aimed to disrupt the parameters of meaning assigned to public places, students also directly reappropriated national heroes long incorporated into the official pantheon. This gesture of reappropriation, however, did not come instinctively. Rather, the revolutionary heroes Emiliano Zapata and 'Pancho' Villa were initially discarded in favor of Che Guevara and Mao Zedong, who served as symbols of revolutionary utopianism around the world. As one participant commented:

> I never thought of Zapata as a student symbol, an emblem. Zapata has become part of the bourgeois ideology; the PRI has appropriated him. Maybe that's why we chose Che as our symbol at demonstrations from the very first. Che was our link with student movements all over the world! We never thought of Pancho Villa either. His name never even crossed our minds![15]

This tactic changed, however, when the official press used such references to international revolution as a pretext for slandering the movement. (A red and black 'strike flag' was controversially raised in place of the Mexican flag in the Zócalo after one demonstration.) Student leaders now pushed for a purging of such symbols and urged the adoption of Mexican symbols and heroes in their place. New orders from the strike committee implored:

> Let's have no more vituperative slogans, no more insults, no more violence. Don't carry red flags. Don't carry placards of Che or Mao! From now on we're going to carry placards with the portraits of Hidalgo, Morelos, Zapata, to shut them up. They're our Heroes. *Viva Zapata! Viva!*[16]

This decision was broadly significant, for it reflected a direct challenge to the PRI's monopoly of the symbolism of Mexico's revolutionary heritage. By parading images of Villa, Zapata, Juárez, and others the students implicitly questioned the government's right to speak in their name, while suggesting that the students themselves had the right to do so.

---

13. Gilabert, *El Hábito*, p. 204. 14. Poniatowska, *Massacre in Mexico*, p. 33.
15. Ibid., p. 32. 16. Ibid., p. 41. See also Gilabert, *El Hábito*, pp. 217–19.

Finally, student strategy involved confronting the legitimacy of the PRI's efforts to contain dissent within a discourse of the 'Revolutionary Family'. Students directly mocked the President's moral authority – as the patriarchal 'father' of the nation – to speak for all Mexicans. Such irreverence took on various forms, including the rewriting of revolutionary *corridos* (popular revolutionary songs), lithographic art, and the liberal use of graffiti, which often incorporated language and slogans drawn from other student movements worldwide.[17] In fact, many students openly expressed their feelings of solidarity with other movements. 'We are conscious of our historical vision: to transform reality, to transform society', a CNH document argued. 'And in this task we are not alone. For the first time youth from around the world are identifying with one another in this common task.'[18]

In one example of this irreverent challenge to the old order, a poster displayed a superimposition of the President's profile (whose jutting jaw and protruding upper teeth lent themselves to caricature) over that of a gorilla donning a riot helmet, thus suggesting the barbarity of state force. Another banner read: 'Free Tuition for Granaderos Enrolling in Literacy Classes.'[19] 'Suddenly the old rules no longer applied', recalled Evelyn Stevens. 'I saw buses speeding down the avenues, their sides painted with the slogan "Death to Díaz Ordaz".'[20] But despite the seriousness of the students' cause, or perhaps because of it, protest was often characterized by 'carnivalesque spectacle',[21] a sight common to the inversion of any hierarchical order. Observing a moment in which the police chief and a *granadero* were burned in effigy while protesters paraded around a coffin labelled 'dead government', Stevens noted that '[i]n spite of the raucousness, there was no violence; the crowd was in excellent humor, in a mood to find each incident hilariously funny, as at a circus'.[22]

The class, generational, and gender diversity of the student movement were its strongest asset. This diversity reflected the more profound impact of student strategizing, which sent upper- and middle-class activists into working-class neighbourhoods and thus,

17. See Carlos Martínez Assad, 'La voz de los muros', in Hermann Bellinghausen (ed.), *Pensar el 68* (Mexico City, 1988), pp. 73–5.
18. 'Respuesta al Apoyo de Intelectuales y Artistas Mexicanos', located in Fondo Particular, 'Movimiento Estudiantil, 1968', Expediente 3, Fichas 101–50, Centro de Estudios Sobre la Universidad, Hermeroteca-UNAM.
19. Poniatowska, *Massacre in Mexico*, p. 47.
20. Stevens, *Protest and Response*, p. 204.   21. Gilabert, *El Hábito*, p. 157.
22. Stevens, *Protest and Response*, p. 214.

in turn, forced a transformation of cultural values in an effort to forge a unified front. Under the pretence of youth solidarity, rigid class lines which traditionally separated one group from another (geographically and socially) were transcended, in turn temporarily masking the realities of economic difference while student organizing took precedence.

As the students' sense of empowerment grew, the regime feared the mounting embarrassment and disruption of public order which characterized the nation's capital. In a dramatic show of force, the army directly occupied the main UNAM campus in mid-September and several days later invaded the Instituto Politécnico Nacional as well, thus definitively violating the constitutional protection of university autonomy. Scores of students were rounded up and imprisoned; many others were forced underground. While the movement remained intact, the heightened repression was clearly taking its toll. Then on 1 October the army withdrew from the UNAM (though remaining at the Instituto Politécnico Nacional). The next day representatives of the CNH met government representatives to discuss a resolution to the conflicts, but the meeting went nowhere and, if anything, proved to be a government tactic to divide the leadership.[23] A march was planned for that afternoon (2 October) to protest against the continued occupation of the Instituto Politécnico Nacional, but word spread of army manœuvres along the planned protest route. To avoid a possible confrontation, at the last moment the march was cancelled in favour of a rally at the 'Plaza of the Three Cultures' instead. This was futile, since the army was waiting for them there too.[24]

The Plaza of the Three Cultures is located in the midst of a massive public housing project called Tlatelolco, a former market site of the Aztec empire. The plaza itself acquired its name because of the juxtaposition of pre-conquest Aztec ruins alongside a colonial-era church, set within the context of modern high-rise apartments. Tlatelolco was and continues to be home to scores of middle-class workers, housewives and children, including students. The meeting that evening drew between 5,000 and 10,000 people, many of whom were simply area residents. As the rally got under way it became increasingly obvious to the leadership that something was wrong. Unidentified people had tried to enter the balcony where the main

23. Gilberto Guevara Niebla, 'Volver al 68', *Nexos* (October 1993), p. 33.
24. According to Guevara Niebla, an infiltrator must have passed along the information that the march was cancelled in favour of a meeting, which presented an ideal situation for a massacre. Ibid., p. 34.

speakers were situated and notes were passed to the speakers that the crowd was full of undercover police posing as spectators. In fact, many members of the 'Olympic Battalion' (trained for security at the Olympics) were scattered throughout the crowd, identifying themselves to one another by holding a white glove in one hand. Suddenly a helicopter circled overhead and two flares were dropped. Within moments shouts ran out from the crowd as army troops filed into the plaza, blocking off the only routes of escape. The soldiers then began firing point blank at the crowd, randomly killing and wounding men, women, and children. The events of that evening have remained etched in the memory of all Mexicans as the Massacre of Tlatelolco.

Accounts of the massacre itself are still largely dependent on oral histories, as the official story remains shrouded in secrecy and denial. It is still unclear, for instance, who ordered in the army, though it is widely assumed that Luis Echeverría, head of Gobernación[25] (and later President from 1970 to 1976), was responsible. Meantime the government circulated the claim that student sharpshooters targeted army troops, hence provoking a response. In fact, armed provocateurs had indeed infiltrated the movement by that point and may have fired on either the army or the crowd. But there is no question as to the preponderance of force used by the military. Foreign journalists on hand for the Olympics put the number of dead at around 200, while official figures admitted to only 49 (including an army captain).[26] Hundreds more were wounded. In the hours afterward, soldiers continued their offensive by conducting apartment-by-apartment searches for those in hiding. In fact, the military cordoned off hospitals and morgues to prevent an accurate count of the dead and wounded; many others were simply 'disappeared'. The arrested were brought first to a military base and then transferred to the Lecumberri prison, filling its cells far beyond capacity.[27] Those not captured went further underground or into exile.

By the time of the massacre at Tlatelolco, the students had generated a considerable base of support for their struggle, reaching into broad sectors of the middle and working classes in the capital.

25. *Gobernación* is usually translated as Minister/Secretary of the Interior. This is a broad remit which encompasses questions of internal security and is a cabinet level position.
26. Cited in Stevens, *Protest and Response*, p. 237. Stevens uses the *New York Times* estimate, which was probably somewhat conservative in its own right.
27. Today the Lecumberri serves as the National Government Archive (Archivo General de la Nación).

For these supporters, the students acted as the moral conscience of the nation, risking confrontation in pursuit of social justice and democracy. But in their efforts to forge a common front with unions and the peasantry the students also discovered the depth of corporativist control and the impact of official propaganda used against them. In fact, while many Mexicans supported the students, many others viewed their actions with alarm and no doubt agreed with newspaper and television reports of agitators, communists, and especially wanton youth. That is, for a broad segment of the population the empowerment of youth had come at the expense of adults' own sense of disempowerment and humiliation. 'This is about a challenge of adults' capacity for comprehension, a defiance of their imagination and of their experience at governing', one editorialist wrote on the eve of the massacre in an article appropriately titled: 'Youth Power: The Parricides'.[28] For many parents, the students' brazen assault on public authority mirrored challenges to patriarchal control in the home. One public employee's comment that 'It's the mini-skirt that's to blame'[29] summed up the attitude of many adults.

One day after the massacre the PRI-controlled Congress voted on a resolution approving the use of force to quell the student movement. Outside the Congress over 500 mothers protested against the army's continued occupation of the plaza at Tlatelolco. Communists and other foreign 'agitators' were readily ascribed blame for the 'disturbances'. The state, writes one author in a recent study, 'made sure there were no victims, only culprits'.[30] Two weeks later, the Olympic games opened with a conservative and compliant press praising Mexico's modernization. As more arrests ensured the effective dissolution of the student movement, it became clear that the government would permit no further organizing against its authority. With no hope of continuing, on 4 December the CNH officially disbanded. But tanks and guns could not easily erase the memory of what had transpired, nor contain the spirit of free speech, democratic values, or the countercultural element of La Onda which the student movement had embodied. The regime succeeded in recapturing the *places* where its institutions and public figures had been mocked and challenged, but it could not as easily contain the continued symbolic resistance to its authority. For, in the words of one Mexican critic, the students had influenced 'the consciousness

---

28. 'El Poder Juvenil-II: Las Parricidas', *El Heraldo Cultural* , 15 September 1968, pp. 8–9.
29. Poniatowska, *Massacre in Mexico*, p. 82.   30. Gilabert, *El Hábito*, p. 161.

of a generation and [signalled] the beginnings of the demystifica-
tion of the country'.[31]

The immediate legacy of the repression was an explosion of
countercultural protest. No longer permitted to demonstrate in the
streets, many youths 'dropped out' in silent protest. As one critic
wrote, a 'hippismo of the left' characterized many youths who had
once been a part of a movement now disintegrated.[32] The development of La Onda as a vehicle for social protest had numerous
apparent contradictions which made it a ready target for leftist
intellectuals as well as conservative forces. Its fashion styles and
musical tastes seemed heavily influenced by foreign models, made
all the more evident when native rock bands began recording their
own music in English. (A massive, two-day rock festival in 1971
reflected the culmination of these rock efforts.) But, lost on critics
at the time – and even down to the present – was the fact that
La Onda offered new symbolic language and gestures for youths
which enabled them to reimagine their identities as Mexicans.
This opened up a critical space for defiance and the flowering of
democratic discourse. Recognizing the threat which La Onda posed
to its legitimacy, the state sought to repress and coopt the movement
during the 1970s, while simultaneously reversing its conservative
economic policies in a burst of populist activism.[33]

Today, the twin legacies of 1968 are the memory of a civil society
which found its voice and a countercultural discourse which continues to resonate among Mexican youth from all social classes.
Together, these legacies have worked toward the forging of a democratic politics in Mexico, one which seeks to build links across socio-
economic divides and remain nationalist in the face of efforts by
the ruling party to coopt, repress, and discredit opposition political
and cultural expression.[34]

31. Carlos Monsiváis, 'Ya nunca nada volverá a ser como antes', *Zona Rosa* (September 1968), pp. 16–17.
32. Javier Molina, 'Los Años Perdidos', in Bellinghausen, *Pensar el 68*, p. 228.
33. This was carried out under the presidency of Luis Echeverría (1970–76), the
very person directly linked in the public's eye with the massacre of 1968.
34. For further reading on the events of 1968 and La Onda, see Roger Hansen,
The Politics of Mexican Development (Baltimore, 1974); Yoram Shapira, 'The impact of
the 1968 student protest on Echeverría's reformism', *Journal of Interamerican Studies
and World Affairs* 19 (1977); and Eric Zolov, *Refried Elvis: The Rise of the Mexican
Counterculture* (Berkeley, Calif., in press).

CHAPTER SEVEN

'Left, Left, Left!': The Vietnam Day Committee, 1965–66

GERARD J. DEGROOT

On 21 May 1965 over ten thousand people gathered on the Berkeley campus of the University of California for Vietnam Day, a twenty-four-hour carnival of anti-war protest. This brilliantly provocative event, organized by the Vietnam Day Committee (VDC), a collection of students and professors disenchanted with liberal America and frightened by the escalating South-East Asian conflict, stunned the University authorities and caused concern in Washington. In the months that followed, however, VDC activists failed to build upon the triumph of 21 May. By its first anniversary the group was a spent force, torn by factionalism and 'respected' only by the far right.[1]

The VDC nevertheless deserves attention because its failure explodes the myth of a single anti-war 'movement' – a seamless progression from the early campus protests through the middle American opposition of the late 1960s and on to the American withdrawal from Vietnam in 1973. Research instead reveals that the VDC was an outgrowth of the New Left political and cultural rebellion and, as such, factious, iconoclastic and ultimately marginalized. This prevented it from serving as a foundation for a popular movement to end the war. Just as the ideals and methods of the New Left alienated 'ordinary' Americans, so too the VDC's moral protest and civil disobedience ran counter to the emergence of a mass opposition to the war. Though the VDC enjoyed brief success within the confines of Berkeley, its effectiveness was limited by the flaws in the New Left approach to politics, namely participatory democracy.

---

1. See House Committee on Un-American Activities, 'Assistance to enemies of US in undeclared war', 89 Cong. (19, 22, 23 Aug. 1966), p. 1111 (hereafter HUAC); also Stephen Smale, 'On the steps of Moscow University', *The Mathematical Intelligencer* 6 (1984), pp. 21–2, and Elinor Langer, 'HUAC inquiry into peace movement has ramifications for academia', *Science* 95 (1966), p. 1087.

In 1964 the Free Speech Movement (FSM) fought the University over the right of students to engage in political protest on campus. The FSM was specifically concerned with civil rights, but its victory in spring 1965 was a boon to activists of all persuasions. Berkeley became a freer, but also more tense, place. University officials, no longer supremely confident in their role *in loco parentis*, feared losing control of the campus to a rebellious student body. Students, in turn, were keen to stretch the limits of their new freedoms. Meanwhile, anti-communists around the country became convinced that Berkeley was the centre of a post-McCarthy communist resurgence.[2]

The VDC bubbled out of this political ferment. The catalyst came in February 1965 when Lyndon Johnson ordered the bombing of North Vietnam. The VDC turned a vague unease over Johnson's policies among disparate individuals in the Berkeley community into a cohesive anti-war movement. The group was the brainchild of Jerry Rubin, later to gain notoriety at the 1968 Democratic Party convention and the Chicago Eight trial. The self-confessed P.T. Barnum of student revolution arrived in Berkeley in January 1964, ostensibly to study, but soon abandoned his books for full-time activism.[3] Rubin first realized his considerable potential as an activist impresario in the VDC. His opportunity came in part because of a leadership vacuum amongst Berkeley radicals, since FSM activists arrested in early December 1964 were still awaiting trial and assuming a low profile.

Rubin approached mathematics professor Stephen Smale in late April with the idea of a massive Vietnam 'teach-in'. The enthusiasm, creativity and 'do it' philosophy of Rubin immediately impressed Smale. The latter, a 'red diaper baby' and veteran of the Young Progressives, the Labour Youth League and the Communist Party, came to Berkeley in 1964, aged 34, a mathematician of international repute. When the USA began to bomb North Vietnam, he was outraged. Determined to protest, and inspired by the FSM, he organized a small anti-war march to coincide with the first teach-in at the University of Michigan in March 1965.[4]

A cadre of activists quickly congregated around Smale and Rubin. The former became the group's organizer, the latter its inspiration. 'We didn't spend much time on analysis and theory,' Smale recalled;

2. See the HUAC investigation and California Legislature, 13th Report of the Senate Fact-Finding Committee on Un-American Activities, 1965.
3. Jerry Rubin, *Do It!* (New York, 1970), preface.
4. Stephen Smale, 'Some autobiographical notes' (unpublished, 1990), pp. 4–17; Smale, interview with the author, 6 Sept. 1991.

'our mode was one of continually doing things, all kinds of things, which would make Vietnam Day into a bigger and sharper anti-war protest . . . It was more like an exciting creative challenge . . . to make Johnson cringe.'[5] Having grown up on television, VDC activists were keenly aware of the power of media and the need to manipulate visual images. Rubin wanted Berkeley to be 'a media symbol for the country'. He later confessed that 'If someone had been making a Hollywood movie, he would not have been able to script the drama of the antiwar movement so theatrically'.[6]

The activists met in Rubin's tiny apartment on Telegraph Avenue, where 'the first decision was to keep the icebox full of beer at all times'.[7] Members competed in proposing 'the biggest, most provocative names' to invite. Ambition knew no bounds. Bertrand Russell, Fidel Castro, Norman Mailer and Jean-Paul Sartre were all mentioned. The mere suggestion of a name – any name – would prompt someone to reach for the telephone. 'Sometimes it worked and the invitations were accepted.'[8] Rubin's strategy was to present the University with a *fait accompli*; he and Smale did not ask permission to stage the event, they instead announced that on 21 May around 50,000 people would attend. How, they enquired, would the University accommodate them?[9] This cockiness is evident in an 11 May letter to the Acting Chancellor, Martin Meyerson:

> we are confident that you will . . . make full use of university facilities available . . . Of course, we require that all the usual regulations regarding limitations on the distribution of literature, fund-raising, speaker's approval, and other political activity be suspended for this period. It is essential that a free atmosphere prevails.[10]

As Smale recalled, 'Luckily, the spectre of the FSM was still haunting the University Administration. A year earlier a Vietnam Day would have been impossible. Now we were not willing to compromise.'[11]

Neil Smelser, special assistant to the Chancellor and a distinguished professor of sociology, advised that the group be given the Sproul Hall steps – the standard venue for medium-sized demonstrations. 'It would be a nice gesture and would not interfere

5. 'Autobiographical notes', p. 18.
6. Jerry Rubin, *Growing (Up) at Thirty-Seven* (New York, 1976), p. 77.
7. *Do It!*, p. 37.   8. 'Autobiographical notes', p. 18.   9. Smale interview.
10. Smale and Rubin to Martin Meyerson, 11 May 1965, Berkeley Chancellor's Files, CU-149, Bancroft Library, University of California, Berkeley (hereafter BCF).
11. 'Autobiographical notes', p. 20.

with classes or business.'[12] Two days later it dawned on Smelser that Vietnam Day was no ordinary protest. After meeting Smale, he agreed to the removal of the fence between the Student Union Plaza and the baseball field (now the site of Zellerbach Hall) and to the construction of an elevated podium. Smale wanted the University to foot the bill for these projects, but Smelser demurred. 'It would not surprise me if there should develop some conflict between the Vietnam people and us', he warned Meyerson.[13]

Morris Hirsch, Smale's friend and maths department colleague, confessed that objectivity was never a prime concern. The VDC had in mind a 'community protest meeting' in the tradition of the American Revolution.[14] This unashamed bias was reason enough for William Bundy, Assistant to the President on Asian Affairs, to turn down an invitation. Bundy's refusal was in keeping with the policy set when the Johnson administration decided not to attend the Michigan teach-in. By ignoring these events, Johnson sought to deprive them of credibility.[15]

Vietnam Day began at noon on 21 May and ended thirty-six hours later. In addition to Mailer, prominent speakers included the controversial paediatrician Benjamin Spock, the leftist journalist I.F. Stone, the comedian Dick Gregory, Yale history professor Staughton Lynd, and Norman Thomas, perennial socialist candidate for President. Bertrand Russell sent a recorded message. It was not all heavy dialectic; the organizers – especially Rubin – wanted a carnival atmosphere, and they achieved just that. Comedians, folksingers and mime artists provided light but relevant relief. The largest crowds came to see The Committee, a San Francisco satirical group, and the folk-singer Phil Ochs. An empty chair on the podium served as a reminder of the absent State Department representative. The big 'names' drew crowds in excess of twelve thousand, with perhaps thirty thousand attending in all.

The list of speakers reflected the umbrella nature of the VDC. Each of the committee's component ideologies had its proportionate representation. The soft left had Alaska Senator Ernest Gruening, the socialists Thomas, and the radical left Isaac Deutscher, biographer of Trotsky. Civil rights activists were represented by Robert Parris of the Student Non-Violent Coordinating Committee,

12. Smelser to Meyerson, 12 May 1965, BCF.
13. Smelser to Meyerson, 18 May 1965, BCF.
14. Morris Hirsch, interview with the author, 6 Sept. 1991.
15. See Sandy Vogelgesang, *The Long Dark Night of the Soul: The American Intellectual Left and the Vietnam War* (New York, 1974), pp. 75–8.

while those from the FSM heard their hero Mario Savio.[16] Given the wide range of political positions, the content of the speeches varied enormously. For instance, Gruening's support for a negotiated peace contrasted sharply with M.S. Arnoni's call for a volunteer force to fight on the side of the North Vietnamese. But differences of opinion did not worry the event's organizers; they had always intended to draw supporters together around a single issue, not a single solution.

Vietnam Day was a major propaganda coup. There were no arrests and the temper was consistently jolly. The *San Francisco Chronicle* – no friend of the left – praised the 'pleasant Chautauqua-like atmosphere'.[17] The event's success can be measured by the panicked ramblings of the right-wing press. The *San Francisco Examiner, Oakland Tribune* and *Berkeley Gazette* all found it necessary to understate the size of the crowd.[18] It was, according to the *Examiner*, 'educational, all right, but in the way dripping acid educates the hand on which it falls'. The paper also felt obligated to point out that 'the ratio of bearded to non-bearded audience members (male) was about 50–50'.[19] To the political right, a beard implied subversive tendencies.

'What next?', everyone wondered. The answer came from Lynd, who, during his speech, had called for 'the creation of civil disobedience so massive and so persistent that the Tuesday Lunch Club that is running this country – Johnson, McNamara, Bundy and Rusk – will forthwith resign'.[20] In the weeks that followed Vietnam Day, the organizers tried to create a mass movement capable of acting upon Lynd's call. In one of its first newsletters, the VDC argued that civil disobedience 'is justified and necessary not only on "moral" grounds, but also on "political" grounds . . . We must say to Johnson, Inc.: "If you want to go on killing Vietnamese, you must jail Americans." '[21] The turn toward civil disobedience was motivated by two conclusions about American politics: first that 'respectable' protest would be ignored by the media, secondly that there was no room in the traditional party system for an anti-war movement since, on the left, liberal Democrats loyally supported Johnson. The VDC consciously decided to have nothing to do with liberal America. 'We didn't

16. A selection of the Vietnam Day speeches is reprinted in *We Accuse* (Berkeley, Calif., 1965).

17. *Chronicle*, 23 May 1965.

18. In their 22 May editions, the *Examiner* put the crowd at 5,000; the *Tribune* at 7,000, and the *Gazette* merely emphasized that 'Less than 300 people greeted the sunrise this morning'.

19. *Examiner*, 22, 25 May 1965.   20. 'Autobiographical notes', p. 26.

21. *Vietnam Day Committee News*, July/Aug. 1965, BCF.

mind alienating liberals,' Smale recalled. 'We didn't need them.'[22] 'They had their own groups,' Hirsch added.[23]

Over the summer of 1965, the membership of the VDC grew to approximately 400, with about two dozen real activists and ten paid staff who worked out of a shabby house at 2407 Fulton Street. An outgrowth of the New Left political culture, the VDC vigorously rejected alliances with Old Left groups like the Communist Party or the Socialist Workers. 'Our way of going about things was not their style,' recalled Hirsch.[24] Old leftists were welcomed with open arms, but only as individuals. Never bound by any single ideology, the committee assumed a pragmatic, present-oriented approach in which the emphasis was upon action, not doctrine.

Like their New Left comrades, the VDC shunned not only orthodox ideologies but also the traditional mechanics of politics. Following in the footsteps of the Students for a Democratic Society (SDS), it placed its faith in participatory democracy.[25] The charter of the SDS, *The Port Huron Statement*, called upon the individual to 'share in the social decisions determining the quality and direction of his life'. Society had to be organized to 'encourage independence in men and provide the media for their common participation'.[26] This was a utopian idea, but also a quintessentially American one in the importance assigned to the individual. It was not enough for the individual to submit to being governed by representatives of his choice, he had instead to participate actively in his own governance. A logical corollary was the belief that all authority was suspect because it quashed individual expression.

Those who believed in participatory democracy extolled the virtues of 'expressive politics' – political choices exercised by individuals in public, rather than imposed from above by anonymous powers. Individual struggle was central to this ideal; through struggle came fulfilment.[27] For instance, during the fight over the FSM, a sense of community developed among protesters as a result of the confrontation with the police and the mass arrests. This eventually became at least as important as the issue over which they were protesting, namely free speech. 'The issue is not the issue' was a popular slogan. 'The purpose of an issue was to create a confrontation in which moderates were radicalized.'[28] But one of the

22. Smale interview.   23. Hirsch interview.   24. Ibid.
25. See Todd Gitlin, *The Sixties: Years of Hope, Days of Rage* (New York, 1987), pp. 102–14, 134–5.
26. Ibid., p. 102.   27. Ibid., pp. 134–5.
28. W.J. Rorabaugh, *Berkeley at War* (Berkeley, Calif., 1989), p. 91.

paradoxes of expressive politics was that style could in theory become more important than substance. Style and substance were supposed to be interlinked, but in practice, as will be seen, they were separated. Participation often achieved nothing beyond mere spectacle.[29]

In its first organizational meeting after the 21 May rally, the VDC delineated three goals:

> The goal is a nationwide peace movement which can coordinate nationwide protest demonstrations.
>
> The goal is mobilization and organization of grassroots anxieties about the war into vigorous opposition, and to work toward participatory democracy.
>
> The goal is to spread the truth about the war – by means of speakers, newspapers, pamphlets, research projects, classes and community meetings – to offset the control of the mass media and the universities by the liberal Establishment's cold war ideology.[30]

Specific plans included door-to-door canvassing, a peace referendum, a speakers' bureau, leafleting of soldiers, an avant-garde film, a play, a book and a research project on University war contracts. All this seems impressive, but with no consistent ideology and little centralized direction, little was actually achieved. Policy was determined not by votes (which were frequent) but by participation. If enough people could be found to take part in a proposed action, it went ahead; if not, it was shelved until the next meeting, no matter how important it might have been.[31]

Participatory democracy could at times work at cross purposes to grass-roots mobilization and organization. It assumed that 'the people' knew where they wanted to go and could get there without firm leadership. Without an ideology, there was no coherent programme for change, no plan for how to convert the enthusiasm generated by a single successful media event into a broad movement. The VDC found no convenient bridge from style to substance. Instead, members were allowed to pursue idiosyncratic goals, some of which were conflicting, if not contradictory. For example, during preparations for a march in November 1965, one group of VDC members drew up plans for a non-violent parade while another equally bona fide faction distributed leaflets calling for a

29. Gitlin, *The Sixties*, p. 135.

30. 'Where is the peace movement in the Bay Area headed?', undated, reprinted in HUAC, p. 1111.

31. Sam Angeloff, 'The antiwar marches and how they happen', *Life* 59 (10 Dec. 1965), pp. 109–24.

distinctly aggressive strategy. ('Bring a picket sign on a *sturdy*, not too short, stick.')[32]

Sam Angeloff, a *Life* reporter who infiltrated the group, soon discovered that 'A VDC vote . . . is never conclusive unless it has been taken several times'.[33] Participatory democracy also meant that the VDC was prey to expert political practitioners – cynics and spies who manipulated the leaderless system. There was no way to tell the difference between a genuine enthusiast and an FBI-sponsored agent provocateur. Hirsch admitted that the biggest mistake of his fellow protesters was that 'We trusted people too much'.[34] 'It remained surprising to me,' wrote Angeloff, 'that a man could wander off the street and join any VDC decision-making body.'[35]

The VDC were not mere bungling anarchists. Many actions were wonderfully imaginative and perfectly planned. For instance, the group discovered that napalm was produced at a nearby plant and trucked to Port Chicago, on the bay. VDC volunteers followed the convoys in a suitably military-looking truck mounted with flashing lights and a boldly lettered sign which read 'DANGER, NAPALM BOMBS AHEAD'.[36] When the VDC found that the Army trained war dogs in Tilden Regional Park, in the hills above Berkeley, it posted signs in the park which read 'Beware of Army War Dogs in the Area. Don't leave any raw meat uncovered or children playing. If dog attacks, wait until handler arrives.'[37] Shortly afterwards, the Army moved to another location.

'In judging what activities to undertake,' a member explained, 'the VDC should use as one major criterion whether or not the activity will increase the number of people who are opposed to the structure and value system of American society.'[38] Toward this end, it sought, by stunts and acts of civil disobedience, 'to create controversy where there is apathy'.[39] 'It was an important policy of the Vietnam Day Committee to make no concessions to respectability, or to weaken the protest',[40] wrote Smale. Or, as Rubin explained more graphically: 'We were fucking obnoxious, and we dug every moment of it.'[41]

32. 'COME TO THE MARCH PREPARED TO DEFEND YOURSELF', undated (Nov. 1965) leaflet, produced by a faction of the VDC. BCF.
33. Angeloff, 'Antiwar marches', p. 113.   34. Hirsch interview.
35. Angeloff, 'Antiwar marches', p. 114.
36. Fred Halstead, *Out Now!* (New York, 1978), p. 85.   37. HUAC, p. 1095.
38. *Daily Californian*, 17 Nov. 1965.
39. VDC press release, 13 Sept. 1965, Social Protest Project, SPP 86/157, Bancroft Library, University of California, Berkeley (hereafter SPP).
40. 'Autobiographical notes', p. 27.   41. *Do It!*, p. 38.

There is no doubt that the VDC created controversy. But it could be argued that controversial acts were not the most effective way to encourage the apathetic to join the movement. An outrageous leaflet on how to avoid the draft advised young men to pretend to be homosexual, a bed-wetter, a 'psycho' or an addict. ('Use a common pin on your arm for a few weeks in advance. Check with your friends who "shoot" to see if the marks look good.') It also suggested that great play should be made of a criminal past: 'Most of us aren't lucky enough to have a felony record, but . . . Suspicion of burglary or robbery or murder are also nice bets.'[42] The VDC seemed unaware (or unconcerned) that such a leaflet might offend those otherwise sympathetic. This was the hazard of a strategy which placed primary emphasis upon arresting attention with shocking stunts (style), rather than upon building a mass movement (substance). Too often the VDC came across as egocentric 'psychic terrorists'.[43]

The most controversial stunt began in July 1965 when the expansion of US ground forces in Vietnam brought trainloads of draftees to the Oakland Army Terminal – via nearby Berkeley. Smale decided that the VDC should attempt to stop the trains, if necessary by blocking the tracks. 'A troop train is not merely a train, it is a symbol; an extension of the war machine', a leaflet proclaimed.[44] A 'telephone tree' was set up which made it possible to summon 1,000 activists within an hour. Spotters as far away as Nevada tracked the trains.[45]

Only on one occasion was a train briefly stopped.[46] But, given that the main goal was publicity, the tactic was successful. The protests focused attention upon the escalation of the war – not to mention upon the VDC. 'This is the way to make news, break through the press blackout,' Smale told an interviewer. 'I think that's what the train demonstrations did. Before that, very little peace activity made the newspapers around here. With the troop train demonstrations the VDC became newsworthy.'[47] He also believes they showed liberals who were anxious about the war how

---

42. 'Brief notes on the ways and means of "beating" and defeating the draft', HUAC, pp. 1133–5.

43. The phrase is Rubin's. *Do It!*, p. 38.   44. 'Stop the Troop Train!', SPP.

45. Smale interview.

46. This occurred on 12 Aug. 1965, when two women protesters suffered broken limbs after attempting to board the train. See Berkeley Police, 'Vietnam Day Committee' (report to City Council), 14 Dec. 1965, Institute of Government Studies Library, University of California, Berkeley, Calif.

47. 'Interview with Stephen Smale, Berkeley Vietnam Day Committee', *Dust* 2 (Winter 1966), p. 48.

to protest. By demonstrating that resistance was possible, 'the VDC gained a huge amount of legitimacy'.[48]

The VDC tried, usually unsuccessfully, to distribute leaflets among the unfortunate passengers of the trains. Starting with the premise that 'the entire war in Vietnam is criminal and immoral', the first leaflet cited the precedent of the Nuremberg trials: 'an individual soldier, even if acting under orders, must bear final legal and moral responsibility for what he does'.[49] This message was never likely to inspire the sympathy and support of the draftees (and their families) to whom it was directed. The insensitivity of these ivory tower existentialists stands out even more markedly in a second leaflet:

> Being young, male and able-bodied is no crime. But we may soon have to pay a heavy price for it. The men in Washington demand that we give up our freedom, our careers, and possibly our lives.
> IF WE VALUE OUR FREEDOM AND OUR LIVES, WE MUST PROTEST THIS 'PHONY WAR'.

The attempt at identification between the predominantly middle-class student protesters and the less privileged soldiers – suggested by the pronoun 'we' – seems inappropriate. If the VDC was trying to establish a fellowship between the protester and the draftee, a bit more sympathy toward the latter was surely merited. It is doubtful, for instance, that the passengers on the troop trains would have agreed wholeheartedly with the VDC that 'It may take more courage to protest than to give in'.[50] The VDC showed little sympathy for the fact that American GIs, like Vietnamese peasants, were victims of this war.

Over the summer of 1965 the VDC organized a second teach-in, scheduled for 15 October, to coincide with the 'International Days of Protest against the Vietnam War'. The VDC had to bear the burden of its own success: in order to appear thriving, it had to improve upon the 21 May extravaganza. Aware of this need, the committee decided to combine the teach-in with a march on the Oakland Army Terminal – a direct and very visual attempt to extend protest into the community.

But the VDC was no longer unobtrusive: the 'establishment' now took the group seriously – perhaps too seriously. Smale noticed how, during the troop train demonstrations, a detective followed him constantly.[51] 'Information obtained from an outside agency'

48. Smale interview.   49. 'Attention all military personnel', n.d., SPP.
50. 'Reservists and men of draft age', 12 Aug. 1965, BCF.
51. 'Interview with Stephen Smale', *Dust* 2, p. 41.

was regularly passed to the campus police who in turn passed it to Smelser.[52] The University was not only better informed, it was more determined 'to prevent, in a fairly careful way, the development of the completely unrestrained and disruptive features that character-ized the Viet Nam Day last May'.[53]

Equally determined were the various public authorities – especially Alameda County. The Deputy District Attorney, Edwin Meese, admitted that 'as the VDC meetings were open to the public, it is not unusual for . . . a young looking police officer to attend'.[54] On 1 October, District Attorney J.F. Coakley, influenced no doubt by the Watts riot of six weeks earlier, warned the Governor Edmund G. (Pat) Brown, that the march would pass through 'sensitive, explos-ive locations of potential racial conflict' and would cause a 'calam-ity'. He asked that units of the National Guard and the California Highway Patrol be made available. 'It is difficult to understand', Coakley pointedly added, 'how such a group as the VDC . . . can be per-mitted by responsible officials to use State property and facilities.'[55]

Coakley was dancing to the tune of his political master, William Knowland, owner of the *Oakland Tribune*, who had the mayor and the council in his pocket. Other prominent California Republicans – among them Ronald Reagan and Senator George Murphy – shared Knowland's determination to use the VDC controversy to embarrass Brown.[56] Aware that 'tension is building up', UC President Clark Kerr warned that 'October 15 and 16 are taking on significance as political testing grounds. The test will be how well law and order is preserved and by whom. After Berkeley and Watts, no one can fail to meet the test fully and promptly.'[57] Brown, due to stand for re-election in 1966, was extremely sensitive to the Republican onslaught. He placed pressure upon Kerr, who in turn bore down upon Roger Heyns, the newly appointed Chancellor.

At a meeting with Heyns, VDC officials promised not to engage in civil disobedience during the march. 'We don't expect to be arrested', Rubin told the *Berkeley Gazette* on 9 October.[58] But, given that the matter of whether or not to arrest marchers was largely up

52. The reference to 'an outside agency' is from a UC Police Report, 6 June 1965, sent to Smelser, BCF.
53. Smelser to Vice-Chancellor Lincoln Constance, 30 July 1965, BCF.
54. HUAC, 1095.
55. J.F. Coakley to Edmund G. Brown (copy), 1 Oct. 1965, BCF.
56. See G. DeGroot, 'Ronald Reagan and student unrest in California, 1966–1970', *Pacific Historical Review* 65 (Feb. 1996).
57. Clark Kerr to Roger Heyns, 3 Oct. 1965, BCF.
58. *Gazette*, 9 Oct. 1965; Heyns to Kerr, 8 Oct. 1965, BCF.

to the Oakland and Berkeley police, there was cold comfort in Rubin's assurance. And, since individual freedom of expression was at the heart of VDC philosophy, it was beyond Rubin's power to predict (or control) the actions of VDC members in a tense confrontation with police.

Another source of tension came from right-wing vigilantes. The Minutemen and the Hell's Angels were both determined to give the VDC a real lesson in civil disobedience. These threats of violence were a boon to Oakland city officials, already convinced that a night-time march would inevitably result in riot. They waited until the eve of the march to deny the VDC a parade permit, thus leaving insufficient time for a legal challenge.[59] Berkeley officials, in contrast, granted a permit. The marchers were thus confronted with the prospect of having to assert their civil rights on the Oakland city line.

The demonstration did not begin well. An impressive list of speakers failed to excite a community which had grown blasé about teach-ins. The crowd was hardly larger, and a good deal less boisterous, than a football rally which occurred simultaneously on the Sproul Hall steps.[60] The entire event seemed headed for disappointment when a larger than expected crowd of about 10,000 gathered for the march on Oakland. This suggests that many were attracted by the prospect of anarchic confrontation, as opposed to the more peaceful discourse of the teach-in.

The march, which stretched thirteen blocks, proceeded down Telegraph Avenue to the city line. There it encountered 650 Oakland police, 400 Highway Patrol and 250 Alameda County sheriffs – all in a nasty temper. Behind them were about 50 Hell's Angels shouting 'America for the Americans', in addition to an assortment of right-wing thugs.[61] In an attempt to outflank the police, the VDC turned right and travelled parallel to the city line. A few blocks on, march monitors ordered a halt. They were confronted with a choice laden with symbolism: to the left lay Oakland and martyrdom, to the right Berkeley and ignominy. 'LEFT, LEFT, LEFT!!!' cried the crowd.[62] For perhaps the first and most important time in its short life the VDC abandoned participatory democracy. The nine members of the executive council decided among themselves how to proceed. Smale and Rubin preferred an immediate sit-down – a

59. *Tribune*, 14 Oct. 1965.
60. *Chronicle*, 15 Oct. 1965; *Daily Californian*, 18 Oct. 1965.
61. *Chronicle*, 15, 16 Oct. 1965.
62. *Tribune*, 16 Oct. 1965; *Do It!*, pp. 40–1; Angeloff, 'Antiwar marches', p. 123.

homage to the tactics of the civil rights movement. They were in the minority. The council voted five to four to turn right.

Thus began the demise of the VDC. The movement split along the fissures evident on the Oakland city line. Many of those who had preferred caution turned to conventional politics, in particular the campaign by the journalist Robert Scheer to unseat the pro-war liberal Democrat Representative Jeffrey Cohelan. What remained of the VDC was hijacked by the extreme left. The group careered down a steep slope to futility and farce. In March 1966, Reagan and Meese made much of a VDC fund-raising dance which they claimed had degenerated into an orgy of drugs and sex.[63] During the following month, a bomb ripped apart the committee's headquarters and a paid VDC official was arrested for parole violation (he was found to have thrown a young girl from a New York roof in 1958).[64] On the first anniversary of Vietnam Day, a teach-in attracted no-name speakers and a tiny crowd. As such it was an accurate reflection of the unrepresentative nature of the extremists who now controlled the group.

The University, ever more confrontational, eventually banned the VDC on the grounds that none of its officers were students.[65] By October 1966 the group had 'shrunken to a dozen Trotskyists with half a dozen letterheads and a mimeograph machine'.[66] But the more ridiculous it became, the more attention the Republican right gave it. During his gubernatorial campaign, Reagan made much of the VDC bogey and the moral decline which it symbolized.[67] In its death throes, the VDC caused more damage to the peace movement than it ever caused, during its heyday, to Johnson's war.

The founders of the VDC long before abandoned ship. Rubin embarked upon new adventures, eventually deciding to run for mayor of Berkeley in order to poke fun at the political system.[68] Hirsch, disillusioned when hard-core politicos took over the group, quit going to meetings after the incident on the Oakland city line.[69]

---

63. See DeGroot, 'Reagan and student unrest', pp. 110–11; and ' "A goddamned electable person": the 1966 California gubernatorial campaign of Ronald Reagan', *History* 82 (July 1997).

64. The bombing occurred on 9 April 1966. Frances M. Medaille, a one-time paid official of the VDC, was arrested on a parole violation by the FBI at a demonstration on 21 April 1966. *Chronicle*, 22 April 1966.

65. J. Lennon (Dean) to Peter Camejo (VDC), 12 Aug. 1966, BCF.

66. *Examiner*, 26 Oct. 1966.

67. See *Tribune*, 22 Oct. 1965; and DeGroot, 'Reagan and student unrest' and 'A goddamned electable person'.

68. *Do It!*, pp. 43–4.   69. Hirsch interview.

Smale, who shared Hirsch's dismay at the way participatory democracy had been trampled by an authoritarian cabal, entered what he called 'a mathematical phase'.[70] Despite his disillusionment, he still insists that the VDC was the advance guard of the movement which ended the war.[71]

It is often the fate of an advance guard to be obliterated long before the main forces engage. So it went with the VDC. Within Berkeley, the group was influential in combating ignorance and apathy about United States policy in South-East Asia. But that is a very limited success. When Jean-Paul Sartre declined his invitation to the May 1965 teach-in, he provided a clue to the group's ultimate failure:

> The problem is not whether or not I would have helped such Americans more or less by going there. The fact is that I cannot help them at all. Because their political weight, unhappily, is nil. . . . These people are totally impotent. One of them wrote me: 'If you do not come to us, if you break off all communication with us, it must be that you regard us as the accursed of the earth!' I do think, in fact, that a man of the American left who has a clear view of the situation, and who sees himself isolated in a land entirely conditioned by the myths of imperialism and anticommunism, such a man, I say, and with all respect, is indeed one of the accursed of the earth. He totally disapproves of the politics carried out in his name and his action is totally ineffective.[72]

The VDC was supposed to be an antidote to radical impotence. But since the moral *angst* of Berkeley radicals was not widely felt across America, this antidote was not in great demand outside the University community. From 1965 to 1967, the vast majority of Americans, including students, supported the war and condemned the 'campus kooks'. If a nascent mass movement against the war existed in 1965, it would surely not be brought to life by anguished references to Nuremberg morality, nor by shocking media stunts. And at this stage neither the draft nor the casualty lists were sufficiently emotive to overcome the automatic tendency of Americans to rally behind the flag during times of war. Triumphant in Berkeley, the VDC became the accursed in wider America.[73]

70. *Sunday Examiner and Chronicle*, 3 Apr. 1966.   71. Smale interview.
72. Halstead, *Out Now!*, pp. 59–60.
73. See E.M. Schreiber, 'Anti-war demonstrations and American public opinion on the Vietnam war', *British Journal of Sociology* 27 (1976); H. Schuman, 'Two sources of antiwar sentiment in America', *American Journal of Sociology* 78 (1972); J.J. Gustainis and D.F. Hahn, 'While the whole world watched: rhetorical failures of anti-war

In the middle of his Vietnam Day speech, Paul Krassner, editor of *The Realist,* cautioned the crowd not to get carried away by the energy generated by the teach-in:

> Don't let your perspective be disjointed here, because when I speak at a college and then I go away, I fly, and I look out. There's a lot of *them.* You know, who really *like* Ed Sullivan. It's very frightening. I mean they aren't the extremists.[74]

The VDC were the extremists, and they revelled in their extremism. They had little interest in or hope for the Ed Sullivan watchers.[75] It might be argued that it was never their intention to break out of Berkeley – though some of their rhetoric suggests the contrary. But a mass movement confined to Berkeley is a contradiction in terms. No matter how vocal the protest in the campus community might have been, as long as it remained quarantined within Berkeley, it could be used by the right as a symbol of moral degradation and extremist excess. The VDC demonstrated that it is impossible to build a genuine mass movement by thumbing one's nose at the masses.

---

protest', *Communication Quarterly* 36 (1988). A poll of 1,200 California residents taken in Nov. 1965 revealed that 87 per cent disapproved of the anti-war demonstrations. *Chronicle,* 12 Nov. 1965.

74. *We Accuse,* p. 26.

75. The Ed Sullivan Show was the most popular variety show on American television in the 1960s.

CHAPTER EIGHT

'The Struggle Continues':
Rudi Dutschke's Long March

INGO CORNILS

Can an anti-authoritarian movement have a leader? Ask Germans over 30 who they think led the student revolt in the late 1960s, and they will answer: 'Rudi Dutschke!' Ask anyone younger and they will ask what a student revolt is. Ask his former comrades, and you will hear that the question is beside the point, that you have been manipulated to mistake the 'character mask' for the diverse social movement of which he was a part.

Rudi Dutschke, mythical figure of the West German student movement, still fires the imagination. Like no other of its young activists, he embodied that curious mixture of ideological zeal and anti-authoritarian practice, romantic idealism and fashionable jargon that has distinguished the West German contribution to the late 1960s cultural revolution. As 'chief ideologist' of the Association of Socialist Students (SDS), the most active and ideologically fertile socialist student organization in West Germany at the time, he led students out of the universities and into the streets. As the victim of an attempted assassination in April 1968, he became martyr and icon of a revolt which, despite its subsequent demise, has had a profound impact on German society to the present day.

Dutschke struggled against authoritarian structures in West Germany's antiquated university system, clashed with the sociologist Jürgen Habermas, befriended the philosophers Herbert Marcuse and Ernst Bloch, confronted a frenzied hate-campaign by the newspaper tycoon Axel Springer, organized a Congress in protest against the Vietnam War in West Berlin (a bulwark of anti-communism), and fused together the 'extra-parliamentary opposition' to the emergency laws in the days of the Grand Coalition of Conservatives and Social Democrats. Badly wounded by an assassin's bullet in his head, he recovered in Italy, was subsequently thrown out of England as a security risk, found a new home in Denmark, and finally re-entered the West German political arena in the mid-1970s as an advocate of a socialist alternative and Green politics. When he died from the long-term effects of his injuries in 1979, he remained optimistic that the people would develop an awareness of their own exploited state and, by way of a 'long march through the institutions', emancipate themselves from their oppressors.

This chapter examines Dutschke's utopian dream, his dogged pursuit of socialist ideals, his problematic role as leader of an anti-authoritarian movement and his contribution to West German politics. It reflects upon his 'message' to current generations, and on the way his present-day admirers, in order to keep his utopian vision alive, have placed him on a pedestal and effectively detached him from his movement.

Setting out

In the latter half of the 1960s, a radical form of idealism developed across Europe. Traditional political parties, it was felt, had failed to provide a vision which extended beyond post-war materialism and wealth creation. Inspired by the American civil rights movement, the revolutionaries in South America and student protesters in Berkeley, young people looked for new values and new ways of living together in solidarity. They demanded a fundamental change of the established economic and political structures, which they perceived to be corrupt and undemocratic. In West Germany this new 'consciousness' also meant dealing with the country's largely unacknowledged Nazi past. Former Nazis were still in positions of power, and the population was still adhering to authoritarian patterns of behaviour in spite of the liberal basic law which everyone in theory supported. West German consciousness was also affected by the fact that East Germany provided a constant reminder of the existence of 'real' socialism. Given the prevalent fear of communism, anyone challenging 'the system' was associated with the 'communist threat' and portrayed as the 'enemy within'.

Dutschke grew up with these contradictions. In his small home town of Luckenfelde in the German Democratic Republic, he experienced the powerlessness of workers and farmers in the 'workers' and farmers' paradise'. A promising athlete, he was barred from studying' sports journalism because of his outspoken criticism of the Stalinist system. He moved to West Berlin shortly before the wall was built, only to encounter what he saw as a similar lack of democracy in the Federal Republic.

As a student of sociology at the Free University, he eagerly devoured the theories of utopian socialists, and soon fancied himself a professional revolutionary fighting for a new and radically different alternative. He joined a small group of disenchanted Munich-based bohemians who advocated radicalizing minorities and seeking confrontation with the state in order to break down traditional mores which prevented individuals from living their own lives as they saw fit. Convinced that the capitalist system as a whole could eventually be brought down, they argued that they had first to destroy the foundations of state authority in order to 'unmask' the state as an instrument of oppression and demonstrate its vulnerability.

Dutschke believed that this process had to start in the universities. Students had the time and the resources to learn about alternatives to the hated culture of the 'establishment', and they had genuine grievances: despite their rising dissatisfaction with overcrowded universities, higher education remained unchanged in its hierarchical structure and authoritarian attitude. Dutschke worked tirelessly to become the 'voice' of student revolt, which he saw as the starting point for a general revolt.

Dutschke joined the SDS in January 1965 with his friend Bernd Rabehl, who had also left the GDR. Dutschke, Rabehl and a cadre of like-minded students attempted to turn the SDS, which lost its status as the youth wing of the Social Democrats in 1961, into a political force, at least in West Berlin. Enlightenment, they hoped, would come through provocation. The importance given to students was a radical departure from the traditional SDS position which was based on the Marxist doctrine that the working class would be the main agent of revolution. They set up study groups in the Free University to read Marx afresh, and formed debating circles. There was no shortage of issues, including the US bombing of North Vietnam, a campaign of 'liberation' supported by the Bundestag in the name of the German people. There was also the issue of the 'formed society', a proto-Thatcherite notion by the conservative Chancellor Ludwig Erhard that class divisions had been erased, and that everyone could join the gravy train. Within the Free University, opposition against 'authoritarian' administrative measures was kindled via teach-ins, resolutions formulated for co-determination and greater democracy, and, in the run-up to Christmas 1966, highly publicized 'walkabout' student demonstrations against the Vietnam war.

The life of a revolutionary meant incessant conflict: the Free University took disciplinary action against Dutschke, and he was criticized by SDS comrades over his reluctance to oust the sensationalist 'political clowns' of the Kommune 1.[1] Their slogans and tactics (like 'What do I care about Vietnam, I'm having problems achieving an orgasm') brought ridicule upon the movement. But the SDS had a more serious problem than internal wrangling: namely the difficulties of organizing students. Turning a diverse and initially apathetic group of middle-class adolescents who were mainly concerned about the countercultural 'lifestyle' revolution and job prospects (50 per cent were destined for the civil service) into a politically effective force proved a serious challenge, requiring a profound optimism on the part of activists.

In newspaper interviews and public debates Dutschke outlined the utopian society the SDS sought, which would be classless and based on principles of direct democracy. He argued that in an age of technological advances and scientific discovery, there was a historic opportunity to reduce working hours. The resultant increased leisure would enable the masses to develop their sensual imagination and a political sense of solidarity with others. People would develop a 'critical awareness' of what governments and authorities were doing in their name, and, for example, stop the arms race. If the people were freed to organize their own affairs according to their needs, they would do away with pointless expenditures, consumption and bureaucracy which stifled the construction of this Garden of Eden.[2] Dutschke also stressed the need for people to become aware of the power of the mass media as 'manipulation centres' which, in his view, colluded with the state in keeping the public from realizing that they could lead creative, self-guided lives, where work, private and public life could form a creative synergy. The blueprint was studiously vague, and intentionally so. Dutschke admitted that he had no 'concrete utopia' to offer. He felt that formulating one was the task of those individuals who had emancipated themselves from authoritarian structures, and could then engage in critical theory.

1. On 1 June 1967 two women and five men moved into a flat in West Berlin to start the project 'Kommune 1'. It was the practical manifestation of a theoretical model discussed by a subset of SDS members, including Dutschke, from 1966. In effect it was a reaction to the theory-heavy debates. The two leading members were Fritz Teufel and Dieter Kunzelmann (formerly of the Subversive Aktion, Munich). 'Kommune 1' became notorious for its unpredictable happenings, and its breaking of social taboos.

2. *Der Spiegel* 29 (1967).

Theory and practice

On 2 June 1967, the student Benno Ohnesorg was 'accidentally' shot dead by a policeman during a demonstration in West Berlin against the visit of the Shah of Iran. Instead of condemning the policeman, Mayor Heinrich Albertz and the Springer press blamed the students for what had happened. Demonstrations were banned, and the truth about the exact chain of events of that night had to be pieced together by the students themselves. In their view, the state had revealed its true colours; they felt shocked, persecuted and alone. This event was the catalyst for student revolt in West Germany and galvanized a previously diverse group, politicizing them in a way no ideology or utopian dream could have.

Dutschke was one of a few hundred students who dared to go out the next day. They organized a meeting on campus to discuss their response. 'Improvising like a jazz musician' (according to his friend Rabehl), he argued that the shooting had not been an accident, and that the time had come to challenge a system that appeared to condone political murder. He wanted a world revolution and a 'free society of free individuals'. It was then decided to march to the Schöneberg town hall. Even though the police put a quick stop to this illegal demonstration, the SDS had revealed itself as the only organization capable of dealing with an emergency and focusing the general feeling of outrage.

After the widely publicized funeral procession from West Berlin to Hanover, Ohnesorg's home town, a conference entitled 'University and Democracy' was hastily convened on 9 June, which was intended to formulate a common strategy for the students, as well as attract further media attention. The conference itself was inconclusive, but is remembered for the clash between Dutschke and the sociologist Jürgen Habermas. In a convoluted speech, Dutschke defended the SDS strategy of provocation, arguing that the material preconditions were ripe for people to take history into their own hands. He felt that by decisive action the students could alert the general public to the dangers of a press monopoly and an authoritarian state. Habermas accepted that students could be catalysts of change, but was sceptical of Dutschke's belief that the struggle for a more open society could be compared with the struggle of South American revolutionaries, and that such an identification would awaken consciousness. When Habermas tried to clarify whether Dutschke would accept violence against the state, and did not get a satisfactory answer (Dutschke had by that time left for West Berlin), he accused him of 'challenging masochistically the institutionalized power', and described his strategy as 'left-wing fascism'. Habermas later withdrew his accusation, admitting that his words had been badly chosen and subsequently misused by the Springer press, which pounced on the opportunity to blacken the students. He perhaps felt that the students were in danger of acting irrationally, getting satisfaction from mere protest.[3]

The next step on Dutschke's path to notoriety was the SDS conference in Frankfurt-on-Main on 7 September 1967. The SDS had found that thousands of students could be mobilized, but had no experience of how to organize or best employ 'the masses' now willing to join. In a clever coup designed to wrong-foot Stalinists in the organization, Dutschke allied with the rival leader of the Frankfurt section of the SDS, Hans-Jürgen Krahl. Together they formulated the keynote speech or 'Grundsatzreferat' which explored the relationship between the authoritarian state and the anti-authoritarian movement. Dutschke and Krahl observed that with the SPD joining the Conservatives in 1966 in a 'Grand Coalition' (with the full support of the unions), there was no longer hope for radical change from the largest opposition party. Opposition groups now had only the street to voice their protest, yet traditional forms of organization in small regional chapters were ineffective to mobilize large numbers of people. In response, Dutschke and Krahl called for loosely structured 'action centres' at all universities. These grassroots-controlled bodies would provide safe havens for 'urban guerrillas' who would confront those in power, expose 'the violence inherent in the system' and thus make the general public aware of their manipulation by the state.

The 'Grundsatzreferat' synthesized Dutschke's hope of transferring the guerrilla struggle into the cities and Krahl's view of the authoritarian state that manipulates, and needs to be confronted. Both ideas were based on the writings of Herbert Marcuse, who had described the advanced industrial state as an instrument of social control by the technocratic elites against the 'real' needs of the people. Representatives of this 'system of rule' were thus the enemy, be they the manipulating press, the parliament which now had the necessary two-thirds majority to change the basic law and introduce 'emergency laws', or the hawks in government and the army who advocated military adventures under the umbrella of NATO.

Drawing on Marcuse's concept of 'the great refusal', expounded in *The One-Dimensional Man*, Dutschke and Krahl argued that students

3. Rolf Wiggershaus, *The Frankfurt School* (Cambridge, 1994), ch. 8.

were now a marginal group, disaffected and persecuted, who would reveal the 'repressive tolerance' of the system by violating the rules of the game. Thinking globally and instinctively identifying with the victims (he worked closely with many students from Third World countries), Dutschke and his comrades saw the Vietnam conflict as a model case that revealed the real nature of 'the system', as well as the gulf between the generations.

On 22 May 1966 Marcuse gave the keynote address at a Vietnam conference organized at the Free University by the SDS. Speculating whether there was a chance for a non-capitalist alternative to the 'repressive technological rationality' of West and East, Marcuse argued this could occur only if the masses refused to swallow the lie that their own freedom was defended in Vietnam. He insisted that American action in Vietnam had to be protested against, even if the protest seemed hopeless, simply to ensure one's survival as a morally intact human being.

In February 1968 the SDS organized a much larger Vietnam conference. For this conference Dutschke and his Chilean friend Gaston Salvatore translated Ernesto Che Guevara's 'Mesaje a la Tricontinental' into German. This pamphlet called for a long and bloody struggle against the 'imperialist' United States by urban guerrillas. These guerrillas – cold killing machines – would take the war back to those who supported it, 'eliminating' capitalism's 'feeding bases' in a spirit of invincibility. While Guevara's programme could be seen as a blueprint for the Red Army Faction[4] (Holger Meins, a film student and later terrorist, produced a short film for the conference on how to make Molotov cocktails), Dutschke was perfectly aware of the fine line between provocation and actual violence against the state.[5] It was this question, how far the students were prepared to go, that exercised and fascinated the media, and that made Dutschke, for a brief period, the centre of attention.

Problems of leadership

Dutschke had become a revolutionary star; the cultural and intellectual elite wanted to talk to him. The Springer press were deeply

4. West Germany's notorious terrorist group, which was formed in 1970. The extent to which disaffected, radical members of the student movement influenced the ideology of the RAF is still debated.
5. On occasion, Dutschke would cross this line himself. Gretchen Dutschke recalls a grotesque scenario when her husband wheeled explosives around West

suspicious of any group advocating any form of socialism in West Berlin. Springer's editors dubbed him 'roter Rädelsführer Rudi' ('red rebel-rouser Rudi') and identified him as Public Enemy Number One. This in turn prompted the SDS to single out Springer as a representative of the 'system' and demand his expropriation.[6] To counter Springer's attack upon him, Dutschke embarked on a series of interviews with the liberal media. The most memorable was broadcast on 3 December 1967 on national television.

His interviewer, Günter Gaus, introduced the 27-year-old Dutschke as the spokesperson of a small minority of young people, 'revolutionaries in a time when one cannot believe in revolutions any more'. Dutschke countered that one could very well believe in revolutions, that it was capitalism that kept people in an unconscious state. Against this, he argued that change was a question of will, that people had the opportunity to revolutionize society. Provocative actions by students would stir them from their unconscious state, and inspire them to 'create their own history':

> We aren't hopeless idiots of history, unable to take our fate into our own hands. . . . We can create a world such as has never been seen before. This world would not know war or hunger anymore, anywhere on this planet. . . . For this we will fight, and have begun to fight.[7]

Gaus was undoubtedly serious in his attempt to understand the West German student movement and to convey that understanding to the public. It was certainly a personal triumph for Dutschke, who had managed to convey to a national audience the students' seriousness. It also shows that Dutschke could present himself as an eloquent and polite young man with strong views who was nevertheless willing to engage in rational debate.[8]

This image contrasts sharply with that adorning the title-page of *Der Spiegel* a week later, on 11 December 1967. The cover shows

---

Berlin, hidden in the pram of his newly-born son. Gretchen Dutschke, *Wir Hatten ein Barbarisches, Schönes Leben: Rudi Dutschke* (Cologne, 1996), p. 180.

6. The thrust of the expropriation demand was that Springer should lose control of his media empire. Even though there was never any open political support by the government for this demand (supported by German intellectuals, writers, etc.), Springer did sell some of his papers in the late 60s to lower his profile.

7. 'Zu Protokoll: Rudi Dutschke', TV Interview with Günter Gaus, Südwestfunk Baden-Baden, 3 December 1967 (translation Ingo Cornils). Transcript in Gretchen Dutschke-Klotz, Hellmut Gollwitzer, Jürgen Miermeister (eds), *Rudi Dutschke: Mein Langer Marsch* (Reinbek, 1980), pp. 42–57.

8. Reading Dutschke's embattled syntax in the transcript, one may be forgiven for dismissing him as a dangerous demagogue, but when watching his delivery on screen, one gets a clear impression why his admirers keep stressing his 'charisma'.

Dutschke as an unshaven fanatic, screaming, with eyes blazing. The article begins:

> The revolution wears a sweater, roughly knitted, with a violent pattern. Coloured stripes over chest and biceps signal the contrariness of the rebel. The sleeves are pushed up in a 'let's do it' manner. The upper body moves back and forth, in time with his speech. His fist, with thumb held up, lies clenched on the table, his lower arms seem to grasp space, as befitting the choreography of a workers' song.[9]

The reader thus gets an impression of Dutschke as a dangerous, caged animal, ready to resort to violence, and very likely controlled by others. The article goes on to acknowledge Dutschke's charisma, but the overall verdict is the same as in the Springer press: Dutschke has no majority, because the majority does not want change.

Students had difficulty learning to use the media to their advantage. While the movement needed the media attention to spread its message, the focus on Dutschke as high-profile rebel brought a reduction of content and serious distortions. Michael Ruetz, then a young photographer in West Berlin following the activities of the extra-parliamentary opposition, accuses *Der Spiegel* of fuelling the hatred against Dutschke. Instead of showing him as a human being, the magazine chose to portray him as a fanatic:

> At the time the media was making Dutschke out to be the reincarnation of not just Hitler, but all of history's monsters. By substituting Hitler with Dutschke, they hoped to stimulate at least a posthumous opposition to the Nazis. . . . Only after he had been turned into a monster, could open season be declared on him.[10]

It is ironic that Ruetz's own pictures of Dutschke have since become the main visual reference for the contemporary reader – and are regularly used by both *Der Spiegel* and the Springer press. These pictures, showing Dutschke with a megaphone at a rally, pushing against police barriers, or captivating an audience in a packed Audimax, convey a sense of great intensity, but never fanaticism. They also suggest that – at least in Ruetz's viewfinder – Dutschke *was* the leading figure of the movement.[11]

Dutschke was well aware of the contradictions of his own role, on the one hand relishing the media attention and trying to use it to further the cause, on the other hand regularly claiming that the

---

9. 'Der Lange Marsch', *Der Spiegel* 51 (1967), p. 52 (translation Cornils).
10. Michael Ruetz, *Sichtbare Zeit/Time Unveiled* (Frankfurt a.M., 1995), p. 251.
11. See also Michael Ruetz, *1968* (Frankfurt a.M., 1998).

anti-authoritarian movement acted by common consent and no member was indispensable to the struggle. He said on many occasions that the movement was looking for the people to lead, but it was obvious that the movement needed leaders. Dutschke, Rabehl, Krahl and a few of their comrades had no problems providing this 'temporary' leadership, very much in the vein of a Leninist avant-garde. Dutschke's own position was on occasion contested, but on the whole these debates were kept under wraps. Oskar Negt, then a young lecturer at the University of Frankfurt and a veteran SDS member, feels that it was SDS's great mistake not to have reorganized itself at the height of its influence to ensure that its leading members had to justify their actions.[12]

Speaking to the television journalist Wolfgang Venohr in the last recorded interview with him before the attempt on his life, Dutschke explained that the 'system' had personalized the struggle in an almost 'total' sense, which had led an authoritarian element to enter the movement. It was his duty to withdraw from the limelight, to allow issues to come to the fore, and to give space for criticism and self-criticism. He himself would go abroad (he had often toyed with the idea of studying with Marcuse in California), and the movement would show the establishment that it did not need a Dutschke to survive.

Interpretations of this 'farewell speech' differ. On a personal level, it must not be overlooked that Dutschke had a new-born son, that his life had been threatened, and that he had led an exhausting existence for a year. His biographer Ulrich Chaussy comments that both content and setting of the interview are full of contradictions: a leader of an anti-authoritarian movement wants to give up his leading role and confirms it at the same time; he did not step down after private consultation with his comrades, but instead spoke to the public via the media like a retiring statesman.[13] In *Der Spiegel* of 22 April 1968, Rabehl tried to control the damage: he claimed that before the assassination attempt, there had been a discussion with Dutschke in the SDS about his function, his role as a person and as chief ideologist, his influence, and his independence within the SDS. While Dutschke, after his recovery, always had a place in the SDS, it was no longer as 'chief ideologist'. However, the movement went into decline soon after his departure, thus confirming how much it really *had* depended on his leadership.

12. Ronald Fraser, *1968: A Student Generation in Revolt* (London, 1988), p. 127.
13. Ulrich Chaussy, *Die Drei Leben des Rudi Dutschke* (Berlin, 1993), p. 228.

The long march

One reason for Dutschke's long staying power in the public consciousness is his slogan of the 'long march through the institutions'. The long march was a strategy to change the system from within, as state and society had shown themselves impervious to any attempt by the *extra*parliamentary opposition to change them from the outside. Dutschke was acutely aware of the danger that the marchers would adapt to the institutions instead of changing them. Therefore, a double strategy of long march and illegal, provocative actions was discussed within the SDS.

Even though the attempt on Dutschke's life stopped any further development of the idea, the slogan with its heroic connotations (Mao Zedong's march across China, Che Guevara's march through Bolivia) made sense for thousands of young people. In all its vagueness the idea of a 'long march through the institutions' was something concrete, something that young people who otherwise felt powerless in the face of a cold system could achieve. Enthusiastically, they entered previously despised institutions and set about changing behaviour patterns and attitudes. In kindergartens, schools and universities, factories, political parties, broadcasting houses and newspaper offices, they hoped to change the relationship between citizen and state, and in the long run to create a counter-public.

The idea of the 'long march' was loosely based on the works of the German philosopher Ernst Bloch. Dutschke met his hero Bloch in Bad Boll in February 1968, and they quickly found common ground: both were yearning for *Heimat*, both had the experience of a partly messianic youth movement, both believed in a paradise on earth, 'where the mindless destruction of capital is ended'. Bloch was aware that Dutschke's aims were vague and that there was little support from the masses, but he was impressed with the young man, who, so he publicly declared, put paid to the hackneyed image of the public enemy with a knife between his teeth. Instead, he recognized in Dutschke the integrity and will to achieve a 'concrete utopia', qualities Bloch himself had described in his book *Das Prinzip Hoffnung.*

Opinions differ on the success of the 'long march through the institutions'. Some see the formation of subcultures, of citizens' initiatives and anti-authoritarian nurseries, as proof of its success, others feel that the institutions proved more adaptable than Dutschke had thought, and that the long march led the students straight into the folds of mainstream society. The notion that the long march was really happening certainly struck terror in the 'establishment'. The SPD (which came to power in 1969) feared it, offering an amnesty for students who had committed minor offences in order to bind them within their own reform-oriented movement (more than 100,000 young people did indeed join the SPD after 1969), and reacting more harshly when it seemed that the students were actually succeeding in their campaign of infiltration. To counter the various communist groups that had formed after the SDS had disbanded, and to stop a subversive sixth column moving into the corridors of power, the 'decree concerning radicals' was announced in 1972.[14]

Dutschke's own long march certainly was an example of tenacity and uncompromising conviction. After the attempt on his life and initial recovery, he encountered difficulty in finding a country in Europe which would allow him extended residence. He planned to read for a Ph.D. at Cambridge, but the Home Office refused him a residence permit on the grounds that his political activism posed a 'potential threat to national security'. In an interview shortly before his request to stay in Britain was turned down by the Appeals Tribunal on 21 February 1971, Dutschke stressed that he was physically incapable of political work, and in any case would be sidelined in England since he could not direct his comrades' struggle from a distance. It is nevertheless significant that, even in what was for him a highly precarious situation (he did not know at this point that he would be granted residence in Denmark), he refused to distance himself from the 'urban guerrillas'.

Dutschke's ambivalent position on the question of violence had long been the open flank of the student movement. He repeatedly stated that violence was a constituent of the ruling 'system', and had therefore to be countered by means of 'demonstrative and provocative counter-violence'. But he also maintained that in Western Europe it was futile to attack prominent members of the establishment, since they were mere 'character masks' and instantly replaceable. What is certain is that his call for an urban guerrilla campaign and his refusal to rule out violence as a political means left him open to suspicion. He knew several members of the emerging Red Army Faction well, and made a point of visiting jailed terrorists. In 1974, his defiant stand at the grave of the terrorist Holger Meins caused a media uproar. Meins had died during a hunger-strike in prison, and Dutschke had exclaimed at the grave: 'Holger, der Kampf geht weiter!' ('Holger, the struggle continues!')

14. See the chapter by A.D. Moses in this volume.

In a letter to *Der Spiegel*, he explained that the struggle for social liberation was the basis of all political action by revolutionary socialists and communists, and that he had wanted to show his solidarity with the cause, in spite of his view that terrorism precluded any process of learning.

It is easy to condemn his show of solidarity with Meins and the common political aims they once shared as politically naive, but in the mid-1970s climate of retrenchment, Dutschke merely voiced the frustration of the New Left, which was becoming ever more marginal to the rest of society. The socialist hopes of a more just and egalitarian society had been disappointed, the university reforms had not brought any real change, and Willy Brandt's promise of more democracy had never been fulfilled.

It was the emerging Green movement in the second half of the seventies that brought new hope. Dutschke initially found it difficult to discern the thrust of this new movement, but instinctively felt that it addressed the broad issues and had the potential for broad support that the student movement had lacked. The Green movement picked up where the student movement failed, arguing that goals in the private sphere of life had to be complemented by the emancipation of individuals as political beings, who would then self-confidently intervene in the public sphere of democratic decision-making. Dutschke felt that his role was to remind his new comrades about social issues, and to warn them not to repeat the mistakes that had been made in the sixties. He freely acknowledged that the students had had their day, that the organization debate was now dominated by broader-based citizens' initiatives, and that the sectarianism of the various communist and socialist groups had all but destroyed the advances the Left had made.

Much has been made of the influence of the student movement on the Green movement. The double strategy of the long march and the urban guerrilla was further developed by the Greens, who achieved a foothold and public forum in the establishment (Dutschke lived to see the first Green representatives enter regional government in Bremen), while still maintaining a strong protest movement outside against sexual discrimination, nuclear power and the arms race. Andrei Markovits and Philip Gorski argue that, even though the Greens have altered the structure and content of what it means to be 'left', their success was built on the achievements of the student movement.[15]

15. Andrei Markovits and Philip Gorski, *The German Left: Red, Green and Beyond* (Oxford, 1993), p. 4.

Myth and reality

Dutschke's long-term impact on West German society is still highly contested. The Springer press, predictably, sees him as the intellectual Pied Piper who caught the media attention while the 'true' representatives of the time (who stayed on the sidelines) were largely ignored. But they have a vested interest in downplaying his significance, since they were (and are) held partially responsible for his attempted assassination.[16]

The student movement has failed, but Dutschke is not associated with its failure. Instead, he has become the object of hero-worship. This has less to do with his ideas of radical socialism than his significance as a symbol of the revolt. His closest friends have written numerous books about him, and even though these have not enjoyed huge sales, they have managed to keep interest in Dutschke alive and have contributed to a modern myth.

Thirty years after the attempt on his life, Dutschke emerges in the liberal press as the 'intellectual and moral heart of the revolt'[17] – we are invited to speculate on what might have been if he had not been shot. Meanwhile, a critical examination of his message is put on hold. This, along with a nagging feeling among the veterans of 1968 that Dutschke took those bullets on behalf of the whole movement, may explain why so many are willing to accept the hero myth. Dutschke has been 'rehabilitated', the public perception of him has changed from sinister revolutionary to moral icon. This does him no justice, but is perhaps a natural by-product of a wider phenomenon: the sixties are now part of our history, even though the frame of reference, after the fall of communism, has changed beyond recognition.

Dutschke's critique of political parties and the lack of democratic practice is now more widely shared, and the pivotal role of student protest in the deepening of democratic engagement in the Federal Republic generally accepted.[18] At the same time, capitalism has reinvented itself in Germany, and fundamental criticism of the 'system' is today very rare indeed. The followers of the long march

16. The students believed that the assassin had been incited by sensationalist headlines in the Springer press urging the population to stop Dutschke. Gretchen Dutschke merely states that on the day of Rudi Dutschke's funeral, Axel Springer's son committed suicide. (G. Dutschke, *Wir Hatten ein Barbarisches, Schönes Leben*, p. 483.)

17. 'Herz der Revolte', *Der Spiegel* 34 (1996), p. 96.

18. Rob Burns (ed.), *German Cultural Studies: An Introduction* (Oxford, 1995), p. 8.

would argue that they have succeeded, while conservatives would cynically point to the many veterans of 1968 who have achieved a comfortable existence and returned to the 'islands of common sense'.

In 1996 two new Dutschke biographies were published in Germany, one by his wife Gretchen and the other by his friend Jürgen Miermeister. While Gretchen Dutschke focuses on her husband's role as a leader who was held back by petty rivalries in the SDS, Miermeister compares him to the philosopher Ernst Bloch and describes him as 'a chosen one, a charismatic leader, a prophet of the new age ... a new, modern, militant messiah'.[19] While it is true that the latest spate of books about Dutschke have the smell of incense, making him larger than life instead of portraying him as one of a number of committed revolutionaries, there is good reason to assign significance to the movement of which he was a part. Its call for 'critical forms of a public sphere' changed the political culture. Authority is no longer unquestioned, nor are the media. But this does not mean that Dutschke and the 1968 generation should be immune to question. After all, their identification with political systems which denied human rights demonstrates that they were as susceptible to manipulation as their conservative counterparts. But he did have a vision, and it can still inspire:

> Our life is more than money. Our life is thinking and living. It's about us, and what we could do in this world ... It is about how we could use technology and all the other things which at the moment are used against the human being. ... My question in life is always how we can destroy things that are against the human being, and how we can find a way of life in which the human being is independent of a world of trouble, a world of anxiety, a world of destruction.[20]

19. Jürgen Miermeister, *Ernst Bloch, Rudi Dutschke* (Hamburg, 1996), p. 14.
20. Richard Davy, 'The life and views of Rudi Dutschke in exile', *The Globe and Mail*, 27 January 1971, p. 7.

PART THREE

Reaction

CHAPTER NINE

Two Responses to Student Protest: Ronald Reagan and Robert Kennedy

CLARE WHITE

We're right at the center of everything. You remember when you're a child and your older brother is the big star, or your big sister is doing all the things? Now it's us, we're right in the center reading about ourselves in the newspaper. It's youth. Everything is youth and us.[1]

Contrary to the usual adolescent experience, students in the sixties found themselves at the centre of events. The boom in birth rates which followed World War II lasted until 1965, and the birth of 76 million babies between 1946 and 1964 had a huge impact upon the United States.[2] There were more people under the age of 25 during the sixties than any previous decade. Fashion, hair and speech styles were increasingly dictated by the young, and imitated by adults. Students in the late fifties and sixties thus had a unique sense of generational identity. A strong sense of cultural importance led naturally to an assumption that they could similarly influence the nation's politics.

In 1960 there were 3,789,000 students in higher education. By 1969 there were 7,852,000 – more students than farmers, construction workers, miners or transport workers.[3] Young people were entering college at a time when the technological demands of the economy and the Great Society's emphasis on education increased the size and importance of universities. Young people were brought together in an environment which stimulated generational identity

I am grateful for the help of all the staff at the John F. Kennedy Library, especially Maura Porter, William Johnston, June Payne and Megan Desnoyers.
    1. Thomas J. Cottle, *Time's Children* (Boston, Mass., 1971), p. 267.
    2. Doug McAdam, *Freedom Summer* (Oxford, 1988), p. 14.
    3. David Steigerwald, *The Sixties and the End of Modern America* (New York, 1995), p. 134.

and cooperation. By the end of the sixties, therefore, students had become a significant force in American politics.[4] No politician campaigning for national office, or for election in a state with a significant student population, could afford to underestimate the importance of student opinion.

During the early sixties student activism meant mainly civil rights agitation, often under the auspices of the Southern Christian Leadership Conference (SCLC) or the Student Non-Violent Coordinating Committee (SNCC). By mid-decade student concern was also focused on university administrations' denial of rights to political activity on campus. Groups such as TOCSIN at Harvard and the Free Speech Movement (FSM) at the University of California at Berkeley challenged the university. Activists also sought to overturn the universities' role, *in loco parentis*, under which university authorities assumed parental power to monitor the social and sexual life of students. By 1965 the burgeoning protest movement was fired by opposition to the Vietnam War. By the end of the decade increasingly radical student groups sought to overturn the standards of their parents' generation. As Wini Breines, a historian of the New Left, later remembered: 'we believed we could achieve an egalitarian, free and participatory society. . . . We believed that we were going to make a revolution. We were convinced that we could transform America through our political activity and insights.'[5]

The rallies, demonstrations and campus wars that were increasingly common by the end of the sixties became a growing concern to older generations of Americans. Put in the context of the urban riots that also marked this period, it was clear that US society had become increasingly fractured and violent. Americans looked to politicians to provide an answer to the fragmentation of their nation.

Both Robert Kennedy and Ronald Reagan had strong opinions about student protest. The ways in which they responded, however, were diametrically opposed. While Kennedy sympathized with and tried to win the direct support of student groups, Reagan climbed to power on the back of student radicals, by assuring the public that he could defeat their supposedly dangerous and unpatriotic challenge. Reagan's stance was largely an electoral strategy. As the

---

4. For a wider discussion of the student protest movement see Tod Gitlin, *The Sixties: Years of Hope, Days of Rage* (New York, 1987); Alan Matusow, *The Unraveling of America* (New York, 1984); James Miller, *Democracy is in the Streets* (New York, 1987); W.J. Rorabaugh, *Berkeley at War* (Berkeley, Calif., 1989); and Kenneth J. Heineman, *Campus Wars* (New York, 1994).

5. McAdam, *Freedom Summer*, p. 19.

Republican candidate for Governor, he recognized that he could benefit from the concern of Californian citizens that radical students were undermining the state university system and threatening social stability. Robert Kennedy, as a Democratic politician, tried to establish a platform to the left of his party from which he could launch his presidential aspirations. He could benefit from student support, and was, in any case, sympathetic towards them. However, his calculations were necessarily more complex than Reagan's, since he also needed to retain the support of those Americans worried about student protest.

That Reagan and Kennedy had such different attitudes to student protest should not be surprising considering their personal and political experience. While Kennedy was born into a wealthy and privileged background, Reagan's beginnings were modest. Their experiences at university were markedly different, with RFK attending Harvard and Virginia Law School and Reagan the provincial and sectarian Eureka College. The difference in their ages was also important. Reagan was 55 in 1966, too old to attempt to represent student concerns. Kennedy was 41, and his youthful looks and attitude, optimized by his longish hair, improved his stature with students.

Politically the two men travelled in opposite directions. As a young man Reagan was a strong supporter of Franklin Roosevelt's New Deal and was later active in the liberal Screen Actors Guild. Although his father was active in Democratic politics, RFK's political views did not conform to standard ideological labels. He had little time for the liberal wing of the Democratic party during the fifties and early sixties. It was not until the assassination of John Kennedy and his own election as Senator from New York (when for the first time, he had to develop his own programme rather than defend that of his brother), that Kennedy began to move to the left of his party. Meanwhile, Reagan was moving steadily rightward. He campaigned for Nixon in 1960, became co-chairman of Barry Goldwater's presidential campaign in 1964 and, shortly afterwards, was persuaded to run against Pat Brown, the Democratic Governor of California in 1966.

There were two ways, however, in which Reagan and Kennedy were similar. First, they represented (or in Reagan's case hoped to represent) large, densely populated and urbanized states with highly sophisticated state university systems. Hence student issues were an important consideration for practically all their constituents, both students enrolled in the universities, and the taxpayers who funded their education. Secondly, both men had their eyes fixed upon the presidency as their ultimate political goal. Both ran for nomination in 1968, although Reagan's challenge was not as serious, or as realistic, as RFK's.

At the start of the 1966 California gubernatorial race Reagan was seen as an outsider even for the Republican nomination. The issue of student protest must have seemed heaven sent. In his autobiography, he maintained that, during question and answer sessions, wherever he campaigned, the public would ask him what action he proposed against campus demonstrators. He replied that 'the students had no business being at the university if they weren't willing to abide by the rules; if they *refused* to obey them, they should go elsewhere'. Invariably, according to Reagan, 'the audience cheered'.[6] He rejected accusations that he had used the issue for his political benefit:

> the opposition tried to make out that I was persecuting the university for political purposes. I wasn't. I had never mentioned Berkeley as an incident, or as an issue, until those question and answer sessions. . . .
> I learned that the people of this state had had a very, very deep and great pride in the university system. Because of that, they were very emotionally involved and disturbed with what was happening to what they thought was the great pride of California. My own position was born of the answers I gave to those questions.[7]

Members of Reagan's campaign team, however, remember differently. The public relations specialist hired by Reagan to run the campaign, Stuart Spencer, later remarked: 'we jumped on [student unrest] as an issue . . . I think Reagan escalated it into an issue and it started showing up in the polls.'[8] When Berkeley activists organized a controversial dance on campus in March 1966, Reagan used reports of the dance to provoke anti-student sentiment. He described a scene of sybaritic students dancing lasciviously, smoking marijuana, and watching films in which 'the nude torsos of men and women were portrayed'.[9] Reagan suggested that the dance

6. Ronald Reagan, *An American Life* (London, 1991), p. 152.

7. Ronald Reagan, 'On becoming Governor', oral history transcript, Bancroft Library, University of California, Berkeley, California, p. 21. For an analysis of Reagan's 1966 campaign see Gerard J. DeGroot, 'Ronald Reagan and student unrest in California, 1966–1970', *Pacific Historical Review* 65 (1996), pp. 107–29, and '"A goddamned electable person": the 1966 California gubernatorial campaign of Ronald Reagan', *History* 82 (1997), pp. 429–48.

8. Stuart Spencer, 'Developing a campaign management organization', oral history transcript, Bancroft Library, p. 31.

9. Cow Palace Speech, 12 May 1966, box 48, Reagan Papers, Hoover Institution Library, Stanford University.

revealed a 'leadership gap' at Berkeley. The dance, he claimed, had been allowed on the grounds of 'academic freedom. What in heaven's name', he asked, 'does "academic freedom" have to do with rioting, with anarchy, with attempts to destroy the primary purpose of the University which is to educate our young people?'[10]

However, Reagan was not merely concerned with students. He criticized faculty as well. By widening the issue to include professors as well as students, Reagan could suggest that the students had been 'indoctrinated' by radical, or 'Communist' professors. This would make his call for strong action seem more appropriate to voters. His tactic, reminiscent of McCarthyism, enabled Reagan both to lambast the UC administration for endangering 'the high and noble purpose of the University' and to criticize Brown for condoning the UC Board of Regents' failure to deal with student behaviour.

Brown was unable to produce an adequate response to Reagan's charges. Frederick Dutton, a Brown appointee to the Board of Regents, believed that 'the person who had the responsibility – Pat – had to see the problem more in grays than his outside political critics. Pat had the grays and Reagan had the black and whites.'[11] Richard Kline, a Brown campaign worker, recalled that 'the university thing drove us nuts . . . It was just utterly strange. All these things happening around us and why couldn't they be controlled? . . . I don't think we understood any of these things.'[12]

Meanwhile Reagan promised a commission, headed by John McCone, formerly head of the CIA, to investigate campus activism, and announced that a faculty code of conduct would be implemented to promote good behaviour. Chancellors, he warned, would be replaced if they did not administer their campus properly.[13] Never mind that the governor did not have this authority; Reagan's supporters were content with a candidate who addressed their fears, even if those fears were largely his creation. The *Sacramento Bee* wrote that:

> the public has been saturated with the misadventures of the few at Berkeley. It has read of beatniks stumping the campus, of LSD parties, of promiscuity, even of the occasional Communist preachment by an infiltrator. It has become so concerned with the one who has

10. Ibid.
11. Frederick Dutton, 'Governor Brown's faithful adviser', oral history transcript, Bancroft Library, pp. 25–6.
12. Richard Kline, 'Governor Brown's faithful adviser', oral history transcript, Bancroft Library, p. 46.
13. *Carpinteria Herald*, 14 July 1966; Cow Palace speech, 12 May 1966.

strayed . . . it has lost sight of the 90 and 9 . . . who represent the real student body on the campus; the solid, responsible core of young pursuing an education at one of the world's best-ranked schools.[14]

In fact, despite the turmoil, the American Council on Education voted Berkeley the 'best balanced distinguished university' in the United States. This news, however, was not as alluring as tales of sex, drugs, and communism.

Three weeks before the election, a Reagan aide in a confidential memo advised that it would be good for their campaign if student unrest bubbled over.[15] In response to the memo Reagan urged the Berkeley branch of SNCC to cancel a speech on campus by the black power advocate Stokely Carmichael, scheduled for 29 October. Carmichael's appearance would, Reagan's news release stated, 'stir strong emotions and . . . possibly do damage to both parties'.[16] SNCC, unsurprisingly, refused to bow to the pressure and went ahead with the rally, thus playing into Reagan's hands. He won the election by just under a million votes.

As Governor, Reagan maintained the populist motif of his election, threatening strong action against California's universities. In 1969 he told a *Sacramento Bee* reporter:

> There are too many in the academic community who consciously, or unconsciously, bare their contempt for the ordinary citizen who may not have had the benefit of a college education, but who is sharing a very heavy tax burden . . .
>
> The same taxpayer . . . is asking why violence and disruption are openly encouraged, or even tolerated, on the campus he finances – in the name of academic freedom. . . . He is wondering . . . why some instructors are able to use their classrooms to indoctrinate and propagandize his children against the traditional values of a free society in this country.[17]

Like most Californians, Reagan did not have a clear understanding of the campus disturbances. He did, however, understand the public's concerns. By addressing them, he profited from them.

Reagan professed support for freedom of speech. But, 'Dissent must stop short of interfering with the rights of other individuals', he maintained.[18] 'Free speech does not require furnishing a podium

14. *Sacramento Bee*, 12 July 1966.
15. BASICO staff to Ronald Reagan, 12 Oct. 1966, box 36, Reagan Papers.
16. Ibid.
17. Transcript of interview with *Sacramento Bee*, 26 Oct. 1969, box 6, Reagan Papers.
18. Transcript of *Face the Nation*, CBS Television, 15 June 1968, Miscellaneous Speeches and Scripts, 1964–74, Reagan Papers.

for the speaker . . . I don't believe you should lend these people the prestige of our University campuses for the presentation of their views.'[19] During an appearance on the CBS programme *Town Meeting of the World* in May 1967, Reagan attempted, rather unsuccessfully, to define the limits of acceptable dissent:

> if government is to mean anything at all, that all of us have a respons-
> ibility, once the action had been decided upon and supposedly by
> the majority will, that we then, while reserving our right to disagree,
> we support the collective or the unified effort of the nation. . . . We
> give up certain individual freedoms in the interest of – well, I sup-
> pose it comes from our own Constitution, our idea that every Amer-
> ican or every person has the right . . . [to] life, liberty and the pursuit
> of happiness. But my pursuit of happiness, if it comes from swinging
> my arm, I must stop swinging my arm just short of the end of your
> nose.[20]

Reagan's limited perception of dissent conveniently provided a check on effective protest. Presumably he believed that one should only express opposing views to government policy in private, thus ignor- ing America's great tradition of dissent. Civil disobedience was ruled out as it impinged on others' rights. The rights of the majority would even be protected 'at the point of a bayonet if necessary'.[21]

Reagan did not just talk about using military might. His response to the People's Park protests of May 1969 resulted in the death of one man, the blinding of another and the injury of hundreds more. Even after an inquiry which found that the force used was inap- propriate, the Governor remained convinced that his actions had been justified: 'there was no alternative. . . . once the dogs of war are unleashed, you must expect that things will happen and that people, being human, will make mistakes on both sides'.[22] Reagan's tough stance aroused popular support. By presenting university unrest as an evil similar to that being fought in South-East Asia, the Governor provoked a sense of crisis on which he capitalized.

19. Reagan press conference, 7 Feb. 1967, Miscellaneous Speeches and Scripts, 1964–74, Reagan Papers.

20. Transcript of *Town Meeting of the World*, 15 May 1967. RFK Senate Papers: Speeches and Press Releases; Subject File, box 3. John F. Kennedy Library (here- after, JFKL). The idea that all men were born with the right to 'life, liberty and the pursuit of happiness' was enunciated in the Declaration of Independence, not the Constitution.

21. Reagan Press Conference, 8 Jan. 1969, box 31, Reagan Papers.

22. Transcript of Reagan meeting with UC Berkeley professors, Sacramento, 21 May 1969, box 178, Reagan Papers.

Reagan repeatedly threatened action against radical professors, or those who participated in demonstrations. He also talked about introducing tuition fees, on the assumption that students who had to pay for their education would be less likely to waste time protesting. Yet he did not bring the campuses under control. Despite his failure, the public continued to support him. Poll ratings rose when the campuses were most active. As the *Sacramento Bee* commented:

> He has firmly attached himself to the public's highly emotional response to the complex problems dominating education and youth. He is not solving these problems. In fact he is not even trying. He is simply making it crystal clear he is opposed to the rude and sometimes violent demonstrations which are so upsetting to the public.[23]

Reagan could not lose: if he won a battle with students, the public were pleased, but if he failed to deal with unrest, his failure merely demonstrated the seriousness of the problem and the need for stronger action. Once Reagan had gained the support of 'middle America', he never lost it. Thus his response to student protest boosted his status nationally, and served his interests well when he later campaigned for the presidency.

Robert Kennedy's approach to student protest was very different. His sympathetic attitude was partly a reflection of his need to attract the New Left in order to forge a following to the left of the Democratic party. Lyndon Johnson occupied the ideological middle ground of the party. As the newly elected Senator for New York, and the figurehead of a 'government in exile', Kennedy realized the need to build a national constituency for a presidential bid. The mutual hostility between the two men precluded Kennedy from presenting himself as Johnson's natural successor. Kennedy regarded Johnson as unfit to be President and almost from the beginning of his senatorial term found ways to disagree with him on policy.[24] Thus RFK moved to the left of the party, urging a radical expansion of the Great Society, and, from 1966 onwards, advocating increasingly doveish policies toward Vietnam. Both stances were popular with student activists, as they reflected two of their main political objectives. Kennedy spoke directly to students on college campuses, often announcing major policy decisions, or new initiatives. (Reagan, in contrast, avoided major universities like Berkeley, speaking

---

23. *Sacramento Bee*, 2 Apr. 1969.
24. For a wider discussion of this issue see Jeff Shesol, *Mutual Contempt: Lyndon Johnson, Robert Kennedy, and the Feud that Defined a Decade* (New York, 1997), and Paul R. Henggeller, *In His Steps: Lyndon Johnson and the Kennedy Mystique* (Chicago, 1991).

instead at second- and third-tier institutions where students were much more conservative.) By early 1967 Kennedy's efforts had clearly paid off. Presidential preference polls taken on campuses throughout the country showed that Kennedy was the students' undisputed hero.[25]

Kennedy's attitude toward student protest, however, was also shaped by his genuine support for most of the ideas students advocated. He identified with students, in part because of his relative youth (he was 39 when he began his senatorial term in 1964). Perhaps in response to the pain of his brother's assassination, he began to read existential literature, deriving comfort from authors like Camus who inspired so many students.[26] Kennedy also believed that students and the young generation had an important role to play in American politics. Joseph Kennedy had instilled his children with a sense of duty towards their country (JFK's Peace Corps had been a manifestation of this belief) and RFK would frequently express this feeling to students in his addresses. Addressing students at Berkeley, he reminded them that they had 'the opportunity and the responsibility to help make the choices which will determine the greatness of this nation. . . . If you shrink from this struggle . . . you will betray the trust which your own position forces upon you.'[27]

Kennedy's response to student dissent was born of these values. He recognized that a democratic society should allow its members to disagree with government policy, and indeed to try to change it. 'It is not enough to allow dissent,' he argued. 'We must demand it. For there is much to dissent from.'[28] He adapted Plato's philosophy that 'the unexamined life is not worth living', telling students that 'a life without criticism is not worth living'.[29] He accepted that many students were not prepared, as Reagan had proposed, to abrogate their right to disagree, in order to support the 'collective or unified effort of the nation' in the face of a policy that they felt morally reprehensible.[30] Kennedy was aware, as few politicians of

25. A poll taken by University of Wisconsin Young Democrats in January 1967 showed 56.5% would not support the President for re-election. Sixty per cent preferred Robert Kennedy as the next Democratic candidate for President. RFK Papers: 1968 Presidential Campaign Papers; Press Division, box 14. JFKL.
26. Apparently RFK had read all of Camus's esays and novels and his copy of *Resistance, Rebellion and Death* had sections underlined on almost every page. Jack Newfield, *Robert Kennedy: A Memoir* (New York, 1969), p. 59.
27. Address by Senator Kennedy, 22 Oct. 1966, University of California at Berkeley. RFK Senate Papers: Speeches and Press Releases; Subject File, box 3. JFKL.
28. Ibid.   29. Ibid. The quote is from Plato, *Apology*.
30. Transcript of *Town Meeting of the World*, 15 May 1967.

his generation were, that conscience was a significant factor in student action. So, whilst he would not condone the use of violence, he refused to brand students who protested against the Vietnam War as traitors:

> I don't think that the mere fact that the United States is involved in the use of force with an adversary makes everything that the United States then does absolutely correct. . . . if there are those within the United States that feel that the struggle could be ended more rapidly with less loss of life, that the terror and the destruction would be less if we took a different course, then I think they should make their views known. I don't think they're less patriotic because they feel that. In fact I think they would be less patriotic if they didn't state their views . . .[31]

Those who believed that Kennedy was merely being opportunistic in order to win student support were quickly won over by the passion of his speeches on issues such as Vietnam and the ghettos. Often Kennedy's addresses were fairly cautious, mostly so as not to offend more moderate supporters, but at question and answer sessions afterwards he often espoused a more radical line. Adam Walinsky, Kennedy's youthful assistant, felt that these sessions showed RFK's most endearing side: 'No matter how hard he would try and protect himself . . . the things that got him into trouble were the things that were just basically right and decent; they would come out time and time again in these impromptu comments.'[32] During one such session at a Catholic girls' college, he conducted a hand-vote on whether or not the bombing in Vietnam should be increased. When a majority voted for escalation, Kennedy reacted angrily: 'Do you understand what that means? . . . It means you are voting to send people, Americans and Vietnamese, to die. . . . Don't you understand that what we are doing to the Vietnamese is not very different than what Hitler did to the Jews?'[33] This kind of comment often brought student crowds to their feet, roaring their support.

Kennedy's focus on the youth of America harmonized with the changing political climate of the late sixties. It was also expedient since the number of students and youths was rising so quickly. By 1968 the median age of Americans was 26, and this, it was calculated, would be lower still by 1972. Kennedy was well aware of

---

31. Ibid.
32. Adam Walinsky, oral history interview with Thomas Johnson, 30 Nov. 1969, 4, RFK Oral History Program, JFKL.
33. John Galloway (ed.), *The Kennedys and Vietnam* (New York, 1971), pp. 101–2.

these trends, as were his key advisers. Dutton, a long-time adviser, advised Kennedy in May 1967 that:

> now, not the early 1970s, is the time to win the loyalty of a large share of the new generation and turn it into a personal following. They now are much taken with you but are also strongly alienated from the Democratic party. If they coalesce politically without you reaching out to them during the critical next several years, they will scatter in their political orientation, and the pieces will likely thereafter not be put back together again. On the other hand, if you could rally a major sector of this huge group of new voters coming along in the next few years, you could decisively affect not only the politics of the 1970s but (because the loyalties then formed would generally be lasting) for most of the balance of this century, as FDR shaped the historic generation of the late 1920s and early 1930s . . . into the political base of American politics for the last four decades.[34]

By November, Dutton had begun to warn Kennedy that his considerable appeal to students was beginning to wane while many older people were alienated by his youthful mannerisms, haircut and speeches.[35] He cautioned Kennedy that he could not afford to alienate students, who were 'increasingly substantive and critical as well as restive', having already estranged so many others.[36] Unfortunately Kennedy's plans had been formulated with the thought that he would run for the presidency in 1972. By the end of 1967, however, student protesters had begun to call for a candidate to challenge Johnson for the Democratic nomination in 1968. Allard Lowenstein, a prominent anti-war activist who had organized a 'dump-Johnson' movement, tried to persuade Kennedy to run, but he declined for two reasons. He knew that a move against Johnson would be viewed by many as ruthless and opportunistic:

> People would say that I was splitting the party out of ambition and envy. No one would believe that I was doing it because of how I felt about Vietnam and poor people. I think that Al [Lowenstein] is doing the right thing, but I think that someone else will have to be the first one to run.[37]

34. Letter from Dutton to RFK, 1 May 1967. RFK Senate Papers: Senate Correspondence; Personal File, 1964–1968, box 3. JFKL.

35. Stewart Alsop reported that the question most frequently asked of Kennedy during the campaign was 'Why don't he get his damned hair cut?' *Saturday Evening Post*, 15 June 1968.

36. Letter from Dutton to RFK, 3 Nov. 1967. Personal Papers of Arthur M. Schlesinger, Jr. Writings: Background Material; 1968 Campaign; RFK's decision to run for President (Folder 1), box W-53. JFKL.

37. Newfield, *Kennedy*, p. 186.

Kennedy also knew, however, that there was very little chance of him winning, and he was enough of a realist not to commit political suicide. If he entered the race students would be his biggest supporters, but most would not be able to vote for him as the voting age was still 21.

Kennedy had moved towards the New Left, but he had not abandoned the old politics entirely. This lost him the respect of many of his former student supporters, who flocked instead to Senator Eugene McCarthy's campaign. Initially supporting Kennedy for his apparent courage and integrity, they turned against him when he refused to stand against the President. At Brooklyn College, RFK was greeted by signs which read: 'BOBBY KENNEDY: HAWK, DOVE OR CHICKEN?'[38] Some of McCarthy's student volunteers started describing Robert Kennedy as 'a moral slob'. As one Cornell senior said, 'we're circulating a dump-Kennedy-'72 letter'.[39]

The Tet Offensive of January 1968 changed the political climate completely. Support for the war, and for Johnson, plummeted. Ironically for Kennedy it was now possible for him to run, knowing that there was a chance of victory. He had agonized for months, knowing that morally he should run, but realistically he could not. When he eventually entered the race just after McCarthy did so well in the New Hampshire primary, many students accused him of opportunism. Though they realized he was the candidate most likely to win the nomination and the election in November, they were angered at the timing of his declaration. Their rejection stung Kennedy. The columnist Mary McGrory wrote: 'He suffers most from the rejection of the college youth, who had found in his brother a champion and idol. The best and the brightest young minds were working across the street for McCarthy . . . No blandishments, and many were offered, could make them cross over. Kennedy had failed them when they needed him.'[40]

The students Kennedy had nurtured since 1964, and for whom he genuinely cared, turned on him in 1968. It is uncertain whether, had he not been assassinated in June 1968, he could have recovered their support. Many of his own aides believed that he would have won them over after a Convention victory. Having made soundings in California universities, Arthur Schlesinger advised RFK on

38. Arthur Schlesinger, Jr., *Robert Kennedy and his Times* (New York, 1978), p. 885.

39. Lewis Chester, Godfrey Hodgson and Bruce Page, *An American Melodrama: The Presidential Campaign of 1968* (London, 1969).

40. Mary McGrory, 'Senator Kennedy vs. Himself', *Chicago Sun Times*, 15 May 1968.

6 May 1968 that, while student support for McCarthy was still overwhelming, this appeared 'to be accompanied in most places by entire friendliness toward you. Most McCarthy people I encountered said they expected in due course to support you with enthusiasm.'[41] With hindsight, student leaders recognized that Kennedy had been the only man in America who could embrace both radical students and blacks, as well as working-class white Americans worried by widening schisms in their country. His ties to old politics won him the support of Democratic voters, not to mention the 'Kennedy Mystique' – so strong since JFK's assassination. But Tom Wicker, a political commentator, while recognizing Kennedy's ability to 'bring us together', voiced a common fear that this was not a 'feasible alliance' in the long term. Kennedy wanted 'to have Mayor Daley's support and the support of the college students. The two are incompatible in the long run.'[42] Tom Hayden concurred:

> In one corner of his [RFK's] very complicated mind, he believed he could use the structure and then destroy it. Use Mayor Daley to become President and, at the same time, encourage the ghetto to rise up against Mayor Daley. . . . It doesn't work. It leads back to embracing the Mayor Daleys and right wingers because they ultimately become the people you must depend on to remain the leader of their power structure.[43]

Ultimately, the difference between Reagan's and Kennedy's approach to student protest was one of scope. Reagan took a short-term view, believing he could profit from the reaction of Californians to student demonstrations. His expert manipulation of the issue was instrumental to his victory in the 1966 election and in his winning re-election. By contrast, Kennedy's strategy towards students was long term. He viewed them as an important part of the coalition he was attempting to build for a presidential bid. RFK failed to win their support through his refusal in late 1967 and early 1968 to stand against Johnson. It is not clear whether he would have won back student support had he lived. But this long-term approach was not, perhaps, fully thought out. Had he lived, RFK might have lost student support in any case. Student protest movements differ from most other pressure groups in that their membership is transitory. Students often lose affinity with their

41. Arthur Schlesinger to Robert Kennedy, 6 May 1968, RFK Senate Paper, Senate Correspondence, Personal File 1964–68, Box No. 11, JFK Library.
42. Interview with Tom Wicker in Jean Stein and George Plimpton (eds), *American Journey: The Life and Times of Robert Kennedy* (New York, 1970), p. 266.
43. Interview with Tom Hayden, ibid., p. 266.

protest groups on graduation, as they enter the job market or gain additional responsibilities. There was a strong possibility, therefore, that many of Kennedy's student supporters would have become more conservative, and fickle.

Kennedy pursued a risky strategy. The mystique attached to his name might have ensured success, but this was by no means certain. Thus Reagan's short-term approach to student protest was rewarded while Kennedy's long-term approach might well have failed. The supporters Reagan won when he attacked students never deserted him. Ironically, however, in the 1980 and 1984 presidential campaigns, Reagan won the support of many of the students he had once criticized so vehemently. Kennedy may have been the students' champion, but Reagan profited, unwittingly, from the transient nature of student protest.

CHAPTER TEN

The Mexican Government and Student Conflict: An Essay

DONALD MABRY

The numerous student strikes in the National Autonomous University of Mexico have involved matters of university governance, fees, and curriculum. They have usually been confined to university precincts, and the national government has rarely had to intervene. Three strikes, in 1929, 1933, and 1968, illustrate how and why the government has become involved in university issues. The key to understanding these three strikes is the role of the government in causing and ending a general strike by the university community. Although the national government played the essential role, its methods varied according to circumstances.

The incidents leading to the general university strike in 1929 were very parochial and limited to the National Preparatory School and the Law School. In February 1929, before the beginning of term, the school director, Antonio Caso, announced that the degree programme would henceforth take three not two years. Angry students tried to get the university administration to rescind the change; it refused. The Secretary of Public Education supported the director. Students then declared a strike and took over the school building, but Caso sent mounted police into the school patios to drive them out. Students could only seethe at the perceived injustice of their treatment. A few months later, the Law School decided to use periodic written instead of oral exams. This policy had been adopted for the university in 1925, but law students had blocked its implementation in their school. The new system not only meant tougher exams but also that students would have to attend class regularly, since 60 per cent attendance was required to gain admission to the first exam and 75 per cent to the other two. The students protested, but university rector Antonio Castro Leal refused to budge.[1]

The students then resorted to violence. On 4 May, a group named a strike committee, authorizing it to attack physically any student who tried to take exams under the new system. That same day, they invaded the national public education building. Then, on 7 May, they took over the law school building, only to be driven out by firemen. President Emilio Portes Gil and Education Secretary Ezequiel Padilla said that, if they had to close the school because students refused to take the examinations, the monies would be diverted to polytechnic or rural schools. This effectively isolated the protesters from potential supporters. Most law students were willing to accept the new exam system and students from the other schools refused to join, for they had experienced written exams for years. Prep students were sympathetic since they had their own grievances against the university administration but they, too, were stymied.[2] Popular sentiment ran against the idea that students should determine what they should study and for how long, and how they would be tested.

Occasional skirmishes between students and public authorities continued over the next few weeks. On 23 May a fierce battle brought the entire university into the strike and forced a showdown with the government. Police fired shots into the air and, along with firemen, fought their way into the law school, driving the students out. The students immediately spread rumours that six of their number had died in the assault and that police were unjustifiably attacking students. Converting the incident into a student versus government issue brought students from other schools into the strike; the exam issue had been irrelevant to them. At once, all 8,154 students at the national university were involved. Students in other institutions also

1. Ciriaco Pacheco Calvo, *La organización estudiantil en México* (Mexico City, 1934), p. 39; Pedro de Alba, 'Las peripecias de nuestro bachillerato', *El Nacional*, 2 Aug. 1933. Emilio Portes Gil, interview in James W. Wilkie and Edna Monzón de Wilkie, *México visto en el siglo XX* (Mexico City, 1969). UNAM, Facultad de Derecho y Ciencias Sociales, *Plan de estudios, programas y reglamentos de reconocimientos en la Facultad de Derecho y Ciencias Sociales* (Mexico City, 1929), pp. 450–1. These and the subsequent events are based on numerous sources; they can be found in the footnotes in Donald J. Mabry, *The Mexican University and the State: Student Conflicts, 1910–1971* (Syracuse, NY, 1982).

2. There is a National Preparatory School in Mexico City, the Escuela Nacional Preparatoria. Prep school students are roughly equivalent to those doing the international baccalaureate in other countries. From the prep school they enter into the professional faculties at university. They are approximately equal in age to high school students in other countries.

expressed sympathy. Suddenly, the movement threatened to spread across the nation.

Troubled by other crises, the Mexican government could not afford to ignore student action. An armed rebellion led by General José Escobar had been quashed in March and April. An end to the three-year-old church–state conflict, which had in places involved armed rebellion, was being negotiated. The special presidential election between Abelardo Rodríguez, the government's candidate, and José Vasconcelos, who had strong support in the university and among intellectuals, was under way. (It had been called because the president-elect had been assassinated the year before by a Catholic fanatic.) Since a number of students, including some of the most prominent strike leaders, were active partisans of Vasconcelos, granting partial autonomy to the university would undercut some of his support from the university community.

Portes Gil removed the university problem by granting it partial autonomy; it became the National Autonomous University of Mexico (UNAM). Portes Gil had attended the national university and had once been a student strike leader. He understood that the faculty and administration as well as most students were not angry because of curricular issues but would welcome making the university an autonomous state agency. So he gave them 'autonomy' but with strings attached – the national government still controlled finances and the appointment of rector. Students were allowed to elect their representatives to school and university councils and to participate in the election of administrators. Both sides could claim victory, leaving Portes Gil to address more important issues.

The 1929 movement set both a precedent and a pattern for subsequent strikes. Numerous young men became prominent political actors in national politics, encouraging later students to try to use university politics to launch political careers. The myth of a national student movement was given credence. Students saw themselves as paladins against an oppressive state. Even conservative students of the 1930s advocated social reform, social justice, and anti-imperialism. Student political activists commonly argued that the state was corrupt, but that 'pure' Mexican youth would fight to save the Mexican Revolution. The 1929 strike became a legend.

Full autonomy came in 1933 when President Abelardo Rodríguez had Congress withdraw funding from UNAM except for a small one-off endowment. He made it an independent university because UNAM refused to support the goals of the Revolution. This decision came because of an internecine fight between those who wanted to preserve academic freedom and those who demanded that all teaching be socialist or Marxist. As part of his presidential campaign in 1933–34, Lázaro Cárdenas supported a constitutional amendment to require socialist education below the prep school level. Some of his supporters wanted it extended to UNAM. Socialist, in this instance, sometimes meant Marxist, but more often meant little more than teaching science, social sciences, and technology, subjects in which traditionalists within UNAM had little interest. Government officials believed that UNAM could not survive the lack of government funding and would come begging once again and, when this happened, the government could dictate the curricula and select the faculty. The traditionalists kept the university going, however, until President Cárdenas, deciding that the university was too important in terms of its educational role and that its alumni were too powerful, arranged a compromise in 1935. In return for a regular appropriation, UNAM accepted Luis Chico Goerne, a strong Cárdenas supporter, as rector. UNAM assumed a pro-Revolutionary posture under the new rector. This rapprochement lasted until 1968. The government also created the Instituto Politécnico Nacional in 1937 to provide the trained personnel the nation so desperately needed. The IPN was totally under government control.[3]

Student political activity changed in the late 1940s because UNAM enrolment increased dramatically in the years after World War II and the government built a modern campus ten miles south of the heart of the city. Student demonstrations on the new campus were less likely to be met by police repression, the spark that created general student strikes, since they were isolated from the bulk of the population. Students were more likely to protest about bus services than they were about curricular issues. Even the increase in student violence in the 1960s had little effect on the city or the nation.

The 1968 strike differed from those of its predecessors because its origins were external to the university. University and city governments had warned for months that student violence, especially by gangs, had to stop or strong measures would be taken. On 22 July 1968, two rival gangs of male adolescent students fought in the Ciudadela neighbourhood of Mexico City. The next day the city

3. On socialist education, see John A. Britton, *Educación y radicalismo en México*, 2 vols (Mexico City, 1976). On the 1933–34 struggle, see Lucio Mendieta y Nuñez, *La reforma universitaria integral* (Mexico City, 1967) and Mabry, *Mexican University*, chs. 4–6.

government responded by sending policemen to stop the attendant vandalism and to arrest the perpetrators. These riot police attacked the students, and pursued them into a school building, whereupon they indiscriminately assaulted everyone, including teachers. A howl of protest arose. The national technical school students staged a protest march on 26 July, which passed by Alameda park in downtown Mexico City, where a pro-Castro group was also holding a rally. The Castroites praised the Cuban Revolution and called for a similar revolt in Mexico. Instead of proceeding to the IPN campus, the marchers stopped to hear the harangues. No one can prove whether students began to vandalize neighbouring businesses (as the government subsequently claimed) or whether police in the area attacked the demonstrators. What is known is that students and police fought each other as students fled through the streets towards the National Palace and then to the old university quarters nearby. They burned a bus and overturned others to form barricades. Students and police were injured and some students were taken to jail. Sporadic fighting continued for days.

The national government called in the army. Much of the fighting was occurring only a few blocks from the National Palace, too close for comfort for those who ruled. Early on 30 July, an army officer, frustrated by the inability of his troops to enter the precincts of the historic National Preparatory School No. 1, which had trained generations of national leaders, ordered the firing of a bazooka to blow down its wooden doors. With that act, the 87,462 students and the thousands of faculty of UNAM who had not been part of the movement closed the university and joined the protests. Strikes and protests quickly spread to other universities in the city and across the nation. To many, it appeared that the government had little regard for human rights or higher education, and that the traditional status of UNAM as a sanctuary off-limits to public security forces had been flouted.

Javier Barros Sierra, rector of UNAM, led a protest march of 100,000 persons through the city on 1 August. That same day, President Díaz Ordaz, speaking from Guadalajara, promised that the government would engage in a dialogue with the students. IPN students and faculty held their own mass march four days later. For the next few weeks, both sides tried to negotiate the agenda and the site of dialogue. To create a united front, students from these institutions and others organized a National Strike Council, an organization so large and unwieldy that it could never effectively represent student interests.

In spite of such actions as protest marches, street theatre, public appeals, fights with police and soldiers, and the takeover of buildings, the students had no hope of winning. The government was too powerful, and it, not students or educational institutions, was guiding the spectacular economic growth which was raising living standards. It represented law and order while the student movement meant disorder. Most people gained nothing from the student movement. Further, the longer the student protest movement lasted, the more it threatened the success of the Olympics, due to open in Mexico in early October. Hosting the Olympiad was a source of great national pride and would generate jobs and income. The public was unlikely to be sympathetic to anyone who threatened to sabotage it, especially to persons who seemed privileged compared to the bulk of the population. So Díaz Ordaz brought the movement to an end. When it became clear that the student movement would not stop, the army was ordered to fire on a protest demonstration being staged in the Tlatelolco apartment complex. Although no one knows for sure how many were killed on the night of 2 October, the military action ended the movement and the Olympics were successfully staged.[4]

The 1968 strike was unprecedented in Mexican history. Never before had hundreds of thousands of demonstrators marched through the capital's streets denouncing the government. Never before had UNAM and IPN cooperated so closely. And never before had the government so blatantly used violence against its elite youth. Squabbles within the university had rarely reached the presidential level, since the President is supposed to be the ultimate mediator of conflict. This traditional role was one reason why the President was never attacked in person, with the notable exception of 1968. As long as he was above the fray, he could be an honest broker – or seem to be.

A comparison of the three strikes examined in this chapter illustrates this point well. In 1929 the decision to use force was made by local officials; Portes Gil, who was out of town when the repression started, was able to mediate the dispute because he had no personal responsibility for what Federal District or National University students had done. In 1935, Cárdenas was in the second year of his presidency, one which pursued leftist policies. Accommodating UNAM, which he could not close, bought support from conservatives. In

---

4. Much has been written about the 1968 movement. See Mabry, *Mexican University*, p. 248 for a long list. A useful collection of documents is Ramón Ramiréz, *El movimiento estudiantil de México: julio–diciembre de 1968*, 2 vols (Mexico City, 1969).

1968, however, Díaz Ordaz could not be the mediator since he was the one who had ordered the army attack on the demonstrators and the university. Recognizing this, the 1968 students demanded public negotiations, which could not be done without the government negating its authority. What the students were demanding was subversive and would invite rebellion. So, in October, the government gave a definitive answer: continuance meant death. Portes Gil would not have used such a tactic, for he was an interim president during an unstable political situation. Díaz Ordaz, however, controlled an authoritarian state which was enjoying a booming economy. Moreover, the sheer magnitude of the 1968 movement, with its hundreds of thousands of participants from virtually every secondary and university-level school in the Federal District, meant that local authorities might not have been able to control events, thus prompting Díaz Ordaz and his government minister, Luis Echeverría, to use the army.

Echeverría (who was President from 1970 to 1976) tried to gain university support but when that failed also took steps to reduce the power of UNAM. The age requirement to be a member of Congress was lowered, increased educational opportunity became a national goal, and Mexico became more leftist in its foreign policy. The government funded new college preparatory schools for UNAM in 1973, partly because of enrolment demand and partly to appease the university. In 1974, the national government created the Autonomous Metropolitan University. It also began subsidizing the private El Colegio de México and built a new campus for it. Both were steps to reduce the power of UNAM.

In spite of the trouble students have caused over the years, they have not tried to overthrow the government, a fact which the latter clearly understands. University student strikes tend to be self-serving. Students rebel when police respond to student behaviour with force, tuition increases are proposed, admission, attendance, or graduation requirements are increased, or when exams are made more rigorous. Most of these rebellions are localized, and, thus, off the national political stage. When a government reacts to student strikes or demonstrations with too much force, the students will call a general strike. As 1968 demonstrates, if the general strike spills into the streets of Mexico City, then it becomes an issue which the President has to resolve. Even in 1968, the political and social criticism was an effort to gain popular support; the effort failed, for the average person did not enjoy the benefits the students had. Moreover, people understood who had the real power in the nation.

Although the students did expose the corrupt nature of the system, corruption got worse. The students had accomplished little.

The government has had to support universities in spite of student behaviour because people want their children to have the chance to enter the professions. The very size of the higher education establishment also means that the universities are a large special interest group which cannot be ignored. This is especially true of UNAM, the premier university. Modest budget increases keep the peace, but the government limits its funding because there are more pressing needs. When the national government wants programmatic changes to meet a national need, however, it funds them and the universities quickly accept the money. Through this modus vivendi, government and higher education have agreed to leave each other alone. The universities understand that it is the national government which ultimately has power. No one could doubt that after the events of 1968.

CHAPTER ELEVEN

The State and the Student Movement in West Germany, 1967–77

A.D. MOSES

The ideological sources of state and student radicalisation

The confrontation between the West German state and the student movement of the 1960s and 1970s is a case of mutual hostility and escalating violence. A feature of the modern state is its monopoly on force, and the student movement set out to resist and disrupt it. But confrontations between police and demonstrators were not capricious exercises in provocation: they were undertaken in support of certain ideals. The ideological legitimization of state and student action is as important as the conflict itself, because in order to win and maintain support, both parties justified themselves by appealing to shared values and generational experiences. A striking feature of the German situation, and the 'structural' factor that led to the ascending spiral of polarization and violence, was the *passion* and *symmetry* of the respective cultural ideologies of the political elite and the student movement.

Both sides were motivated by a moral and political imperative to ensure that Nazism, or its equivalent, would never again blight German soil. They sought to implement the perceived lessons of Germany's past, in particular, those of the Weimar Republic (1919–33) and the subsequent Nazi period (1933–45). Whether 'Bonn was Weimar' was the burning question of the day, and the respective cultural ideologies of the West German state and its opponents sought, in their divergent ways, to prevent an affirmative answer.[1]

1. Fritz R. Allemann, *Bonn ist nicht Weimar* (Munich, 1956); Karl Dietrich Bracher, 'Wird Bonn doch Weimar?', *Der Spiegel* (13 March 1967), pp. 60f.; Hans Schuster, 'Wird Bonn doch Weimar?', *Merkur* (June 1969), pp. 501–14.

Reflecting radically different generational experiences, both sides drew symmetrically opposed conclusions from the catastrophic past. The political class – the founders of the new West German state – had personally experienced Weimar, the Second World War (1939–45), and the Soviet incorporation of the eastern German provinces (*Länder*).[2] They based their historical analysis on the theory of totalitarianism, which dominated Western thinking during the Cold War. The weakness of Weimar was twofold: first, its 'value neutrality' tolerated large numbers of Nazis and communists, whose explicit goal was to abolish the parliamentary system and replace it with right or left-wing dictatorships; second, there were too few 'militant democrats' prepared to defend the constitutional order against such extremism. Weimar had been torn asunder by totalitarian ideological polarization, while the state had failed to control paramilitary organizations of the right and left.[3] This view was shared by social democrats (SPD), many of whom had been persecuted by the Nazi regime, and then similarly oppressed after the war by Soviet officials in their occupation zone. In this way, the theory of totalitarianism became the unofficial legitimating ideology of the Federal Republic, which was seen by its elites and allies alike as the bulwark against perceived Soviet aggression.[4]

The conclusive answer to totalitarianism was liberal democracy, and the founders of the new West German state defended the new Bonn republic with the policy of 'belligerent democracy' (*streitbare Demokratie*) – the resolute protection of the 'free democratic basic order' (*freiheitliche demokratische Grundordnung*), the 'state of law' (*Rechtsstaat*), and the 'anti-totalitarian consensus' against perceived security threats.[5] Fascism and communism were thus understood as directed *against* the liberal state. In 1950 and 1951, at the height of

2. Jeffrey Herf, *Divided Memory: The Nazi Past in the Two Germanys* (Cambridge, Mass., 1997).

3. Richard Löwenthal, 'Widerstand im totalitären Staat', in Richard Löwenthal and Patrik von zur Mühlen, *Widerstand und Verweigerung in Deutschland, 1933 bis 1945* (Bonn, 1984), pp. 11–24. A recent intellectual history of totalitarianism is Abbot Gleason, *Totalitarianism: The Inner History of the Cold War* (Oxford and New York, 1995).

4. It should be noted, though, that the SPD did not support entry into NATO until 1960. See Stephen J. Artner, *A Change of Course: The West German Social Democrats and NATO* (Westport, Conn., 1985).

5. Eckhard Jesse, *Streitbare Demokratie: Theorie, Praxis, und Herausforderung in der Bundesrepublik* (Berlin, 1980); Erhard Denninger *et al.*, *Freiheitliche demokratische Grundordnung: Materialien zum Staatsverständnis und zur Verfassungswirklichkeit in der Bundesrepublik*, 2 vols. (Frankfurt a.M., 1977). The term 'free democratic basic order' is mentioned in those articles of the *Basic Law* (18, 21:2, and 91) that deal with 'enemies of the state'.

the Korean War, the legal and institutional rudiments of an inner security apparatus were established, including the laws in the penal code (*Strafgesetzbuch*, StGB) adumbrated in the section 'Dangers to the State'. Communists were persecuted because they opposed the rearming of West Germany and its entry into the Western military alliance.

Such laws distinguished West Germany from its neighbours by their preventative character. By targeting oppositional activity before it could become organized, they sought to obviate what government ministers called 'intellectual sabotage' and 'ideological subversion'.[6] The Federal Republic, unlike the established Western liberal democracies, so the argument went, could not afford the luxury of tolerating radical critics and 'inner enemies', because its own democratic roots were still shallow and its international position at the forefront of the Cold War was precarious. The point was to prevent the Weimar scenario: an alternative public sphere or extra-parliamentary centre of political loyalty. The most significant manifestations of this posture were the banning of the Communist Party (KPD) in 1956 and the controversial 'Emergency Laws' (passed on 28 June 1968), which invested the state with the coercive means to stabilize the polity during times of crisis.

Liberal and parliamentary though 'belligerent democracy' was, its prophylactic and system-stabilizing aims lent the Federal Republic a conservative, at times even authoritarian, tenor, which perpetuated traditions of heavy-handed 'statism'. Haunted by the spectre of 'ungovernability' – another legacy of Weimar – governmental elites opposed civil disobedience that challenged the technocratic administration of affairs.[7] In the siege mentality of the Cold War, protest against government policy was interpreted as hazardous to the system as a whole. The liberal sociologist Ralf Dahrendorf assailed the fear of conflict among German elites as a 'cartel of anxiety'.[8]

Without doubt, the 'traditionalism' of the early Federal Republic aided the integration of the tens of millions of Germans who had supported Hitler. And yet, precisely for this reason, 'belligerent

6. Cited in Sebastian Cobler, *Law, Order and Politics in West Germany* (New York, 1978), pp. 52f., 74ff. Typical is law §90a StGB, which made it a crime to 'defame the state and its symbols'. Law §129 StGB targets criminal organizations and their support, and was later amended to include 'ideological' support: for example, the sale of books that popularize terrorist texts.

7. Cobler, *Law, Order and Politics in West Germany*, p. 82. See also Peter Katzenstein, *West Germany's Internal Security Policy: State and Violence in the 1970s and 1980s* (Cornell, NY, 1990).

8. Ralf Dahrendorf, *State and Democracy in Germany* (New York, 1967), pp. 261f.

democracy' was less than compelling for the younger generation. The point of the 'anti-totalitarian consensus' was to prevent extra-parliamentary opposition to the 'free democratic basic order' and *Rechtsstaat*. But in conservative hands, these ideals stifled critique, dissent, and difference *per se*, radicalizing the younger generation, which saw the seedbed of fascism precisely in the absence of critique, dissent, and difference. In the end, 'belligerent democracy' created the rod that beat its back: the government's campaign for the 'Emergency Laws' actually *produced* the 'inner enemy' they were meant to check.

How was this possible? The younger generation, born around 1945 (referred to in Germany as the '68ers'), did not share the totalitarian experience of their parents, whose democratic commitment they doubted.[9] Had they not cheered for Hitler, or at least failed to resist his regime? Worse still, were there not many former Nazis in positions of power? The older generation seemed to find the anti-communism of West Germany, which mirrored that of the Nazi state, more attractive than its democratic pretensions.[10] Hopes of reform were dashed when the SPD joined the ruling Christian Democrats (CDU) in a Grand Coalition in 1966. Without an effective parliamentary opposition, it was feared, Germany would once again slide into dictatorship. Consequently, the 68ers joined older left-liberal intellectuals in the 'Extra-Parliamentary Opposition' (APO), to resist the proposed 'Emergency Laws', seeing in them the attempt to establish an anti-constitutional, authoritarian regime like Franco's Spain, Salazar's Portugal, or even Hitler's 'Third Reich'.[11]

Sections of the student movement were not content with mere protest or resistance. Adhering to Marxist-inspired 'fascism theory', they understood national socialism as a form of 'bourgeois dictatorship', which the ruling class instituted in times of crisis to maintain its domination.[12] Identifying with 'Third World' struggles against global capitalism, they condemned West Germany's economic and military links with the USA, which was regarded as pursuing a

9. Heinz Bude, 'The German *Kriegskinder*: origins and impact of the generation of 1968', in Mark Roseman (ed.), *Generations in Conflict: Youth Revolt and Generation Formation in Germany, 1770–1968* (Cambridge, 1995).

10. Hans Magnus Enzensberger, 'Berliner Gemeinplätze', *Kursbuch*, 11 (January 1968), p. 155; Kurt L. Shell, 'Extraparliamentary opposition in postwar Germany', *Comparative Politics* 4 (July 1970), pp. 652–80.

11. Iring Fetscher, *Terrorismus und Reaktion in der Bundesrepublik Deutschland* (Frankfurt a.M., 1977); Horst Mewes, 'The German New Left', *New German Critique*, 1 (1974), pp. 22–41.

12. Wolfgang Wipperman, 'The post-war German left and fascism', *Journal of Contemporary History*, 11 (1976), pp. 185–209.

genocidal war in Vietnam, reminiscent of the Nazis' imperialism. The working class would be radicalized, it was naively believed, when student provocation revealed the 'true' fascist face of the capitalist state. In stark contrast to 'belligerent democracy', fascism was seen to emanate *from* the state. Opposition to and critique of the system, not its affirmation, was the imperative of the past.

Both sides understood themselves as 'mastering the past', but came to diametrically opposite conclusions. By viewing the other as representing the fatal errors of the past, they set in motion a cycle of escalation: the greater the efforts of the state to quash radical dissent, the more the state seemed to students the authoritarian or fascist object of odium they assumed it to be. Likewise, the more the students defied and resisted the state, the more they appeared to politicians and security forces as the much-feared 'inner enemy'. The symmetry of the respective cultural ideologies was an in-built mechanism of radicalization.[13] Unless the vicious circle was broken by virtuous gestures of reconciliation and the stereotypes of the other shattered, the logic of each ideology led to the metaphorical or even physical annihilation of the other.

The escalation

In the beginning was the death of Benno Ohnesorg, shot by a policeman in Berlin during a demonstration against the visit of the Shah of Iran on 2 June 1967. Hitherto the students had employed tactics of limited illegality (sit-ins, teach-ins, etc.) – generally non-violent and novel types of demonstrative activity, for which the police were unprepared. Now it appeared that the state was prepared to use murderous violence against the APO. The West Berlin-based student movement spread throughout the Federal Republic, and a debate ensued about the efficacy of 'violent defence'. Violence against property rather than people was thought the best means of politicizing a population rendered docile by consumerism and an exaggerated communist threat.[14] While revolutionary

13. Fritz Sack and Heinz Steinert, *Protest und Reaktion* (Opladen, 1984); Antonia Grunenberg, 'Anti-totalitarianism vs. anti-fascism: two legacies of the past in Germany', *German Politics and Society* 15 (1997), pp. 110–24; A.D. Moses, 'Cultural ideologies and historical legitimation', ibid., pp. 125–30.

14. Donatella Della Porta, *Social Movements, Political Violence, and the State: A Comparative Analysis of Germany and Italy* (Cambridge, 1995), pp. 37f.; Karl Otto, *APO: Die ausserparlamentarische Opposition in Quellen und Dokumenten, 1961–1970* (Cologne, 1989).

rhetoric intensified, the future core members of the major terrorist group, the Red Army Faction (RAF), Andreas Baader, Gudrun Ensslin and two others, took matters into their own hands by fire-bombing two Frankfurt department stores on 2 April 1968.[15] On 11 April, Rudi Dutschke, the charismatic student leader, was shot and severely wounded by an angry citizen, who judged him a threat to democracy. Students blamed the press, especially the populist newspapers owned by Axel Springer, which portrayed them as anarchic criminals.[16] During demonstrations against the attack on Dutschke and the Emergency Laws, involving some 300,000 protesters nationwide, the Springer building in Berlin was besieged and 27 policemen injured.

Such was the polarization of students and the state in 1969. Whither the revolution? It had become apparent that the state would not relinquish its control of the streets, and that the wider population did not share the students' revolutionary ambitions. There were two alternatives: transform or destroy the state. Unable to negotiate between moderates and radicals, the principal student organization, the 'Socialist German Student League' (*Sozialistischer deutscher Studentenbund*, SDS) dissolved itself in 1970, whereafter it is impossible to speak of a unified student movement.[17] And yet, the idealistic ardour of the 68ers was by no means spent. The vast majority of them heeded Dutschke's peaceful, though radically reformist, call to 'march through the institutions'. Leftist university graduates, eager to actualize the reform promise of the social–liberal coalition government (SPD–FDP) led by Willy Brandt (1969–74), joined the SPD and became teachers and journalists.

Terrorism, by contrast, took the 'anti-fascist' analysis to its logical conclusion by attacking what Che Guevara called 'the heart of the beast'. After terrorist training in the Middle East, the RAF returned to West Germany to begin the 'armed struggle' against US military bases, establishment figures, and the Springer press. The high point of the early 1970s was the 'May Offensive' of 1972 – a response to US bombing in Vietnam – in which the American military head-quarters in Heidelberg was attacked and soldiers killed in Frank-furt. Although reviled by the wider population, the RAF appeared

---

15. On the RAF, see Stefan Aust, *Der Baader Meinhof Komplex*, 2nd edn (Hamburg, 1997).

16. Rob Burns and Wilfried van der Will, *Protest and Democracy in West Germany: Extra-Parliamentary Opposition and the Democratic Agenda* (London, 1988), pp. 110ff.

17. Tilman Fichter and Siegward Lönnendonker, *Kleine Geschichte des SDS* (Berlin, 1977).

to enjoy some support in the new youth milieu ('the scene') – the counter-cultural left-wing opposition to bourgeois (*bürgerlich*) Germany. Based on and around university campuses, home to a bewildering array of communist and anarchist groups (*K-Gruppen*, '*Spontis*'), and with its own press and tightly knit social life, 'the scene' deeply alarmed the state. An Allensbacher Institute opinion poll reported that 20 per cent of Germans said they would shelter RAF members from police pursuit. By 1 June 1972, however,the inner core of the RAF had been captured in massive security operations.[18]

The reaction of the state

The state was not a unified entity. On the one hand, the social–liberal coalition, which ruled in Bonn and most provinces throughout the 1970s, wanted to reintegrate the younger generation, avoid open displays of force, and thaw relations with the communist countries in the east (*Ostpolitik*). On the other hand, conservative Christian Democrats (CDU), who held power in the federal upper house (*Bundesrat*) and some provincial governments, accused opponents of being soft on communism abroad and 'extremists' at home.

In 1970, the social democratic chancellor, Willy Brandt, defused the tense situation by declaring that his government would 'dare more democracy' and grant amnesty from prosecution to about 10,000 protesters, who had broken demonstration laws. Yet fear grew in SPD circles that by remaining within the system hardliners would hijack key institutions, including the SPD itself. The growing youth wing of the SPD (*Jungsozialisten* or *Jusos*), after all, had explicitly stated its intention to 're-ideologize' the party.[19] In response to the large number of communists entering the teaching profession in Hamburg, the city senate resolved, in late 1971, to require all applicants for civil service positions to guarantee their loyalty to the 'free democratic basic order'. By the following January, the central government and all provinces had agreed to institute and coordinate similar selection and disciplinary policies. Applicants for civil service jobs would be vetted by the secret service agency, the *Verfassungsschutz* (Office for the Protection of the Constitution).

18. S.D. Hoffmann-Axthelm *et al.*, *Zweikulturen* (Munich, 1979); Wanda von Baeyer-Katte *et al.*, *Gruppenprozesse* (Opladen, 1982); Wolfgang Kraushaar, *Autonomie oder Getto?* (Frankfurt a.M., 1978); Andrei S. Markovits and Philip S. Gorski, *The German Left: Red, Green and Beyond* (Oxford, 1993), pp. 81ff.
19. Markovits and Gorski, *The German Left*, pp. 94f.

Called the *Extremistenbeschluss* or *Radikalenerlass* (Decision on Extremists, Decree on Radicals) by the state, and the *Berufsverbot* (Ban on Careers) by the left, the policy gave great disciplinary power to the state, and in due course the *Verfassungsschutz* gathered some two million files on suspected 'inner enemies'.[20] Although only relatively few were actually dismissed or refused employment, leftist students and intellectuals felt intimidated and campaigned vigorously against the policy. Once again, it was thought, the state resorts to authoritarian measures when democratic forces attempt its reform.[21]

No less significant was the state's reaction to terrorism. As of 1970, the new federal government bolstered the Federal Criminal Investigation Bureau (*Bundeskriminalamt*, BKA) with massive budget and personnel increases, and appointed Horst Herold to oversee its operations. A modernizer and 'security intellectual', he was convinced that the fight against terrorism would only succeed with the most advanced information-gathering and computer technology, and the coordination of different state agencies under the command of the BKA. Such measures were instituted as part of the policy of 'Inner Security' in 1972.[22] In response to the RAF's 'May Offensive' that year, the state was able to mobilize 150,000 police and border guards and capture the RAF leadership.[23]

The nightmare of terrorism, however, had only just begun. Loosely organized but potent *Rote Zellen* (Red Cells) of two or three persons committed 132 bombing and arson attacks by 1982.[24] Moreover, the incarceration of terrorists triggered a cycle of escalation, which repeated itself over subsequent years. RAF prisoners were isolated from other prisoners, according to some sources, in windowless cells with constant artificial light. These conditions were interpreted as 'isolation torture' by 'the scene', and prisoners went on hunger-strike.[25] A 'second generation' of terrorists was born, and henceforth the RAF gave high priority to freeing its captured members. The day after the hunger-striker Holger Meins died on 9 November 1974, Günter von Drenkmann, a judge, was shot by

20. Gerhard Braunthal, *Political Loyalty and Public Service in West Germany: The 1972 Decree against Radicals and its Consequences* (Amherst, Mass., 1990), p. 166; Gregg O. Kvistad, 'Radicals and the state: the political demands on West German civil servants', *Comparative Political Studies* 21 (1988), pp. 99–125.

21. Horst Bethge and Erich Roßmann (eds), *Der Kampf gegen das Berufsverbot* (Cologne, 1973).

22. Erhard Blankenburg (ed.), *Politik der inneren Sicherheit* (Frankfurt a.M., 1980).

23. Enno Brand, *Staatsgewalt: Politische Unterdrückung und Innere Sicherheit in der Bundesrepublik* (Göttingen, 1988), p. 118.

24. Markovits and Gorski, *The German Left*, pp. 73–5.

25. See 'Torture in the FRG', in *Kursbuch* 32 (August 1973).

the 'Movement of 2 June', another group formed specifically to free terrorists. In response, later that month, the BKA undertook 'Operation Winter Journey', a search for terrorists. Some 96 apartments were raided in 15 cities.[26] In the lead-up to the trial of the RAF leadership in 1975, the RAF occupied the German embassy in Stockholm in the hope of exchanging 'prisoners'. Several hostages were killed in the ensuing raid, and an RAF member was badly wounded. He later died in police custody, confirming 'the 'scene's' view that the state murdered political prisoners.

While terrorism dominated the headlines, far greater numbers were involved in other confrontations with the police, namely in massive demonstrations against the construction of atomic energy plants. In response to the occupation in February 1975 of a building site at Whyl, the minister-president of Baden-Wurttemberg, Hans Filbinger, complained that 'If it becomes normal for any large-scale project to be faced with opposition from people with ideological or other interests who will use force directly or indirectly, this country will become ungovernable.'[27] At subsequent protests, at Brockdorf in October 1976, and Grohde in March 1977, thousands of policemen in riot gear, reinforced by helicopters and water cannons, confronted tens of thousands of demonstrators. Yet despite the physical confrontations, the provocation of communist hardliners, and massive numbers involved, no more martyrs in the mould of Ohnesorg were created. Herold's modernization of the police and security forces had succeeded.[28]

The tension between the state and protest movements culminated in the worst case of violent escalation: the notorious 'German Autumn' of 1977.[29] With their leadership sentenced to life imprisonment, the RAF shot the man they held responsible, the federal attorney-general, Siegfried Buback, and his driver, in April. Conservative politicians called for the introduction of the death penalty, and the Bavarian minister-president Franz-Josef Strauss went so far as to suggest that several prisoners be executed for every RAF victim. After the shooting of the Dresdner Bank chief Jürgen Pont in a bungled abduction attempt, and a failed rocket attack on

26. Markovits and Gorski, *The German Left*, p. 123.
27. Cited in Cobler, *Law, Order and Politics in West Germany*, p. 85.
28. Heiner Busch *et al.*, *Die Polizei in der Bundesrepublik* (Frankfurt a.M., 1985), pp. 319–56.
29. Margit Mayer, 'The German October of 1977', *New German Critique* 13 (Winter 1978), pp. 155–64; Geoffrey Pridham, 'Terrorism and the state in West Germany during the 1970s', in Juliet Lodge (ed.), *Terrorism: A Challenge to the State* (Oxford, 1981), pp. 11–56.

the Federal Court building in Karlsruhe, the RAF succeeded in kidnapping the president of the major employer association and former Nazi officer Hans-Martin Schleyer in August, killing four of his bodyguards in the process. Once again, they wanted an 'exchange of prisoners', but since the exchange of the leading CDU politician Konrad Lenz in 1975, the government had decided to refuse further negotiations. Palestinian terrorists hijacked a Lufthansa jet to increase the pressure. In the ensuing public hysteria, a media blackout was ordered and thousands of police and border guards lined city streets. Members of 'the scene' and left-liberal intellectuals were denounced by conservative politicians, like Filbinger, for 'sympathizing' with, if not actually causing, terrorism, an accusation which was lent plausibility for many Germans by the notorious 'Mescelaro Affair' in the summer, in which an anarchist student had publicly confessed 'secret joy' at the murder of Buback.[30] Only a month earlier, in September, 70,000 protesters had faced 10,000 police at Kalkar, in yet another violent encounter over an atomic energy plant. West Germany was dangerously polarized. The tension was finally released on 18 October when special German forces raided the stricken Lufthansa jet, freeing all hostages and killing the hijackers. That night, four of the RAF's 'first generation', including Baader and Ensslin, committed suicide in their Stammheim cells.

Conclusion

The 'German Autumn' of 1977 is remembered in the Federal Republic as a time of dangerous ideological division. Leftists contended that the state undermined its commitment to the *Rechtsstaat* in hastily passed laws, which dramatically extended police powers and restricted civil liberties: the paradox of a virtual police state ('creeping fascism', some called it) to protect democracy.[31] Conservatives and many social democrats, like the political scientist Kurt Sontheimer, retorted that without terrorism and utopian criticism of the Federal Republic, such a reaction would never have occurred.[32] Fortunately for West Germany, the crisis management

30. See the response of Jürgen Habermas, 'A test for popular justice: the accusation against the intellectuals', *New German Critique* 12 (1977), pp. 11–13.

31. Freimut Duve *et al.* (eds), *Briefe zur Verteidigung der Republik* (Reinbeck, 1977).

32. Kurt Sontheimer, *Die verunsicherte Republik: Die Bundesrepublik nach dreissig Jahren* (Munich, 1979).

of the social democratic chancellor Helmut Schmidt (1974–82) averted the civil war measures for which conservatives had called, and which would have played into the terrorists' hands. Social democratic provinces de-escalated the situation by a less strict application of the *Radikalenerlass.*

It had become apparent that 'belligerent democracy' was insufficient when not balanced by tolerance for a loyal *non-parliamentary* opposition. Citizens wanted to be more than obedient objects of government policy. But then the left needed to commit itself to the Federal Republic's liberal institutions. The founding of the Green Party in 1977 marked a positive beginning, even if it regarded itself as an 'anti-party party'. Although the left still clashed violently with police during the early 1980s over nuclear weapons and squatting issues, the disturbing polarization of 1977 was not repeated. Conservatives, for their part, had to temper their rhetoric when Filbinger was forced to resign in disgrace on 7 August 1978, after the writer Rolf Hochhuth revealed that he had served as a judge under the Nazis and had sentenced servicemen to death in the last days of the war. He had not shown the generosity to leftists in the 1970s that had been granted him after the war.[33] But it was precisely such generosity that the country needed to break out of the vicious circle of escalating violence.

33. On the integration of Nazi elites in the Federal Republic, see Ulrich Herbert, 'NS-Eliten in der Bundesrepublik. Bestrafung – Tolerierung – Integration', in Karl Teppe and Hans-Ulrich Thamer (eds), *50 Jahre Nordrhein-Westfalen – Land im Wandel* (Münster, 1997), pp. 7–22.

PART FOUR

Reverberations

CHAPTER TWELVE

Reforming the University: Student Protests and the Demand for a 'Relevant' Curriculum

JULIE A. REUBEN

Almost no students value activity as citizens. . . . But apathy is not simply an attitude; it is a product of social institutions, and of the structure and organization of higher education itself.
Port Huron Statement, Students for Democratic Society, 1962.

In the early 1960s, small groups of students formed in American colleges and universities to encourage political activism among their peers. Inspired by the student civil rights agitation in the South and disturbed by the apathy that reigned on campus, these students blamed the institutions they attended for the widespread complacency of their fellow students. They argued that the nature of university education – its abstract curriculum that ignored contemporary social issues, its devotion to the ideal of objectivity and distrust of commitment and engagement, its authoritarian style of instruction that encouraged passivity rather than participation, and its campus rules that unnecessarily restricted students' freedom – produced uninvolved, self-centred students and graduates.[1]

Although efforts to promote greater activism initially produced little change, by mid-decade, the rising tide of social protest, combined with the notoriety of the Free Speech Movement at the University of California, Berkeley, made a national student movement viable. Activists wanted to take advantage of this new mood to

The author would like to thank Lisa Lovett for her comments on earlier drafts of this essay, Julie Stewart for research assistance on women's studies, Alan Divack and Idelle Nissila-Stone at the Ford Foundation Archives, and the Spencer Foundation for their generous funding of this research.
  1. Mitchell Cohen and Dennis Hale (eds), *The New Student Left: An Anthology* (Boston, Mass., 1966).

institute permanent changes on university campuses, which would abolish traditional practices believed to inhibit student involvement. They wanted a new, 'relevant' education, which would encourage students' active participation in their own education and in their society.

Students first tried to reform the university indirectly, by creating alternative 'free universities' – intended as models for what the university should become. But, as the decade progressed, militancy increased and students tried to change the university directly, demanding new programmes that would link curricula to political movements. Black students led this second phase with calls for black studies programmes. They were followed by other ethnic groups and by women, seeking curricula to further their own liberation. In each case, a 'relevant' curriculum was defined as one that addressed subject matter related to political and social causes *and* rejected traditional academic practices. Militants wanted instructors to abandon political neutrality and objective scholarship. They demanded a blurring of distinctions between faculty and students, with more participatory pedagogy, giving students control over programme development. Finally, they wanted the classroom opened to community members and non-traditional students, and to teachers without academic qualifications.

In some respects, these attempts to transform the curriculum were successful. For example, by the early 1970s, 800 colleges and universities had established black studies programmes. Although the number has since decreased to about 375, black studies, as well as other ethnic studies and women's studies programmes, have become prominent and apparently permanent parts of American higher education. But, despite this success, activists were unable to impose broader changes in academic practices which they believed essential to a 'relevant' curriculum.[2]

Phase One: the free university movement

The Students for Democratic Society (SDS), one of the most dynamic sources of campus activism, encouraged its members to relate political change – the fight against racism, poverty, the war in Vietnam – to institutional change in universities and colleges. On the most basic level, SDS leaders argued that universities served the status quo by failing to graduate independent, engaged, critical

2. Thomas J. La Belle and Christopher Ward, *Ethnic Studies and Multiculturalism* (Albany, NY, 1996), p. 78.

citizens. They seemed instead to produce the opposite – conformist, satisfied adults who sustained the 'system' without knowing it. 'When we consider the fact that *our universities are already chief agents for social change in the direction of [Orwell's] 1984*,' explained Carl Davidson to a national SDS convention, 'I think we can see why it is imperative that we organize the campuses.' According to this view, university reform was a precondition for wider change in the political consciousness of the nation.[3]

SDS and other activist groups on campuses thought that universities needed to offer courses that dealt directly with contemporary political and social issues and encouraged activism. They faced a dilemma: they wanted to transform the curriculum but they had no control over the content or structure of courses offered. The Vietnam teach-ins, organized by students and faculty at a number of universities in 1965, offered a potential solution – alternative political education outside the regular course of study. At the 1965 national convention, SDS delegates proposed parallel institutions that could offer the kind of education they thought universities should provide. 'Free universities', they argued, could provide a model for university reform. As students woke up to the possibility of a 'true' education, they would demand institutional changes.[4]

Over the next few years, students at hundreds of institutions founded free universities, created to 'destroy the irrelevant university'. Although these varied widely, certain common features emerged. Students controlled their own education, and chose courses they wanted to take. They assumed that they knew best what they needed to learn. The authority of the instructor was decreased, with faculty encouraged to think of themselves as facilitators and to use pedagogical techniques that promoted active learning and relied on students' experiences. Although regular faculty could teach at free universities, organizers welcomed students, community activists, and others as instructors.[5]

Organizers also rejected the model of political neutrality. Although various ideological positions were accepted, political courses were designed to engage students in a cause, not simply offer a dispassionate analysis of events. Free universities, such as the Experimental

3. Carl Davidson, 'University reform revisited', address to the 1966 SDS National Convention at Clear Lake, Iowa. Published as an SDS pamphlet, reprinted in *Educational Record* 48 (1967), p. 8.
4. Paul Lauter and Florence Howe, *The Conspiracy of the Young* (New York, 1970), ch. 4.
5. Ann Arbor Free University, January 1966, quoted ibid., p. 108.

College at San Francisco State, included courses on 'organizing', that included direct involvement in community projects. The Free University of Pennsylvania organizers described their curriculum as 'too contemporary, controversial, broad or narrow to be part of the university curriculum', and included courses on 'Black Power', 'The New Left', 'Contemporary Education', and 'American Youth in Revolt'.[6]

Free universities were open to everyone. Students rejected the idea that special qualifications were needed to attend university. They also eschewed grades and other mechanisms of evaluation judged irrelevant to learning. Student activists argued that grades only served the interests of corporate capitalism, which needed easy ways to divide and rank people. Some organizers, however, sought to have their courses recognized by the university and granted credit – the first step in transforming the regular university.

At a number of institutions students were allowed to take free university courses for credit. San Francisco State, for example, permitted students to earn independent study credit for alternative classes and even gave credit to groups of students rather than just individuals. Some departments even counted these courses when calculating staff teaching loads. The University of California, Berkeley created the Board of Educational Development to sponsor courses outside regular departments which would not require approval of faculty committees. These classes could be initiated by faculty or students, although student-initiated courses required a faculty sponsor in order to be granted credit. This policy effectively institutionalized Berkeley's Free University. Although not all universities went this far, many tolerated free universities and gave them some official sanction.[7]

After discovering that universities could easily coexist with free universities without changing core education programmes, militant students changed their views on alternative curricula as an instrument of university reform. Once enthusiastic supporters, they came to despair of the power of free universities to transform higher education. Carl Davidson explained to fellow SDS members: 'We may feel liberated in our Free Universities; but, in the meantime, the "unfree" university we left goes on cranking out corporate liberals.

6. James W. Brann, 'San Francisco students run own "college"', *Chronicle of Higher Education* 1 (21 Dec. 1966), pp. 1, 4–5; Free University of Pennsylvania brochure quoted in Lauter and Howe, *Conspiracy of the Young*, p. 105.
7. Brann, 'San Francisco students', p. 5; Nathan Glazer, '"Student power" in Berkeley', in Daniel Bell and Irving Kristol (eds), *Confrontation: The Student Rebellion and the Universities* (New York, 1968), p. 12; Lauter and Howe, *Conspiracy of the Young*, pp. 110–11.

In fact, they have it easier since we aren't around making trouble.' Activists decided to confront universities directly and force them to change.[8]

Phase Two: black studies and other liberation curricula

At the same time that SDS rejected free universities as a mechanism of change, black students began to take the lead in campus protests. Courses on black history and politics had been part of the free university curricula. Picking up on SDS leaders' perception that indirect curricular reform was ineffective, black activists demanded that universities create black studies programmes which would provide a 'relevant' education that furthered black empowerment. Activists argued that adding classes on 'the black experience' would not suffice; the university needed to fundamentally change standard academic practices. After 1968, black studies, rather than free universities, became the most dynamic model for university reform.

Black activists argued that the education offered by the university was racist and perpetuated the subjugation of non-whites. 'If the university has traditionally trained the leadership of this country, then it is teaching racism, for that leadership has been responsible for creating and perpetuating unabated racism domestically and internationally', argued William Sales, Jr., a student at Columbia. Students maintained that universities stripped blacks of their cultural identity by insisting that they adopt white cultural mores in order to succeed. As a consequence, black elites had become alienated from themselves and from the larger black community. Students hoped that black studies would heal this estrangement. 'Colleges', Elliott Moorman, a Princeton student, insisted, 'must create a black leadership group that readily and permanently identifies with, and is culturally proud of, other black Americans. . . . Hence the need for Afro-American studies.' Black studies was not supposed to be 'just another academic department within the University'; according to Harvard students it would be 'uncomparable to other University departments because it is the first legitimized academic structure created specifically to enable Black students . . . to broaden *knowledge of self*'.[9]

8. Davidson, 'University reform revisited', p. 8.
9. William W. Sales, Jr., 'Response to a "Negro negative"', in Immanuel Wallerstein and Paul Starr (eds), *The University Crisis Reader: The Liberal University Under Attack*

Radical black students and their allies saw ties to the black community as a critical feature of the programmes they sought. Community programmes would help students overcome the alienation felt in the university, and help struggling black communities by bringing the resources, expertise and money of universities to the deeper problems of urban ghettos. They warned, however, of the danger of patronizing these communities. Gerald McWorter, a militant sociologist at Spellman, argued that universities should not assume their usual attitude of 'We've got something and we're going to put it in there'. Instead, they must define 'some kind of cooperative arrangement' with black communities.[10]

Community-based programmes would, it was also hoped, ensure that black studies were rooted in an authentic 'black perspective'. Students expected black studies to provide an antidote to the white values that pervaded their education, and wanted, therefore, a guarantee that new programmes did not just offer a few more courses in Afro-American history or literature. They wanted programmes that embodied 'black consciousness' and sought ways to make black studies truly 'black'. This meant that the programmes must be controlled by black administrators and faculty. But, as students frequently pointed out, black leaders had been trained to 'whiten' themselves and, therefore, many internalized the perspective of their 'colonizers'. So black leadership, while a necessary precondition, was insufficient insurance of a 'black perspective'. Cooperative programmes with black community organizations would help orient black studies toward black rather than white culture, since blacks in segregated communities were assumed to be more isolated from white values, and closer to a true black culture.[11]

Students offered additional strategies for affirming a black perspective. Donald Ogilvie, a Yale student, explained the need for hiring faculty based on their experience rather than their education:

> We want an opportunity to learn about the things that are relevant to our existence and we want to learn in the best possible ways,

(New York, 1971), p. 371; Elliott Duane Moorman, 'The benefit of anger', ibid., p. 336; 'As the Afro-American Studies Department was born out of student struggle, continued student participation and support are essential to its survival', HUF 124.171.4, ca. 1971, Harvard University Archives.

10. Gerald A. McWorter, 'Deck the ivy racist halls: the case of Black Studies', in Armstead L. Robinson *et al.* (eds), *Black Studies in the University: A Symposium* (New Haven, Conn., 1969), p. 63.

11. Troy Duster, 'The third world college and the colonial analogy', in *The University Crisis Reader*, pp. 340–3.

experiencing the expertise of *all* those who have something to offer. This means exposure in the classroom to men of controversial qualification – on the one hand, eminently qualified to instruct because of *what* they know; yet, on the other hand, grossly underqualified because of *how* they came to know it.

Students also set themselves up as bulwarks against false consciousness. At many institutions, radicals demanded a role in the governance of black studies departments. They believed that if they could control course development and faculty selection, they could assure that programmes would contribute to self-understanding and black empowerment.[12]

Proponents of black studies believed that they could develop alternative forms of scholarship that would breach the gap between knowledge and action, and serve as levers for general academic reform. Ronald Walters, a political scientist at Howard, explained that one of the promises of black studies was that it would 'revolutionize an institution that needed shaking from its lethargic sense of existence. I had hoped that scholars would begin to see their disciplines in new ways and that the university would make the administrative changes to facilitate this process.' It was hoped that students' role in governance would spread to other departments, creating a new alliance between students and faculty, which would wrest control away from trustees and administrators who did the bidding of industry and government. Instead of preparing students to be 'cogs' in the system, universities could then provide a truly liberating education. Black studies, explained Nathan Hare, then head of black studies at San Francisco State, 'will have an impact ultimately on the whites. The white student will use it as a basis for demanding a change in his own curriculum, as he is doing now, and we can bring about an impact, if we are successful, on the entire cemetery of American education as it exists today.'[13]

Black studies became a model for other groups seeking to use the university to further liberation movements. In the West and South-West, a Chicano student movement emerged and formed campus organizations, such as MEChA (El Movimiento Estudiantil Chicano de Aztlàn), which pressed for Chicano studies programmes. A group of graduate students organized a conference at the University of

---

12. Donald H. Ogilvie, 'A student's reflections', in *Black Studies in the University*, p. 81.
13. Ronald Walters, Letter to Dr Walter Leonard, Executive Secretary, Review Committee, Afro-American Studies Department, 21 Dec. 1971, Harvard University Archives. Hare, p. 117.

California, Santa Barbara in April 1969, which produced a blueprint
for the development of Chicano studies, *El Plan de Santa Barbara*.
It echoed many themes of the black studies movement: Chicano
control, close ties to the community, action-oriented scholarship,
political empowerment, and 'a rebirth of pride and confidence'. In
the late 1960s and early 1970s, Puerto Rican students in New York,
Native Americans in the South-West, and Asian Americans in California also agitated for programmes designed to serve their distinct
political and cultural needs.[14]

Feminists also looked to black studies as a model for women's
studies programmes that linked group/personal liberation and
university reform. Women's studies was seen as the 'academic arm'
of the Women's Liberation Movement. In order to fulfil this function, it could 'not become another area for pure academic study',
but should instead support 'action against patriarchy' and help
women develop 'a strong sense of an inner core of self'. As Elaine
Showalter explained in 1971: 'teaching about women means total
involvement: importing life and struggle into the classroom; creating new relationships between students and teachers, urging ties
between study and action'.[15]

Early women's studies programmes tied political goals to new
forms of governance. For example, the original plan for the Women's
Studies College at the State University of New York, Buffalo emphasized the importance of egalitarian control:

> Since the rights of women require change in the structure of society,
> the way we work together is one form of practice to achieve this
> change. In determining the structure of the college our goals are
> many: to ensure participation of all concerned with the college, to
> change traditional hierarchical forms, to develop group responsibil-
> ity and to break down the traditional distinctions between clerical or
> secretarial roles and decision-making roles.

In addition to non-hierarchical governance structures, a number of
programmes tried to engage 'outsiders', including faculty wives,
female workers in the university, and feminists not affiliated with
the institution, as students, instructors, and organizers.[16]

14. Carlos Muñoz, Jr., 'The quest for paradigm: the development of Chicano studies
and intellectuals', in Antonia Darder *et al.* (eds), *Latinos and Education: A Critical
Reader* (New York, 1997), pp. 442–4; La Belle and Ward, *Ethnic Studies*, pp. 81–7.

15. Marilyn Salzman-Webb, 'Goddard College', *Female Studies* 3 (1971), p. 156; Elaine
Showalter, 'Introduction: teaching about women', *Female Studies* 1 (Dec. 1971), p. xii.

16. Christine Grahl *et al.*, 'Women's studies: a case in point', *Feminist Studies* 1
(Fall 1972), p. 111.

The curriculum also reflected political aims. Courses offered a feminist perspective on traditional academic disciplines, such as the history of women, women in literature, and the psychology of women. They also included classes that focused on feminism or issues raised by the feminist movement, such as 'The Politics of Health', 'Women and the Welfare System', and 'Sexism, Racism and the Courts'. All courses sought to raise consciousness about 'the role and status of women' and to challenge stereotypes that, in the words of one programme coordinator, 'assign us to "our place" and keep us there'. Some programmes also offered 'skills' courses, such as car mechanics, in order to give women tools to 'control their lives, change society, or become independent'.[17]

Organizers paid particular attention to classroom dynamics. At Sacramento State College, for example, each instructor was asked 'how she structures her class as to allow maximal student self-direction' and was expected to agree that the 'lecture/exam/research paper orientation' was not 'a valid approach to a women's studies class'. The feminist classroom would reject traditional power and authority relations, and should strive to overcome women's traditional socialization. This meant 'validating' students' experience and helping them find their 'voice'. Feminists hoped that they could, in their own classes and throughout the university, challenge practices that were 'heavily oriented toward male performance, male dominance, and toward the perpetuation of male hegemony in the definition of professional standards and values'. Feminists hoped that women's studies could provide a model of non-sexist, egalitarian education that would ultimately transform the university.[18]

Institutionalization

Although conceived as instruments of university reform, black, ethnic and women's studies muted their challenge to traditional academic practices as they became established. University faculty and administrators were willing to introduce courses that addressed these groups' experiences, but rejected the more extensive changes

17. Ibid., p. 113; Anne Beuf, 'College of thematic studies: Women's Studies [University of Pennsylvania]', *Female Studies* 7 (1973), p. 226; 'Chicago liberation school for women', *Female Studies* 3 (1971), p. 149.

18. Karen Kennedy, 'Sacramento State College', *Female Studies* 3 (1971), p. 171; Marcia Landy, 'University of Pittsburgh', *Female Studies* 3 (1971), p. 161. See also Adrienne Rich, 'Toward a woman-centered university' (1973–74), in *On Lies, Secrets, and Silence* (New York, 1979), pp. 125–55.

in governance, pedagogy and scholarship that activists considered essential to a 'relevant' education.

This pattern of partial success is most starkly illustrated by the fight for black studies. University administrators and faculty managed, through a variety of strategies, to institute programmes that conformed to traditional academic standards. At some institutions, savvy administrators responded to demands quickly, purposefully taking the initiative away from radical students. Elsewhere, administrators, after fighting long battles with radical students and refusing to give in to their demands, created their own more traditional programmes. Still other institutions acceded to demands initially, but later exerted control over the programmes, reorienting them along more traditional lines. Yale, Howard and Harvard offer examples of these three different patterns.

In all three cases, institutions relied heavily on faculty committed to the scholarly study of African Americans to formulate alternatives to radical students' demands. These faculty participated in campus debates, positioning themselves between conservative colleagues, who did not accept the need or legitimacy of black studies, and radical students. They argued vigorously for more scholarship on blacks, but dismissed many of the particular demands of black militants. They rejected the notion that black studies could be taught only by blacks and that it would primarily serve the psychological and social needs of black students, arguing that white students had as much or more to gain from black studies. Although they welcomed student input, they thought that faculty control of curriculum and staff was essential to prevent politicization of the programme. They viewed interdisciplinary area studies programmes that had been set up in the 1950s as an appropriate model for black studies, arguing that this organization would ensure that the new programmes would have strong ties to traditional academic disciplines. In some cases, these faculty created uneasy, but successful, alliances with students, but often students distrusted them more than conservative opponents. In either case, these faculty, rather than radical students, determined the ultimate shape of new programmes.

Moderate faculty found an important ally in the Ford Foundation. McGeorge Bundy, then Foundation president, took an early interest in black studies, participating in a symposium organized by the Black Student Alliance at Yale in 1968. There, he expressed support for new scholarship on blacks, but insisted the field should be organized like other academic areas, without racial exclusivity or particular political philosophy. If black studies 'is to be in a university', he told the audience, 'it will be studied by men and women without regard to nationality or color or specific commitment to a particular political cause'. Soon after, the Foundation offered grants to help selected institutions start black studies programmes. The Foundation sought an alternative to the 'hastily conceived and academically unsound courses' designed in response to students' demands. The Foundation believed it could 'make an important contribution to the orderly development of this hitherto-neglected field of studies by helping a few strategic institutions get off on the right foot'. It hoped that 'the courses developed under these grants may set some standards of quality by which other institutions can measure and eventually revise their own offerings'. Yale and Howard were among the first grant recipients.[19]

Yale responded quickly to student demands for a black studies programme. President Kingman Brewster established a joint faculty – student committee on Afro-American studies, led by the political scientist Robert Dahl. It drafted a proposal for an interdisciplinary major, which was approved by the faculty on 12 December 1968, making Yale the first major university to offer a degree in the new field. Yale acted before demands for black studies became too heated and avoided much of the strife other institutions experienced. The programme required that students concentrate on a discipline relevant to Afro-American studies. In their junior year, they would take a seminar introducing them to the field, and in their senior year would write a research paper in conjunction with a colloquium. In addition to the courses required by their discipline, students were expected to take six courses in other disciplines, from a list with an Afro-American focus. Courses were taught by both black and white faculty.[20]

The Ford Foundation judged the Yale programme the strongest they supported. In particular, they praised its interdisciplinary structure: 'high faculty standards are ensured by the requirement that teachers in the Afro-American Studies program must be approved by both the director of the program and the head of the department of his or her academic specialty'. The programme made some

19. McGeorge Bundy, 'Some thoughts on Afro-American studies', in *Black Studies in the University*, p. 176; Memo from F. Champion Ward to McGeorge Bundy, *re*: 'Grants totaling $747,667 for support of Afro-American studies programs at six colleges and universities', 20 May 1969, Ford Foundation Archives, reel 2004, grant 69–0518.

20. 'Yale plans major in Afro-American studies next year', *Chronicle of Higher Education* 3 (23 Dec. 1968), p. 3.

concessions to radical conceptions of black studies – for example, the original plan for the junior colloquium included a community service component. In general, however, it conformed to the ideals of faculty moderates, emphasizing 'serious academic study and teaching'.[21]

Other universities were not as successful at containing students' demands for black studies. Howard University was disrupted by a series of student protests before it decided to establish a department of Afro-American Studies. Radical students wanted an autonomous school of black studies but the administration rejected their demands, refusing to countenance 'a center of black provincialism, separatism or propaganda'. Instead, the faculty voted to create a department of Afro-American studies 'to meet the legitimate needs of students in this area, and to ensure that a sound academic program in Negro studies is developed'. What emerged was a compromise between radical students' plans for a college of black studies and those faculty who considered Howard's already extensive course offerings in Africa and African American areas sufficient. Like the Yale programme, it made some concessions to student demands, including an extensive 'community development component'. But the director was careful to justify this on academic grounds: '[it] not only meets the students' intense desire for "relevant" activity, but it is also a legitimate teaching strategy that has been largely ignored by conventional curriculum designers'.[22]

Both Howard and Yale, although under different degrees of pressure, instituted black studies programmes that resisted radical challenges to academic norms. Other institutions, however, agreed to student demands, creating programmes which challenged university practices. But in many cases, these programmes were eventually re-formed and brought back into the academic mould. Harvard provides an example. Like Yale, Harvard had hoped to take the initiative for black studies out of students' hands. Franklin Ford,

21. Jack Bass, *Widening the Mainstream of American Culture: A Ford Foundation Report on Ethnic Studies* (New York, 1978), p. 8. Committee quoted in 'Yale plans major', p. 3. The junior year colloquium is described in Yale's report to the Ford Foundation, Ford Foundation Archives, reel 2004, grant 690–0523. The community outreach element was reduced over time. For views of influential Yale faculty, see David Brion Davis, 'Reflections', in *Black Studies in the University*, pp. 215–24; C. Vann Woodward, 'Clio with soul', in *Black Studies: Myths and Realities* (New York, 1969), pp. 16–31, and John W. Blassingame, 'Black Studies: an intellectual crisis', and 'Introduction' and 'Appendix' in John W. Blassingame (ed.), *New Perspectives on Black Studies* (Urbana, Ill., 1971).

22. Quoted from 'Proposal for support of a new department of Afro-American studies at Howard University', Ford Foundation Archives, reel 2004, grant 69–0518.

the Dean, appointed a committee of faculty, with the economist Henry Rosovsky as chair, to study the question of Afro-American and African studies. The committee published its report in January 1969, recommending, among other things, the creation of an inter-disciplinary major in Afro-American studies, similar to Yale's.[23]

Faculty accepted these recommendations in February. The committee then designed a preliminary curriculum for the new major and presented it to interested students in early April. The new major would require students to fulfil the condition of con-centration in one of a few designated disciplines and supplement those courses with a few additional core Afro-American studies classes. Students were enraged by this proposal, which in their view did little to change the current curriculum. They argued further that the very structure for the major – requiring concentration in an established discipline – 'presupposes that Afro-American Studies is less than a legitimate and valid intellectual endeavor', and insisted that 'Afro-American Studies needs no support from so-called "allied" fields'. An alternative proposal was put before the faculty. It created an ad hoc committee made up of six interested students and six faculty. This committee would hire faculty for the Afro-American Studies Department. Once at least four faculty were hired, an ex-ecutive committee, made up of four faculty and four students, would define the curriculum, hire further faculty and run the department. The student proposal created turmoil within the faculty, but was approved on 22 April 1969.[24]

The ad hoc committee hired Ewart Guinier to chair the new department. Guinier, along with the newly formed executive com-mittee, developed a department with many of the attributes desired by militants. Although most of the faculty had doctorates, they had nevertheless 'been involved with innovation and purposeful change all their lives'. This, Guinier asserted, brought students 'a breadth of vision ordinarily unavailable in academia'. The department also adopted a 'black perspective'. Guinier explained:

> Its purpose is the development and use of appropriate tools with which to examine the Black experience in Africa and the New World in all its aspects and from a Black perspective. We hope to assess and to build on past and present theories of the Black experience and the strategies and tactics employed in the liberation of Black

23. *The Report of the Faculty Committee on African and Afro-American Studies* (Cam-bridge, Mass., 1969).
24. 'No Title [AFRO Speech and Motions for the 22 April 1969 Faculty Meeting Regarding Afro-American Studies]', 1969, Harvard University Archives.

peoples. The Afro-American Studies programme at Harvard stresses
the relationship between the Black experience and the Third World
experience in general. It encourages students to compare the Black
American experience with that of other colonized peoples in Africa,
Asia, Latin America and the Caribbean. These tasks are accomplished
by combining study and teaching with action.

In order to place the black experience in the context of the Third
World experience, Guinier tried to expand the department's scope
to include a course on Mexican Americans. Community-based activities were also encouraged.[25]

Three years after Harvard created the department, it was re-
viewed by a committee appointed by President Derek Bok. This
committee found little to praise. It concluded that the department
should focus solely on Afro-Americans' experience and leave the
study of Africa and other groups to other departments, and also
suggested that community programmes be minimized. Most importantly, it recommended that the department's governance structure
should henceforth match established practice, i.e. that the executive committee be dissolved and that students be explicitly excluded
from hiring decisions. The Dean was urged to appoint a committee
of senior faculty in allied fields to search for additional tenured
faculty, and when a new tenured faculty member was appointed, he
or she should take over as chair.[26]

The Harvard faculty accepted these recommendations, but the
transformation to traditional norms was delayed by the need to
find new individuals with a different vision of black studies. Finally,
in 1980, Harvard hired Nathan Huggins to chair the struggling
department. Huggins thought that the department had been 'highly
political, radical, and contentious'. Unlike Guinier and militant
students, he felt that black studies should have strong relations
with the disciplines and should be organized like area studies. He
believed that all faculty should have joint appointments in other
departments to ensure the intellectual integrity of the programme.[27]

Other institutions went through similar processes of re-forming
black studies departments originally established on the militant
model. Reviews of black studies in the late 1970s and early 1980s

25. *Report of the Afro-American Studies Department*, 1970, Harvard University Archives,
p. 1.

26. *Report of the Committee to Review the Department of Afro-American Studies*, 1972,
Harvard University Archives.

27. Nathan Huggins, *Afro-American Studies: A Report to the Ford Foundation* (New
York, 1985), p. 54.

reported that faculty without traditional academic qualifications were being replaced by those with Ph.Ds, and that community outreach programmes were no longer a priority. At some institutions, such as the University of California, Berkeley, these changes re-ignited student protests. At others, little notice was taken.[28]

Although the battle between militant students and moderate faculty was particularly pronounced in black studies, similar struggles affected other programmes. One of the most dramatic conflicts involving women's studies occurred at San Diego State College. Roberta Salper, one of the organizers of women's studies there, accused SDSC of trying to 'coopt' women's studies and diffuse its radical potential. Approached by a group of feminists planning a women's studies programme, the administration encouraged them to seek outside funding from the Ford Foundation. During the application process, the administration, according to Salper, tried to destroy the collective governance of the programme by insisting that one person act as the official representative. The administration also wanted the women's studies committee to give up control over the grant proposal, allowing their representative to work out details with Foundation officials. The committee refused to support this plan, and left the college to establish a community women's studies programme at the San Diego YWCA. Salper explained their decision:

> Had the San Diego State Women's Studies Program come under the control of one of the corporate foundations we could expect the results of the policies so clearly articulated by McGeorge Bundy; the program would be devoid of any study of the political, economic and social aspects of the American power structure, of that dangerous business of 'mixing the "political" and "historical" view of a set of events', and of any interaction between movements for social change around the school and those outside it.

Salper's experience illustrates the hazards feminists faced when they tried to cooperate with the institution they were seeking to change.[29]

The SDSC case did not convince feminists to abandon the university, but it did fuel sharp debates about the structure of women's programmes and their relation to the feminist movement. These debates came to a head in 1973 at the West Coast Women's Studies

28. Karen K. Miller, 'Race, power and the emergence of Black Studies in higher education', *American Studies* 31 (1990), pp. 83–99; Elias Blake, Jr. and Henry Cobb, *Black Studies: Issues in Their Institutional Survival* (Washington, DC, 1976).
29. Roberta Salper, 'Women's Studies', *Female Studies* 5 (1972), p. 103.

Conference, where a group of feminists disrupted the Conference and accused its organizers of divorcing women's studies from the radical feminist movement. These confrontations weakened the ties between feminists on and off campuses, and strengthened the academic orientation of women's studies. By mid-decade, the political debates subsided and gave way to more pragmatic concerns about institutional survival. Discussions among leaders of women's studies shifted from how to change academia to how to become better established as an academic discipline.[30]

Conclusion

Black, ethnic and women's studies have their roots in student activists' efforts to make their education more relevant. Their ultimate goal was to transform academic practices that seemed to inhibit political activism. To some extent, these programmes have kept alive students' vision. They have brought political and social issues into the curriculum. Faculty in these fields continue to challenge aspects of the academic life that students questioned, such as the ideal of objective scholarship. But these changes have been divorced from other reforms students sought, such as opening the boundaries between the community and the university, and greater student control over their education. As faculty and administrators established new programmes in the university, they accommodated them to traditional academic norms, making them more like the education students opposed than the one they envisaged.

30. Marilyn J. Boxer, 'For and about women: the theory and practice of Women's Studies in the United States', in Elizabeth Minnich *et al.* (eds), *Reconstructing the Academy: Women's Education and Women's Studies* (Chicago, 1988), pp. 77–9.

CHAPTER THIRTEEN

Coming of Age Under Protest: African American College Students in the 1960s

SANDRA HOLLIN FLOWERS

As heirs apparent to the legal battles and non-violent protests that began the desegregation of American schools in the 1950s, it would seem that African American college students of the 1960s would have followed the example of political activism set by their elders. And, initially, they did. During the late 1950s, black college and high school students alike participated in demonstrations and 'sit-ins' (occupying and refusing to relinquish seats reserved for white patrons) led by civil rights organizations such as the National Association for the Advancement of Colored People (NAACP), the Congress of Racial Equality (CORE), and the Southern Christian Leadership Conference (SCLC). The pivotal events were the lunch counter sit-ins at Greensboro, North Carolina. Initiated by four North Carolina A&T[1] College students on 1 February 1960, the Greensboro sit-ins inspired black students at fifteen southern colleges to conduct similar demonstrations before the month ended.[2]

This initial phase of the black student movement was characterized by three features which distinguish it from the activity of later years:

The first was the target: Southern social and governmental institutions and the mores of Southern society generally, and not the administrations of universities or any agency widely respected outside the South. Secondly, the participants were black and white, working

1. 'A&T' stands for 'Agricultural and Technical', a common designation for predominantly black colleges in early twentieth-century America and an indication of the curricular and social mission of these institutions with regard to their constituency.
2. Durward Long, 'Black protest', in Julian Foster and Durward Long (eds), PRO-TEST! Student Activism in America (New York, 1970), pp. 459–60.

together. . . . Thirdly, the style was non-violent. Influenced by the Christian pacifism of Martin Luther King, the civil rights workers employed marches, pickets, boycotts and sit-ins to dramatize racial injustice and stir the conscience of the public. When arrested, they submitted, when attacked, they seldom retaliated; their strategy was one of moral superiority, with its attendant costs in suffering and occasional martyrdom.[3]

Despite their placid demeanour, the students often encountered rioting and violent physical assaults by white spectators. The ensuing media coverage left white philanthropists 'both amazed and angered to discover that [private] schools supported by their money spawn[ed] "agitators" and "troublemakers"'. Similarly, state officials pressured public institutions with threat of closure if they failed to control their students. Consequently, although a few college presidents supported their students' political activity, it was more common for students whose conduct jeopardized the financial well-being of their institutions to find themselves expelled.[4] The irony of this outcome is perhaps best articulated by Carson Clayborne's conclusion that, 'Rather than indicating the existence of radicalism on black college campuses, the decision of black students to engage in protest was the outgrowth of guilt and frustration owing to their previous failure to take effective action against the humiliating Jim Crow system.'[5]

However, the sixties were scarcely underway when radicalism became the preferred form of protest for thousands of black college youth. Howard Zinn captured the ascendant mood in observing that 'there is a part of the South impermeable by the ordinary activities of nonviolent direct action, a monolith south completely controlled by politicians, police, dogs, and prodsticks. And for this South, special tactics are required.'[6] Zinn identified two such 'special tactics': (1) armed revolt, and (2) aggressive action on the part of the federal government against local and state governments which defied federal desegregation mandates. While Zinn preferred the latter, students and other young people increasingly chose the former.

3. Ibid., p. 461.
4. Louis Lomax, *The Negro Revolt* (New York, 1962), pp. 208–10.
5. Clayborne Carson, *In Struggle: SNCC and the Black Awakening of the 1960s* (Cambridge, Mass., 1981), p. 15. 'Jim Crow' refers to the restrictive laws and code of conduct which, following the Civil War, replaced slavery as the means of relegating African Americans to the most lowly positions in the socio-economic order. The classic text is C. Vann Woodard's *The Strange Career of Jim Crow* (New York, 1957).
6. Howard Zinn, 'The limits of nonviolence', *Freedom Ways, A Quarterly Review of the Negro Freedom Movement* 4 (1964), p. 144.

Thus, within a matter of years, the tenor of protest among African American college students progressed from an accommodationist stance to one of militancy. This chapter traces that transformation.

The fruits of segregation

African Americans neither were nor are the only oppressed minority group in America. In fact, the ideation of the common oppression shared by peoples of colour was a unifying theme in the late-sixties ferment over campus politics. It was an exciting time to be non-white in America, for not since the nineteenth-century decimation of the Native American had any ethnic group dared to mount sustained mass resistance to racial oppression in the United States. Consequently, as the black student movement became increasingly nationalist, it served as a model for other ethnic groups to form political organizations and articulate the demands of their constituencies.

To be sure, racial oppression had been challenged before the 1960s. As early as 1917, African Americans were taking to the streets to protest against social atrocities such as lynchings, as was the case with a 10,000-person march led by the NAACP in New York City. Ensuing decades witnessed continuing protest of varying degrees.[7] Significantly, though, while interracial civil rights organizations had been at the forefront of mass resistance for most of the twentieth century, it was segregation itself that gave rise to the black student movement of the 1960s. In the more than 200 years from the founding in 1636 of America's first university, Harvard, until the outbreak of the Civil War in 1861, only 28 black people graduated from American colleges. By 1900, 47 segregated institutions had been founded, chiefly in the South, to provide higher education for African Americans. Until the 1950s, most black college graduates came from these schools, although only since World War II have the schools provided graduate and professional programmes.[8]

Eventually more than 100 such institutions came to be known as Historically Black Colleges and Universities (HBCU). Along with schools classified as predominantly black (those with black enrolments greater than 50 per cent), these schools enrolled

7. Tom Cowan and Jack Mcguire, *Timelines of African-American History: 500 Years of Black Achievement* (New York, 1994), pp. 152–201.

8. Patricia Gurin and Edgar Epps, *Black Consciousness, Identity, and Achievement: A Study of Students in Historically Black Colleges* (New York, 1975), pp. 19–23.

96 per cent of all black college students as late as 1960 and 82 per cent in 1965.[9] Although the proportion of black students enrolled at HBCUs and predominantly black institutions has declined steadily since the mid-1960s, the historical contribution these schools made to American education remains significant, given the economic and material deprivation under which they have operated. Rather than enjoying the deference generally given to college presidents, leaders of HBCUs might have found themselves publicly humiliated by white benefactors. Lomax, for instance, relates the poignant tale of one president granting an elderly white woman's request to 'sing a few verses of "Swing Low, Sweet Chariot"' as a prelude to his successful negotiations for a library for his campus.[10] 'I do not envy these men,' Lomax writes. 'Only with reluctance do I sing their praise. Yet praiseworthy they are. They fashioned us into the rebels we are.'[11]

For virtually all black Americans in the first half of the twentieth century, the segregated collegiate experience was preceded by a segregated elementary and high school education far below the American middle-class norm. These experiences inspired a world-view which teachers would pass on to young pupils, who would in turn grow up to become the black student activists of the 1960s. Given the social and political isolation which for so long shaped the intellectual development of black America, then, it is superbly ironic that the very schools established to keep the races separate should be the birthplace of America's student protest movement of the sixties. However, before coming of age, the movement would undergo a period of incubation that affiliated it for a time with a church-based civil rights organization.

Conflicts in an evolving political consciousness

Founded in 1957 following the year-long boycott that resulted in the desegregation of Montgomery's bus system, the SCLC assumed

9. James R. Mingle, 'Black enrollment in higher education: trends in the nation and the south' (Atlanta, Ga., 1978), p. 8.
10. Lomax, *Negro Revolt*, pp. 207–8.
11. Ibid., p. 212. This is not to say that the institutions or all of their leaders were inherently nationalist. On the contrary, they were often vilified and satirized for upholding white middle-class values and inculcating the same into their students. E. Franklin Frazier's 'Education of the black bourgeoisie' is the classic pre-Civil Rights Movement critique of the black college (in his *Black Bourgeoisie: The Rise of a New Middle Class in the United States* (London, 1957), pp. 56–76). For a contemporary

a prominent position in the nascent civil rights movement under the presidency of Martin Luther King, Jr. One of SCLC's founding members described it as 'an organization that would do the same thing [as the NAACP] and yet be called a Christian organization'.[12] This was a shrewd strategy to pursue in the South, commonly referred to as 'the Bible Belt', because of the pervasiveness of the church in the region. Where appeals to social conscience failed, those to the Christian ethic of brotherly love might succeed more readily.

SCLC's Baptist ministerial leadership and the assumptions of tolerance inherent in the organization's name went far toward establishing it as the pre-eminent organization for non-violent protest. As such, it could be simultaneously a subversive force and an upholder of constitutional values. In its subversive manifestation, SCLC exposed the nation's underlying racism by putting masses of black men, women, and children on city streets to be jailed and brutally manhandled for peacefully pursuing their rights as American citizens. In its role as an upholder of constitutional values, the organization affirmed and worked through judicial channels to secure the American ideals of liberty, justice, freedom, and equal opportunity. Given this profile and the fact that many students were strongly attracted to SCLC's Christian and Gandhian ideologies, SCLC emerged as a logical vehicle for organizing and, to some extent, sponsoring the burgeoning black student movement.

That this movement did need organizing was a common perception according to Juan Williams, who notes the displeasure of civil rights leaders with the maverick character of the student movement. Consisting of hastily formed and widely dispersed college associations, the student movement had no overriding ideology or national identity as did the civil rights organizations. Nonetheless, the students' persistence, defiant attitude, and youthful impatience quickly led to their media coverage overshadowing that of the established organizations. Thus, when Ella Baker, SCLC's executive secretary, suggested sponsoring a student conference, SCLC leaders agreed in hopes of persuading the students to work under their direction.

---

view of the black college from the perspective of students, see 'Howard University: 1967–1968: "You saw the silhouette of her afro"', in Henry Hampton, Steve Fayer, and Sarah Flynn (eds), *Voices of Freedom: An Oral History of the Civil Rights Movement from the 1950s through the 1980s* (New York, 1990), pp. 425–48.

12. T.J. Jemison, quoted in Juan Williams, *Eyes on the Prize: America's Civil Rights Years, 1954–1965* (New York, 1987), p. 89.

While most students opposed becoming 'a youth arm of the SCLC', the two generations did come together at a contentious April 1960 conference. The students, resisting pressure from the civil rights organizations to submit to their authority, emerged from the conference with a temporary group called the Student Nonviolent Coordinating Committee (SNCC, pronounced 'snick'),[13] which by October had recruited a small staff paid subsistence wages. With this staff, the organization established an administrative office and 'acted primarily as a coordinating agency for the Southern protest groups [whose representatives] met every two months to discuss plans'.[14] The organization was on the way to becoming what one of its historians has called 'a broad and sustained movement to achieve major social reforms',[15] the first such student organization of its kind.

While SNCC and its member organizations asserted their autonomy from SCLC, the group's first headquarters was, in fact, in SCLC's Atlanta office. Not only did this arrangement seem to place SNCC under the auspices of SCLC, but the new student organization also began its existence in complete harmony with the SCLC philosophy, as evident in the wording of its first call for a student conference. 'We are . . . convinced', the fall 1960 announcement read, 'that only mass action is strong enough to force all of America to assume responsibility and that nonviolent direct action alone is strong enough to enable all of America to understand the responsibility she must assume.'[16] With such a firm initial commitment to non-violence, how, then, did SNCC become the vanguard of the most radical black student movement America has known?

Association and assimilation

SNCC came into being just months before the continent of Africa erupted in revolution. Though Sudan and Ghana had become independent nations in 1956 and 1957 respectively, in the three months between 30 June and 1 October 1960, eleven other African nations won their independence from European colonizers. The impact of these emerging nations on the formation of African American political consciousness is perhaps best appreciated in the context of a government report which noted that,

13. Ibid., pp. 136–7.
14. James Forman, *The Making of Black Revolutionaries* (New York, 1985), p. 220.
15. Carson, *In Struggle*, p. 19.   16. Ibid., p. 27.

Among Blacks, a strong feeling of identification with Africa, with Africans, and with people of African descent all over the world, is emerging. Under the context of 'Pan-Africanism', this identification is being explored in many forms: dress, hair styles, learning African languages; learning and appreciating African art, music, and other artistic expression; attending Pan-African Conferences; and developing new methods to express their African goals and aspirations.[17]

Several years would pass between the birth of the black student movement and this extensive identification with African heritage. Almost immediately, however, America's black student movement became associated with leftist ideology, not a surprising development, given that leftist ideals and agencies were consistent with those of the newly emerging African nations. The movement did not have to go out of its way to come in contact with leftist ideology, for among those who answered SNCC's call for the 1960 conference were organizations such as the Socialist Party (and its Young People's Socialist League), along with the Students for a Democratic Society.

Association with leftist ideology and African independence struggles made the nascent black student movement all the more vulnerable to the tactics of the Federal Bureau of Investigation (FBI) which some credit with a major role in destroying the American student movement of the 1960s.[18] Nonetheless, SNCC most assuredly would have become an FBI target even without such threatening associations, given that black Americans, since 1919, had ranked second only to communists on the FBI's most-spied-upon list. By 1968, in fact, SNCC was firmly entrenched in the FBI's infamous 'Rabble Rouser/Agitator Index', a hall of fame reserved for 'the most violent and radical groups and their leaders'.[19]

From its infancy, then, even before it had sorted out its own political currents, SNCC had some degree of affinity with the leftist ideology that ultimately would woo it from the side and philosophy of SCLC and the civil rights movement in general and toward militant confrontation. Commenting on the transformations which took place in black political activism from the pre-student movement

17. President's Commission on Campus Unrest, 'The black student movement', in *The Report of the President's Commission on Campus Unrest* (Washington, DC, 1970), p. 104.
18. See, for example, *COINTELPRO Revisited – US Domestic Covert Operations*, particularly 'How COINTELPRO helped destroy the movements of the 1960s', http://www.accessone.com/~rivero/POLITICS/COINTELPRO/USDomCovOps1.html. 7 July 1997.
19. Kenneth O'Reilly, *'Racial Matters': The FBI's Secret File on Black America, 1960–1972* (New York, 1989), p. 277.

period to the mid-1960s, the sociologist Lewis Killian notes that internal and external factors often work to distort a movement's original vision, broadening it to include increasingly more object-ives. Eventually, 'vagueness and inconsistency in the specific goals may develop so that the total program becomes very diffuse and often contains contradictory propositions'.[20]

Perhaps the greatest 'contradictory proposition' faced by the black student movement was the fact that it placed its faith in a system that simultaneously repressed it while appearing to be its ally. For example, in much of the rural South – largely populated by uneducated labourers and agrarians – the primary objective was to change the balance of electoral power through increasing the numbers of black registered voters and office holders. These were achievable aims, since many parts of the South were (and remain) predominantly black, a characteristic which leads to the region being known as 'the Black Belt'. With a governing body of their peers, southern black people could look forward to what other Americans took for granted: revitalized infrastructures in the areas where they lived; decent schools, textbooks, and per capita expenditure for their children's education; accessible health care; more lucrative and secure employment; better housing; and humane treatment from the law enforcement and criminal justice systems.

However, the prerequisite to all these outcomes – a fully enfranch-ised black electorate – had to be wrested from a region ruled by white supremacists who had the full cooperation of law enforce-ment officials in repressing the black population. Consequently, when CORE volunteers made forays into the South via the 1961 'Freedom Rides', it took intervention from the federal government to force white southerners to yield ground. The Freedom Rides were a re-enactment of CORE's 1947 expedition testing a Supreme Court ruling against segregation in interstate transportation. The riders planned to travel from Washington, DC, to Louisiana, a journey through six southern states encompassing nearly half the eastern seaboard of the United States. Defeated by mob violence, they finished the last leg of their journey by airplane. However, stu-dents from CORE and SNCC immediately resumed the challenge. Encountering everything from sieges, to arrest, to beatings with baseball bats and pipes, the students battled their way through the South throughout the month of May. Before the summer ended,

20. Lewis M. Killian, *The Impossible Revolution? Black Power and the American Dream* (New York, 1968), p. 127.

300 Freedom Riders had made the same journey; and in September the Interstate Commerce Commission mandated stronger regulation of interstate transportation.[21]

While the students were mounting their challenge to segregated interstate travel, voter registration drives were being undertaken with some success by NAACP chapters scattered throughout the South. No sooner had the Freedom Rides ended when, joined by their white counterparts and under the leadership of SNCC, black students began flooding rural communities to register the disenfranchised. However, even some southerners underestimated the privation, danger, and terror they would experience in this new venture. For instance, in 1963, Anne Moody, a Mississippi native attending Jackson State College, joined CORE's voter education drive in one of Mississippi's more virulent rural counties. Initially, Moody was exhilarated by the experience of seeing 'white folks actually tremble with fear' at the sight and sound of hundreds of black people filling city streets with protest marches. After a month, however, the students had had little success registering the county's black residents. Moody recalls that, after a woman and her two small sons were shot at from a passing car,

> Negro participation dropped off to almost nothing, and things got so rough we were afraid to walk the streets. In addition, our money was cut off. We were being paid twenty dollars a week by the Voter Education Project, a Southern agency which supported voter registration for Negroes. They said that since we were not producing registered voters, they could not continue to put money into the area. . . . We sometimes went for days without a meal.[22]

But when one organization faltered in its support of the students, other organizations or lone individuals stepped to the fore. Paula Giddings, for example, cites the pressure black women exerted on their churches to open their doors to the activists when ministers were reluctant to do so. Further, as Giddings reports,

> Wherever the SNCC volunteers stationed themselves in the rural South, such women were invaluable allies . . . [who] could be counted on to welcome SNCC workers into their homes – a courageous act in itself.
>
> Those who sheltered the students could expect to be jailed, burned out, or subjected to the crudest violence. Nevertheless, these women adjusted to the situation and did what they had to do. [On the day a] Mrs. Johnson of Mississippi was to be jailed. . . . she got up early

21. Williams, *Eyes on the Prize*, pp. 145–60.
22. Anne Moody, *Coming of Age in Mississippi* (New York, 1978), ch. 23.

enough to fix breakfast for her family and the students before turning herself in.[23]

This Mississippi woman's dedication to the southern struggle speaks
volumes for the communal spirit of the civil rights movement and
its widespread, interracial appeal. Initially, this interracial aspect
was highly prized because the white students the movement attracted
were from respected schools and affluent, influential families who
could move federal government to take action on their behalf if
necessary. However, white student involvement increasingly became
a source of contention within SNCC, since the students brought
with them organizational experience and leadership which undermined SNCC's attempts to develop indigenous black leadership. As
Carson notes, 'That SNCC had become a magnet for northern white
students was apparent by the spring of 1963 when they comprised
one-third of the participants at SNCC's annual conference. . . . By
the fall of 1963, 20 percent of SNCC's staff were white.' Sensitive
to the effects of this shift in its racial composition, SNCC hired
recruiters to increase involvement from students at black colleges,
but the effort met little success.[24]

Racial tension within the movement was exacerbated following
the 1964 murders of three civil rights workers – James Chaney, a
black Mississippian, and Michael Schwerner and Andrew Goodman,
white students from New York. In its investigation of these deaths,
the FBI increased its Mississippi contingent tenfold, a move that
created resentment throughout the movement because it appeared
that the increased protection was a result of the deaths of the white
students, whereas black civil rights workers were routinely brutal-
ized and murdered with scant federal notice.[25] Given the internal
stresses which the movement was experiencing, the interracial tensions simply brought to the forefront a developing trend within
SNCC and the black student movement in general: black nationalism, which manifested itself initially in a transitional phase known
as black power.

The black power watershed

Before he became SNCC chairman in 1966, the former Howard
University student Stokely Carmichael had already achieved notoriety

23. Paula Giddings, *When and Where I Enter: The Impact of Black Women on Race and
Sex in America* (New York, 1984), p. 284.
24. Ibid., p. 100.   25. Ibid., p. 115.

for popularizing the 'black power' slogan. That slogan is credited with everything from radicalizing the black movement to generating a white backlash against black people. It has been traced to the 1950s and to black icons like Richard Wright, Paul Robeson, and Adam Clayton Powell.[26] Carmichael attempted to clarify and capitalize on the slogan, in particular in his book on the subject, co-authored with Charles Hamilton. Critics, however, frequently judge the book so ambiguous as to lend itself to competing political ends. For instance, in the statement 'Black Power . . . means the creation of power bases, of strength, from which black people can press to change local or nation-wide patterns of oppression',[27] one finds justification for reformist politics as well as for armed aggressive action against the government.

Although the black power slogan was not enthusiastically embraced by civil rights leaders, it nonetheless echoed earlier calls for developing indigenous black leadership throughout the South. The concept of black power also encouraged efforts at empowerment, focused as it was on economic development and control of community resources ranging from schools to banks. Militants, on the other hand, saw in the black power concept the necessary mindset for taking a more aggressive stance against racism. In this viewpoint, it was no longer admirable to 'turn the other cheek' in the face of white violence or to live as an intimidated people. Indeed, the slogan implied, those who continued terrorizing black people would do so at a great cost to property and life.

This defiant attitude was perhaps the one most associated with the black power concept, for, as Carmichael said,

> The advocates of Black Power reject the old slogans and meaningless rhetoric of previous years in the civil rights struggle. . . . One of the tragedies of the struggle against racism is that up to this point there has been no national organization which could speak to the growing militancy of young black people in the urban ghettos and the black-belt South.[28]

While black power as a concept offered no such organization, it nonetheless created a permanent and unmistakable demarcation between the old order and the new and ushered in the final phase of the black student movement.

26. Carson, *In Struggle*, pp. 209–10.
27. Stokely Carmichael and Charles V. Hamilton, *Black Power: The Politics of Liberation in America* (New York, 1967), p. 46.
28. Ibid., p. 50.

Nationalism comes to campus

In the early to mid 1960s, the South was the destination of pre-ference for black students seeking activist involvement during the summer or for those inclined to take a year out of school and devote themselves fully to the movement (as SNCC encouraged its workers to do). Until Lyndon Johnson's War on Poverty, there was no organized effort to improve conditions for the masses of black people, and certainly no effort rooted in the power of the people themselves. Consequently, the southern movement – with its 'direct action' assault on racist traditions, its grass-roots organizing, and its highly publicized successes and dangers – was an attractive outlet for politically minded black students.

At mid-decade, though, black students began turning their attention to and focusing their energies on their own localities. According to Anthony Odum, this 'transformation of black student protest' occurred on four fronts: a move from a parochial to a mass movement; from expressive to instrumental behaviour; from religious to political ideology; and from integrationist to separatist goals.[29] Among the factors contributing to this transformation was the frag-mentation that had always characterized the movement because of its diverse and far-flung composition and varied ideologies. More-over, as the movement grew from regional to national proportions, students returning from their southern experiences discovered newly politicized communities at home. Unfortunately, however, many of these emerging political associations were fragile and easily pro-voked into violence, as was the case with a deadly shooting invol-ving black students of competing political factions at the University of California at Los Angeles.

This change in focus developed in tandem with the spread of nationalist ideology in the nation as a whole. As old as black polit-ical thought itself, African American nationalism is a multi-faceted ideology which experienced its first significant flowering in Marcus Garvey's Universal Negro Improvement Association, a 1920s separ-atist movement committed to repatriating black people to Africa. While African American nationalism has nearly a dozen variants (including economic, cultural, educational, to name a few), they all have in common a conviction that black people have both the right and the need to define themselves in their own terms and to foster

29. Anthony Odum, *Black Students in Protest: A Study of the Origins of the Black Student Movement* (Urbana, Ill., 1972), pp. 76–8.

respect for self and love of one's racial group. Where the variants differ is in their instrumental expression – the lifestyle and political choices one adopts as a result of the conviction.

Thus, for example, members of the Nation of Islam adopted separatism as a life choice. Others, those who styled themselves revolutionary nationalists, studied the writings of African and other Third World dissidents and armed themselves against the United States Government. Still others proclaimed their nationalist sentiment through African-influenced modes of dress and artifacts or, following the example of the Nation of Islam, cast aside Western personal names for African ones. Even the entertainment industry – particularly 'soul music', with its roots in gospel and blues and its aggressive expressions of ethnic pride – became nationalist in a sudden and extraordinary way. Songs such as James Brown's 'I'm Black and I'm Proud', the Temptations' 'Message to a Black Man', and The Impressions' 'We're a Winner' established both a political foundation and a distinctive sound that set black popular music apart from all other forms and became the preferred expression for a generation and its descendants.

Arguably the most eloquent advocate of 1960s African American nationalism was Malcolm X, a popular speaker on American campuses in the years before his death. In a study of his appeal to students, one sociologist asserts that his ideas were 'precursors to the development of sociological interpretive tools' for black students and that the students, in turn, were the interpreters of these ideas to rural black communities during the 1960s and 1970s.[30]

White segregationists would agree with this assessment, since they held that the defiance of previously docile southern blacks was attributable to the influence of 'outside agitators'. Whatever the source of nationalist influence among black students, research conducted at ten HBCUs from 1964 to 1970 found that

> Very few Afro-American or Black student unions existed on either southern or northern campuses in 1964 ... by 1970, every school in [the] study had one. . . . The demonstrations were over; they had led nowhere; they had simply subjected Black people to brutality without producing enough change. . . . [Thus, nationalism became] an energizing force through which students came to accept group identification and collective concern as positive elements in their personal identities.[31]

30. Donald Cunnigen, 'Malcolm X's influence on the black nationalist movement of southern black college students', *The Western Journal of Black Studies* 17 (1993).
31. Gurin and Epps, *Black Consciousness*, pp. 207–9.

In its incipient stage, campus nationalism adopted the term 'black power' to describe its emphasis on self-pride and empowerment. One of its earliest manifestations occurred at Howard University in Washington, DC. In 1966, Howard students elected as home-coming queen Robin Gregory, a woman who ran on a black power platform and wore the emerging afro hairstyle in defiance of the school's prevailing white American look and world-view. Following Gregory's election, nationalist organizations proliferated at Howard. In 1967, a Black Power Committee issued a 'Black Power Manifesto' calling for 'the overthrow of the Negro college' and its replace-ment by 'a militant black university which will counteract the white-washing black students now receive in "Negro" and white institutions'. The manifesto failed to achieve its objectives. However, its substance set the tone for subsequent student–administration confrontations and was the prelude to disruptions at Howard which led to the first student takeover of a black campus.[32]

Students at other black campuses quickly followed suit. Summar-izing the findings of a survey of his peers, an academic affairs vice-president reported student protest over issues such as food services, dormitory regulations (in an age of curfews and sex-segregated dorms), disciplinary practices, and social privileges. Tactics, like grievances, shared a similarity from campus to campus: demonstra-tions, boycotting of classes, pressuring administrators, and destruc-tion of both campus and community property.[33]

While the issues may appear mundane and self-serving compared to the world-changing mission of the activists of the early sixties, they were essentially directed toward the same goal: personal dig-nity. Speaking, for instance, of campus unrest in general, the pres-idential commission report asserted that 'student rebellion is not merely a crisis at the university. It is equally a crisis *of* the university itself – of its corporate identity, its purposes, and its justification.'[34] To black students such as those who drafted the Howard manifesto, it was also time for the university – at least the black manifestation of it – to justify its very existence. Was the black college as an institution of the black community free to set its own intellectual and political agendas, or was it not? Would the black academy invest materially in its immediate and surrounding environs, or were inadequate,

---

32. Lawrence B. de Graaf, 'Howard: the evolution of a black student revolt', in Foster and Long (eds), *PROTEST!*, pp. 319–44.

33. E.C. Harrison, 'Student unrest on the black college campus', *The Journal of Negro Education* 41 (Spring 1972), pp. 113–15.

34. *President's Commission on Campus Unrest*, pp. 74–5.

deteriorating facilities and services the measure of the value it placed on its constituency? In short, relative to the black pride which had swept the nation, where did the black college stand?

These were the kinds of issues which arose on black campuses as a result of the rise of nationalist consciousness. However, nationalist agitation was by no means limited to southern schools. As one observer noted, when black student enrolment at predominantly white institutions grew to as few as 50 to 100 students, even those few students could pressure administrations into making concessions.[35] Consequently, campuses from Harvard to Berkeley and at all points in between witnessed the rise of black student unions, demands for black studies programmes, black faculty, modified recruitment and admissions policies for black students, and the separatist self-segregation of all-black dorms on predominantly white campuses. These and other demands were invariably met. Black political activists were included among the campus schedule of speakers, leftist radicals such as Angela Davis were hired on faculties, African as well as African American studies degree programmes were developed, and students were given a greater role in campus judiciary procedures.

While black student organizations around the nation became more focused on conditions in their own environs, SNCC was faltering and desperately seeking revitalization. During 1967 and 1968, it tried to effect a merger with the Black Panther Party for Self-Defense which two California college students, Huey Newton and Bobby Seale, had founded in 1966. At the height of their popularity, the Panthers had 29 chapters nationwide. Their reputation eventually eclipsed that of SNCC, since they appealed not only to college students but to urban ghetto youth as well. However, by 1970, the Panthers had been destroyed by internecine warfare and government suppression; and SNCC – racked by rancorous and chaotic power struggles, membership purges, and ideological permutations – had dwindled to a tragic remnant of the organization which had inspired the American student movement of the 1960s. So, for all practical purposes, ended the black youth movement of the century.

A generation's legacy

During the florescence of 1960s black nationalism, ideologues frequently equated the increasingly militant movement with the

35. Mingle, 'Black enrollment', p. 7.

American tradition of resistance to tyranny. Those who opposed this comparison were apt to call the black power or nationalist agenda 'treason' because it was aimed at American policies. However, as Alain Locke, one of the chief architects of the 1920s cultural phenomenon known as the Harlem Renaissance, said,

> Every generation . . . will have its creed, and that of the present is the belief in the efficacy of collective effort, in race co-operation . . . This deep feeling of race is at present the mainspring of Negro life. It seems to be the outcome of the reaction to proscription and prejudice; an attempt . . . to convert a defensive into an offensive position. . . . It is radical in tone, but not in purpose and only the most stupid forms of opposition, misunderstanding or prosecution could make it otherwise. Of course, the thinking Negro has shifted a little toward the left with the world-trend, and there is an increasing group who affiliate with radical and liberal movements. But fundamentally for the present the Negro is radical on race matters, conservative on others, in other words, a 'forced radical,' a social protestant rather than a genuine radical.[36]

At the time of Locke's observation, Jim Crow laws, lynching, and the Ku Klux Klan were commonplace throughout the South; and both the franchise and higher education for black people were the prerogative of the 'Talented Tenth', as W.E.B. DuBois dubbed that portion of the African American populace which he deemed worthy of leadership. Forty years after Locke's observation, when the black college generation of the sixties proclaimed its creed, little had actually changed for black Americans except for some slight modification in the face of the nation's racism. Consequently, for any who had lived through the Harlem Renaissance, the black awakening of the 1960s must have seemed like political déjà vu.

Like that of its predecessors, the creed of the new generation of college students was rooted in race consciousness and collective effort and took the offensive in preference to the defensive. For its time, it, too, was radical. A people who had been told for centuries to content themselves with substandard citizenship stood forth boldly and said, 'No. Not any more.' In this standing forth lies the true gauge of radicalism and the true gauge of the achievement of America's black college students of the sixties: to offer up one's life in exchange for the civil liberties and dignities which America itself

36. Alain Locke, 'The New Negro' (1925), reprinted in *Studies in American Negro Life* (New York, 1980), p. 11.

proclaims as a national creed. And in this regard, the 1960s was the era in which black Americans came of age as Americans. The legacy they left for every succeeding generation is no less than the legacy upon which they built their own movement. It is nothing less than the legacy of America in its best moments.

CHAPTER FOURTEEN

The Refiner's Fire: Anti-War Activism and Emerging Feminism in the Late 1960s

BARBARA L. TISCHLER

The importance of women's efforts on college campuses to end the Vietnam War has been obscured by the tendency on the part of some commentators to suggest that many women abruptly abandoned the anti-war movement to take up the new feminist cause and never looked back. This teleological approach tends to diminish the positive influence of organizational, theoretical, and personal insights gained in the anti-war movement upon the emergence of a highly structured, theoretically nuanced, and personally impassioned women's movement, whose constituent groups, however diverse, shared the idea of liberation from male authority.

This chapter seeks to reconnect the new feminist movement of the late 1960s and early 1970s with the anti-war movement that helped inspire its creation. On college campuses all over the USA, women honed their skills and came to understand their rage at the objective conditions of their lives. Following the lead of the historian Sara Evans,[1] it is now possible to reflect, not simply on the origins of the feminist movement in the anti-war movement, but also on the importance of women's roles in that movement as a self-contained historical phenomenon *and* as an inspiration to the new feminist movement.

In 1979, Evans published a seminal study of the origins of the new feminist movement. Locating the spirit that activated the feminist movement in the struggles for civil rights and against the devastating war in South-East Asia, she sought historical continuity as

1. Sara Evans, *Personal Politics: The Roots of Women's Liberation in the Civil Rights Movement and the New Left* (New York, 1992).

186

well as transcendence for new feminism. Her narrative evoked women's contradictory feelings of dehistoricized isolation rooted in the imperatives of the historical moment as well as an emerging, if not perfectly defined, sense of connectedness to the 'usable past' of earlier women activists. Evans's work on the roots of contemporary feminism is typical of the strain of 1960s scholarship that eschews the top-down focus of more traditional historical writing. Recognizing the limitations of 'great man', 'great woman', or even 'great movement' theories of development, she and others have offered analyses and remembrances of the loosely structured but symbolically powerful activism of this period.

Simply put, women proved themselves able, active participants in both the civil rights and anti-war movements. In performing the tasks required of them and in challenging the post-World War II version of the proper 'woman's sphere', women activists acquired essential organizational skills and sharpened their analytical approach to advocacy. In doing so, they perceived the need for action *as women* and were consequently prepared with the skills and ideological framework to become their own advocates. It is intuitively correct, and, as Evans demonstrated, empirically clear that the women who formed the early feminist collectives and launched the first consciousness-raising groups garnered much of their organizational know-how from their service as 'grunts' of the civil rights and anti-war movements. More important, as Evans argues, the creative energy, repressed anger and outright rage of many feminists in the late 1960s and early 1970s was inspired in general by the inequities of American society and in particular by their perceived betrayal by brothers, comrades, lovers, and friends. Many women, genuinely committed to the struggles in which they had begun their political work, faced the reality that their voices in radical movements were frequently not heard or routinely ignored.

The civilian anti-war movement is often identified with the generic spirit of activism on college campuses which started in the early 1960s with civil rights sit-ins, participation in the Freedom Summer of 1964, Berkeley's Free Speech Movement of the same year, and teach-ins against the Vietnam War. In the effort to end the war, young American women worked alongside male activists. For instance, women were present among the 200–300 University of California students who walked seven and a half miles from their campus to the Oakland Army Terminal in 1965. They sought to stop the trains carrying newly inducted troops destined for Vietnam – one woman even sat on the tracks and was pulled from in front of

a speeding train by a policeman.[2] Women also marched to the
Oakland Induction Center to urge (unsuccessfully) young civilian
men to resist induction into the military. When tear gas canisters
flew, standards of chivalry that would ordinarily have exempted
women from harm did not apply. Women who exercised their right
as citizens to express their anti-war views were equal-opportunity
recipients of police brutality.

Acutely aware of 'generation gap' politics that demanded their
participation in a war over which they had no control, young men
and women, according to the historian Ruth Rosen, 'expressed
contempt for the military and economic "establishment", vowed to
change "the system", and favored direct action over the stodgy,
hierarchical, bureaucratic ways of the adult world'.[3] But women
in the student cohort of the mid-1960s, Rosen argues, faced not
one generation gap but two. In addition to being ignored because
of their youth, and legally disempowered, women faced the
infantilization of their sex.[4] Protected by families and the state from
the privileges and demands of adult status, white middle-class 'girls'
were presumed to be spending their teenage and young adult years
waiting for the husband who would continue to protect them from
the real world.

'Good girl' images of themselves at first made it difficult for
many women to recognize their exploitation within the anti-war
movement. Margery Tabankin, a student anti-war activist at the
University of Wisconsin from 1965 to 1969, described this dynamic:

> Part of being a woman was this psychology of proving I was such a
> good radical, 'better than the men'. We felt we were motivated by
> something higher because we didn't have to go to war ourselves.
> Most guys didn't take women seriously, however. They were things to
> fuck. . . . You went through this intense experience [at demonstra-
> tions], and you went back and had sex. It [sex] was much more on
> men's terms.[5]

2. See Mark Kitchell (director), *Berkeley in the Sixties* (film), (San Francisco, 1990).
3. Ruth Rosen, 'The female generation gap: daughters of the fifties and the
origins of contemporary American feminism', in Alice Kessler-Harris *et al.*, *US History
as Women's History: New Feminist Essays* (Chapel Hill, NC, 1995), p. 315.
4. The voting age was not reduced to 18 until 1972. Women of all ages faced
restrictive laws relating to credit and their legal status as property holders as well as
discrimination in employment and other aspects of society and culture based on
pervasive and long-held assumptions about their ability to function as fully responsible adults.
5. Myra MacPherson, *Long Time Passing: Vietnam and the Haunted Generation* (New
York, 1984), p. 552.

Tabankin was so taken with the organizer Tom Hayden that she even did his laundry when he visited Madison to speak. For women raised to value their ability to serve men, sexually and personally, old patterns were difficult to break. Creating another model for participation in the anti-war movement, a model based on comradeship and equality rather than sexual servility, involved radical changes in men's attitudes about women and women's attitudes about themselves.

By the mid-sixties, young women began to challenge what they had learned from their mothers about appropriate roles for women in society, first in practice in the civil rights and anti-war movements and then in a more theoretical framework with the development of new feminism. Marches not marriage, teach-ins not PTA meetings, and getting arrested for civil disobedience not disciplining children, all became subjects of discussion and action for women who sought an identity beyond husband, home, and children. The expected and very real ambivalence of this generation of women regarding the extent to which they were willing to reject the paradigm of their mothers deserves deeper investigation. Suffice it to say, for many college women, the imperative of reforming society exerted a strong claim on their time, energy, and skill.

While the anti-war movement is most strongly identified with white, middle-class college students, it also provided a voice for African Americans. Black GIs formed their own anti-war groups, and African American women saw themselves, through opposition to the war, as standing in solidarity with revolutionary women of colour throughout the world. A female member of the Black Panther Party noted in 1969:

> Vietnamese women are out there fighting with their brothers, fighting against American imperialism, with its advanced technology. They can shoot. They're out there with their babies on their backs ... and they're participating in the revolution wholeheartedly just as the Vietnamese men are participating in the revolution, in the national liberation struggle. The success of their national liberation struggle is just as much dependent upon the women continuing the struggle as it is dependent on the Vietnamese men.[6]

Women whose revolutionary activity was a life and death matter provided inspiration for young American women who were beginning to identify with the liberation struggles of others but were not yet ready to articulate a revolutionary ideology of their own.

6. Interview cited in G. Louis Heath (ed.), *Off the Pigs! The History and Literature of the Black Panther Party* (Metuchen, NJ, 1976), p. 342.

Many college women identified themselves with the New Left, the loose coalition that challenged the ideals and institutions at the bedrock of American liberalism and world power after World War II. Although women were participants and organizers in various New Left organizations, the critique of American capitalism espoused by the Students for a Democratic Society (SDS) and other groups rarely extended to sexism. The rigid hierarchical structures and 'party line' of the Old Left had given way to a theory of human nature that valued multi-dimensionality and the empowerment of the individual in every area of expression from speech to sexuality. In 1962, the SDS leader Tom Hayden had declared that 'the time has come for a reassertion of the personal'.[7] Abbie Hoffman articulated a political and cultural vision based not on theory and hierarchical organization but on fulfilling individual desires:

> I don't like the concept of a movement built on sacrifice, dedication, responsibility, anger, frustration, and guilt. All those down things. I would say, Look, you want to have more fun, you want to get laid more, you want to turn on with your friends, you want an outlet for your creativity, then get out of school, quit your job. Come on out and help build the society you want. Stop trying to organize everybody but yourself. Begin to live your vision.[8]

Hoffman's ideas represented perhaps the most radical (or anarchistic) approach to creating a new societal paradigm. Nevertheless, self-actualization in its most individualistic form influenced movements throughout American culture as well as the society at large.

In spite of the emerging emphasis on the individual as a creative contributor to the new, liberated society, the New Left at its inception embraced many of society's most insidious and widely held assumptions about the inherent limitations of women. The New Left had rejected the Old Left demand that the individual subordinate himself *or* herself to the needs of the group. But while it valorized the creativity and expressiveness of the individual, it failed to comprehend the value of women's individual or collective contributions to the struggle.

Thus, women activists had to work harder to be heard in the very movements that seemed to value the individual. In the case of the anti-war movement, they often had to struggle for legitimacy. One

---

7. Tom Hayden, March 1962 speech at the University of Michigan, cited in Evans, *Personal Politics*, p. 104.
   8. Abbie Hoffman, *Revolution for the Hell of It* (New York, 1968), pp. 61–2.

1972 female Harvard graduate described her experience, which included having her skull beaten by a policeman during a demonstration, as 'weird'. After all, she was a *girl* in a protest movement to prevent the slaughter of young men – 'Our life was never on the line, *we* weren't going to war . . . as women, we were slightly less credible.'[9] The experience of young people in general but women in particular in the New Left was one of learning, growing, and transformation. Through their experiences, women were well-prepared for the organizational task of creating the new feminist movement. 'In the midst of sexist movements, women were having experiences that transformed their consciousness and changed their lives,' Wini Breines has noted. 'When women acquired the experience and skills that enabled them to feel strong enough to move out on their own, it was with political ideas that they had inherited from the sixties.'[10]

Very soon, powerful and critical voices emerged which articulated a theory of political reform and revolution which not only assumed the validity of a women's perspective, but asserted the *superiority* of women's theoretical understanding, basic assumptions about the world, and modes of action. In June 1968, Valerie Solanis published the SCUM (Society for Cutting Up Men) Manifesto in *The Berkeley Barb*. She cast her argument in blatantly sexual terms and asserted, in effect, that the presence of men was detrimental to the development of true revolutionary politics:

> The male's inability to relate to anybody or anything makes his life pointless and meaningless. The ultimate male insight is that life is absurd, so he invented philosophy and religion. Being empty, he looks outward, not only for guidance and control, but for salvation and for the meaning of life. Happiness is impossible on this earth, so he invented Heaven . . . A woman not only takes her identity and individuality for granted, but knows instinctively that the only wrong is to hurt others and the meaning of life is love . . . No genuine social revolution can be accomplished by the male, as the male on top wants the status quo, and the male on the bottom wants to be the male on top . . . The male changes only when forced to do so by technology, when he has no choice, when 'society' reaches the stage when he must change or die. We're at that stage now; if women don't fast get their asses in gear, we may very well all die.[11]

9. MacPherson, *Long Time Passing*, p. 539.

10. Wini Breines, 'Review essay', *Feminist Studies* 5 (1979), pp. 504–5.

11. Valerie Solanis, 'S.C.U.M. Manifesto' in 'The Berkeley Barb' (7–13 June 1968), in Judith Albert and Stewart Albert, *The Sixties Papers: Documents of a Rebellious Decade* (New York, 1984), pp. 463–4.

The language is one of frustration and disgust: men have failed to end the war or to create a more humane society. For the women of SCUM, there was no alternative but to challenge men to move out of the way.

Despite the appearance of Solanis's 'Manifesto' in 1968, it is interesting that so many women remained active in the anti-war movement into the 1970s, even as their frustration inspired them to found a movement of their own. However, the extent to which 'women's issues' became contested terrain between men and women (and even among women) within these organizations cannot be underestimated. Women radicalized by the anti-war movement were at the same time marginalized by their comrades in that same movement.

Among the prominent student organizations that committed themselves to the anti-war movement, SDS was perhaps the most visible and influential in terms of setting the stage for feminist activism. Kirkpatrick Sale underscored the importance of SDS to the women's movement when he called the organization 'the seedbed for the women's liberation movement – sometimes, to be sure, as much by inadvertence as intention'.[12] Women challenged SDS members to consider issues of participation and leadership, but with no theoretical analysis of the role of women in radical politics, the group was ill-equipped to hear these challenges and act upon them. The Port Huron Statement, the manifesto of SDS written in August 1962, articulated a generational perspective on materialism, democracy, and the role of the university as an instrument of social reform, but said nothing at all about women.

With its dramatic expansion after the American escalation of the Vietnam War in 1965, SDS fixed its sights firmly on the struggle to revolutionize American society. But efforts to raise women's issues as a distinct political agenda were met with the assertion that women's concerns were peripheral to the broader political agenda: ending the war. Nevertheless, as early as December 1965, the SDS National Council included a workshop on 'Women in the Movement' which issued a statement that 'the problem of participation by women is a special problem – one that reflects not only inadequacies within SDS but one that also reflects greater societal problems, namely the problem of the role of women in American society'.[13] Although SDS women were not able to get the National Council to act upon the problem of women in the movement, their analysis

12. Kirkpatrick Sale, *SDS: The Rise and Development of Students for a Democratic Society* (New York, 1973), pp. 9–10.
    13. Ibid., p. 252.

was broad-ranging and cultural, refined in the same fire as that in which SDS had shaped its critique of the war, racism, imperialism, and American society itself.

The National Council resolution subsumed women's issues under the broader rubric of 'building the anti-imperialist movement in this country',[14] much to the dissatisfaction of women who were coming to see women's liberation as distinct from anti-imperialism or the movement to end the war. This same resolution placed the responsibility of taking the initiative to 'discourage male supremacism in interpersonal relationships with both men and women'.[15] The message was particularly offensive to women activists because it appeared to trivialize the issue of male supremacism by making it simply an issue between and among individuals. Further, it placed the burden of dealing with sexism on women rather than on SDS as a whole.

In June 1967, at the Women's Liberation Workshop of the SDS national convention, participants formulated an analysis of women's position in the United States, in the movement, and in their closest working and personal relationships with male colleagues:

> As we analyze the position of women in capitalist society and especially in the United States we find that women are in a colonial relationship to men and we recognize ourselves as part of the Third World. Women, because of their colonial relationship to men, have to fight for their own independence. This fight for our own independence will lead to the growth and development of the revolutionary movement in this country. Only the independent woman can be truly effective in the larger revolutionary struggle. We seek the liberation of all human beings. The struggle for liberation of women must be part of the larger fight for human freedom. We recognize the difficulty our brothers will have in dealing with male chauvinism and we will assume full responsibility in helping to resolve the contradiction. Freedom now! we love you![16]

Even though many women remained active in SDS and other movement groups for a few more years, by 1967 the die had been cast for activist women who sensed an irresolvable tension between mainstream movement participation and articulating grievances of their own.

In 1968, the SDS national convention endorsed the concept of equal pay for equal work, but a more comprehensive statement

---

14. Cited in Alice Echols, *Daring to Be Bad: Radical Feminism in America, 1967–1975* (Minneapolis, Minn., 1989), p. 121.
15. Ibid., p. 122.
16. *New Left Notes* (10 July 1967), in Evans, *Personal Politics*, pp. 190–1.

about women's liberation sparked, according to the historian Mari Jo Buhle, a 'raucous denunciation similar to what Socialist women had endured [earlier in the century] when they dared to compare women's liberation with that of the Proletariat'.[17] While the national SDS organization debated relatively bland statements of support of women's rights and struggled with internal dissent, individual women subsumed the feminist critique of the organization into a broader analysis of women in American society. In March 1968, Naomi Jaffe and Bernadine Dohrn argued powerfully against the pervasive sexism in mainstream consumer culture while also taking aim at the movement that defined women through men:

> Over the past few months, small groups have been coming together in various cities to meet around the realization that as women radicals we are not radical women – that we are unfree within the Movement and in personal relationships, as in the society at large. We realize that women are organized into the Movement by men and continue to relate to it through men. We find that the difficulty women have in taking initiative and in acting and speaking in a political context is the consequence of internalizing the view that men define reality and women are defined in terms of men. We are coming together not in a defensive posture to rage at our exploited status *vis a vis* men, but rather in the process of developing our own autonomy . . .[18]

While Jaffe and Dohrn articulated an institutional perspective rooted more in revolutionary struggle than in women's liberation, women forming their own groups emanating out of SDS were less complacent about the gap between SDS policy and practice. In early 1969, one SDS woman wrote:

> We were still the movement secretaries and the shit-workers; we served the food, prepared the mailings and made the best posters; we were the earth mothers and the sex objects for the movement men. We were the free movement 'chicks' – free to screw any man who demanded it, or if we chose not to – free to be called hung-up, middle-class, and up-tight. We were free to keep quiet at meetings – or if we chose not to, we were free to speak up in men's terms. . . . We found ourselves unable to influence the direction and scope of projects. We were dependent on the male for direction and recognition.[19]

17. Mari Jo Buhle, *Women and American Socialism* (Urbana, Ill., 1983), p. 324.

18. Naomi Jaffe and Bernadine Dohrn, 'The look is you', *New Left Notes* (18 March 1968), in Albert, *Sixties Papers*, p. 228.

19. Sale, *SDS*, p. 526.

Though she decried sexism in the movement and in society, Dohrn did not accept the centrality of women's issues in a revolutionary context. In March, she responded that, 'Most of the women's groups are bourgeois, unconscious, or unconcerned with class struggle and the exploitation of working class women . . .'.[20] The rift was becoming pronounced for many women activists, as the very movement that had espoused freedom and creativity, especially in terms of individual expression and sexuality, now trivialized their concerns as less than central to the real issues of the class struggle and the Vietnam War. Increasingly, women activists came to feel that there was no return to mainstream radical politics.

Women in SDS and throughout the anti-war movement began to challenge the premise that a broad-ranging attack on American capitalism and imperialism would mitigate the need for ending male supremacy. They refused to accept that women's issues were marginal, but this refusal came at no small price. Women often had to choose between continuing alliances with men and the need to raise critical issues which the Movement had failed to acknowledge. They themselves were often split on the issue of 'which was more important – ending the war or ending sexism'. Worst of all, women who spoke out in support of women's issues were attacked with a discourse laden with sexist and near-pornographic imagery. Coming from comrades in the anti-war struggle, this was painful indeed. The activist Ellen Willis reflected:

> It's hard to convey to people who didn't go through that experience how radical, how unpopular and difficult it was just to get up and say, 'Men oppress women. Men have oppressed *me*. Men must take responsibility for their actions instead of blaming them on capitalism. And, yes, that means *you*.' We were laughed at, patronized, called frigid, emotionally disturbed man-haters and – worst insult of all on the left! – apolitical.[21]

By 1969, the ninth (and last) SDS National Convention, meeting in Chicago, passed a resolution declaring that sexism was a problem faced by all women and that the battle against male supremacism 'doesn't stand apart from the fight against capitalism in our society, but rather is an integral part of that fight'. The resolution went further than earlier documents to focus on the importance of women to the movement and the need to recognize and eradicate sexism:

20. Ibid.
21. Ellen Willis, 'Radical feminism and feminist radicalism', in Sohnya Sayres *et al.* (eds), *The '60s Without Apology* (Minneapolis, Minn., 1984), p. 94.

blatant examples of chauvinism within the movement [are] a clear indication that we don't understand how chauvinism works against us. Chauvinist ideas, that women are scatter-brained, that they are mere sexual objects, that they are physically weak and not fighters, hold women back – keep women politically undeveloped, and thus rob the movement of half of its fighting force.

Nevertheless, the issue of sexism was submerged in a broader political analysis that presupposed that women were soldiers in the New Left whose basic goal was the overthrow of capitalism. The text of the resolution ends:

In the last analysis, we must realize that as long as the material base for male chauvinism exists, it cannot be completely defeated. Therefore, the primary fight must be against this capitalist system of exploitation. In the same light, we must also see that the end of capitalism is not an instant guarantee to the end of chauvinism and that the struggles against it (like racism) must continue to be waged by women and men.[22]

Though the resolution was never passed by the SDS membership because of the factional struggle tearing SDS apart, this was not in any case the political analysis that movement women wanted to hear from their comrades.

The factional struggle and subsequent demise of SDS enabled many women to assert the importance of women's issues in various groups which would later become allied, however tenuously, in the new feminist movement.[23] Nevertheless, many women remained loyal to established anti-war groups. They believed fully in the causes for which they worked but did not yet fully believe in themselves. The author Marge Piercy pointed out that 'it is pitifully easy for radical women to accept their own exploitation in the name of some larger justice (which includes half the world) because we are taught from childhood to immolate ourselves to the male and the family'.[24] A similar theme emerged in the open letter written by 'A Berkeley Sister' to 'A White Male Radical'. This essay stresses the importance of personal connection in political relationships. The woman veteran of the movement is willing to go her own way in order to avoid becoming oppressed by male comrades in the anti-war

22. 'The fight for women's liberation is basic to defeating imperialism!', *New Left Notes* 5 (30 June 1969), p. 7.
23. See Echols, *Daring to Be Bad*, p. 122.
24. Marge Piercy, 'Grand coolie damn', in Robin Morgan (ed.), *Sisterhood is Powerful: An Anthology of Writings from the Women's Liberation Movement* (New York, 1970), pp. 436–7.

cause, a cause which, for many men, was defined in specifically masculine terms:

> I ... will not accept your ridiculous role of self-reliance; it is inhuman, counterrevolutionary and opposed to the goals of Women's Liberation. Your reluctance to be close and open when all is said and done indicates that you make a rather limited socialist after all. Refusing vulnerability you are refusing friendship. Refusing acts of sharing you seem so sadly alone. Long ago, earlier feminists wanted to be tough like you. Only fifty years later did they realize how they had assumed the role of the oppressor. Like many Blacks they had silently slipped into the oppressor's habits and therefore truly failed.
> That is why you are an enemy.[25]

As Evans noted, women who moved tentatively toward their own organization 'kept trying to find a way to be equal within the very insurgency that had built the very foundation for their growing self-consciousness'.[26]

For many women anti-war activists, membership in a movement in which they faced marginalization created increasing personal and organizational tension and became progressively difficult to maintain. Yet, for others who saw the struggle for women's liberation in a larger revolutionary context, connections remained powerful. Writing in response to Robin Morgan's 'Goodbye to All That', in which she railed against male activists for their oppression of women and, worse yet, for their lack of understanding and support for women's issues, Genie Plamondon, Minister of Communication of the White Panther Party, wrote powerfully of the need to stay the anti-war, revolutionary course:

> I'm gonna raise my head and my *fist* in anger and love, and join my brothers and sisters in demanding and working and fighting for *Freedom now* – *by any means necessary* – I'm not going to join any women who want a 'genderless society' – they can have their own genderless tribe, I'm not down on that – I love to fuck, I love being a woman, and I love *men* – oh yes I do – Nor am I going to join any woman, any body, who wants to 'take over the movement' – bullshit – I align myself with all revolutionary people who are dedicated to serving the people and liberating the planet from *all* oppressive forces – the White Panther Party is dedicated, Rising Up Angry is dedicated, the Young Patriots and Young Lords are dedicated, the Weathermen are dedicated, the Vietnamese are dedicated, the Koreans, the Cubans

25. A Berkeley Sister, 'To a white radical', and 'The Berkeley tribe' (15–22 May 1970), p. 8, in Albert, *Sixties Papers*, p. 518.
26. Evans, *Personal Politics*, p. 189.

the Chinese and Africans are dedicated – and we are all *revolutionaries,*
we are all for *change* – on the planet and within ourselves, anybody
not prepared to change will *die,* and I won't waste my time saying
goodbye . . . *Seize the time outlaws!!!!!*[27]

Plamondon's perspective was shared by a minority of women who
began their revolutionary activities in the anti-war movement and
found their path to personal and women's liberation in a revolutionary movement cause.

Women did not always lobby for recognition of their issues from
within established movement groups; some preferred instead to
stage anti-war events with a women's focus. For example, in February 1966, Berkeley women held a rally and protest at the Oakland
Army Induction Center four days after two army nurses were killed
in a helicopter crash in Vietnam. Making the connection between
their own need for a separate movement and that of African American activists in SNCC, the women declared that 'parallels can be
drawn between treatment of Negroes and treatment of women in
our society as a whole'.[28]

Often, new feminist activism took the form of publishing position
papers in which the mainstream radical had little interest. The result
was a variety of new feminist newspapers. For example, the alternative
paper, *off our backs,* first appeared in 1970. According to the editors,

> the name *off our backs* was chosen because it reflects our understand-
> ing of the dual nature of the women's movement. Women need to
> be free of men's domination to find their real identities, redefine
> their lives, and fight for the creation of a society in which they
> can lead decent lives as human beings. At the same time, women
> must become aware that there would be no oppressor without the
> oppressed, that we carry the responsibility for withdrawing the con-
> sent to be oppressed. We must strive to get off our backs, and with
> the help of our sisters to oppose and destroy that system which for-
> tifies the supremacy of men while exploiting the mass for the profit
> of the few.[29]

Drawing on their experience in the anti-war movement as well as
their radical political language and perspective, the women of *oob*

27. Genie Plamondon, 'Hello to all that', 'The Berkeley tribe', in Albert, *Sixties
Papers,* pp. 522–3.
28. Cited in Charles DeBenedetti, *An American Ordeal: The Anti-War Movement of
the Vietnam Era* (Syracuse, NY, 1990), p. 146.
29. See Carol Douglas and Fran Moira, '*Off Our Backs*: the first decade (1970–
1980)', in Ken Wachsberger (ed.), *Voices for the Underground, Volume I: Insider Histories
of the Vietnam Era Underground Press* (Tempe, Ariz., 1993), pp. 107–30.

made connections with women from all over the world, including Vietnam, to promote women's liberation. *Oob* went through its own growing pains, factionalism, and splits, but it survived into the 1990s as a vehicle for radical feminist expression.

Some of the women who split from *oob* joined the radical lesbian collective that published *The Furies*. The original organizers had come from the anti-war and mainstream women's movements, but were unwilling to see women's issues as anything less than central to the broader revolution and accepted no compromise in the articulation of their oppression:

> The base of our ideological thought is: Sexism is the root of all other oppressions, and Lesbian and women oppression will not end by smashing capitalism, racism and imperialism. . . . Lesbians must get out of the straight women's movement and form their own movement in order to be taken seriously . . .[30]

The movement they sought was to be a women's movement, but also a worldwide movement that would expose and attack problems, not as aspects of capitalism or imperialism, but as a function of pervasive sexism and anti-woman biases:

> We want to build a movement in this country and in the world which can effectively stop the violent, sick, oppressive acts of male supremacy. We want to build a movement which makes all people free. For the Chinese women whose feet were bound and crippled; for the Ibibos of Africa whose clitori were mutilated; for every woman who has ever been raped, physically, economically, psychologically, we take the name of *The Furies*, Goddesses of Vengeance and protectors of women.[31]

More than twenty-five years after the publication of this declaration, it can be difficult to comprehend the courage it took for women (and men) to 'come out' in a culture which was ignorant about and hostile to homosexuality.

It should come as no surprise that women who participated in the anti-war movement often describe the experience in transformational terms. The female Harvard graduate who described her search for credibility as a 'girl' in a male-dominated movement, commented that 'the war and the movement to stop it changed my life – in the way I questioned everything, in the sense of involvement in something greater than myself, and in the sense of my

30. Cited in Ginny Berson, 'The Furies: Goddesses of Vengeance', ibid., p. 315.
31. Ibid., p. 321.

outrage'.[32] Whether or not that sense of outrage led individual women into feminist groups, it was a major contributing factor in keeping women connected to the revolutionary enterprise in one form or another.

This chapter has presented examples of the ways in which women who chose to step forward in the struggle of the 1960s and early 1970s for a more just society discovered the need to become advocates for their own rights. Advocacy for others contributed to a greater understanding of the collective power of women. The new feminism has drawn its sustenance from myriad sources, a few of which are described here. No linear tale of 'progress' from one movement to another, the story of new feminism is a complex tapestry of interconnections and apparent disconnections. When viewed from a feminist perspective, these experiences make sense. Even sisterhood that derived its roots from other compelling causes can be powerful, and, as Evans suggested in 1979, this sisterhood has the potential to realize that power in varieties of activism both highly visible and as yet unrealized.

32. MacPherson, *Long Time Passing*, p. 543.

CHAPTER FIFTEEN

Germany 1968 and 1989: The Marginalized Intelligentsia Against the Cold War

GÜNTER MINNERUP

Both the West German student rebellion of 1968 and the East German citizens' movement of 1989 were parts of wider international phenomena in their respective power blocs, and for this reason they are usually subsumed into the general discussion of the West European and North American student movements of the 1960s or of the anti-Stalinist uprisings in Eastern Europe of the 1980s, respectively. This chapter, by contrast, sets out to explore their specifically German features. The two decades separating them, the fundamental systemic differences between West and East, and not least the fact that 1968 was very predominantly a student phenomenon, while students played virtually no part in 1989, should warn us from the outset against any easy symmetry between the two.[1]

Despite the sociological and historical differences, however, there are nevertheless direct threads linking 1968 with 1989. It will be argued that these can be found not only in the close cultural links that obviously existed between the two German states, but also and especially in the particularly oppressive and deforming effect that the Cold War had on them both. Seen in this light, 1968 and 1989 were 'very German' (in the sense that they could not have occurred in this form anywhere else but in Germany) ideological rebellions by sectors of the intelligentsia in the Federal Republic and the GDR against specific deformations of their societies, and many of the

---

1. To avoid tedious repetition, 'the West German student movement of 1968' and 'the East German citizens' movement of 1989' will be abbreviated throughout the rest of this chapter as '1968' and '1989' respectively, except where these abbreviations would give rise to confusion.

features that set these movements apart from similar events in other countries can be explained in these terms.

What were the common features distinguishing the West German *Außerparlamentarische Opposition* (APO) of 1968 from, for example, the French and Italian student rebellions of the same year, and the East German citizens' movement of 1989 from, say, the Polish or Czech anti-Stalinist revolts? The principal one was undoubtedly their common isolation from any genuinely broad-based popular social or political opposition movements. Where the French or Italian students could relate, however problematically, their protest strategies to powerful domestic currents of working-class militancy (and even in the USA there were the black rebellion and the growing anti-war sentiment to draw on), the West German students met only with hostility and incomprehension in the streets and outside the factory gates. East German activists might not have met with such hostility from the population at large, but (unlike their counterparts elsewhere in Eastern Europe) they were certainly isolated, at least until the wave of popular mobilizations which quickly washed over them.

The isolation of both movements was only in part due to the fact that comparatively high living standards gave little cause for mass social unrest. Even more crucial was the extent to which the status of both Germanies as frontline states at the epicentre of the Cold War had deformed their political cultures. This was not just a question of repression, although the prohibition and persecution of communism in the Federal Republic and the activities of the GDR's State Security (*Stasi*) were significant enough. Even the potential opposition forces had internalized the exigencies of the East–West confrontation: the SPD (*Sozialdemokratische Partei Deutschlands*) opposition in Bonn became virtually indistinguishable from the governing CDU (*Christlich-Demokratische Union*) well before the formation of the Grand Coalition of 1966–69, and dissident communists inside and outside the SED (*Sozialistische Einheitspartei Deutschlands*) were afraid to provoke open splits which might endanger the survival of the GDR.

Both in the 1960s and the 1980s, therefore, the protest movements found themselves confronting apparently monolithic ruling blocs. Their places in history are owed to the fact that, against all the apparent odds, they succeeded in opening up deep cracks in these monoliths, even if the eventual outcome of their protests turned out to be quite different from what most of their activists had desired.

1968

Student protest in Germany preceded similar revolts in other European countries and students in West Berlin were mobilized earlier and more massively than in the rest of the Federal Republic. Before the May Events of Paris 1968, West Berlin was the undisputed centre of student protest in Europe both in terms of numbers participating and in the radicalism of thought and action displayed. The pioneering role of West Berlin was no accident: the divided city had been at the heart of the Cold War for two decades, and it was there that the conflicting ideologies of 'communism' and the 'free world' were most immediately confronting each other. West Berlin, with its cheap housing and the exemption of its residents from military service, had an unusually large student population and a vigorous student subculture. Until the early 1960s, West Berlin students had generally shared in the virulently anti-communist consensus prevailing in the city, but from 1964 onwards an increasingly large number of students became involved in protest actions over a variety of issues but which always focused on the core issue of free speech. These included the controversies over the invitation of the liberal journalist Erich Kuby to address students at the Free University, the dismissal of the assistant lecturer Ekkehard Krippendorf in 1965, the visit of the Congolese prime minister Moise Tshombe in 1964, of the US vice-president Hubert Humphrey 1967 and, most fatefully, of the Shah of Iran in June of the same year.[2]

These early clashes defined the key battleground between the student movement and what the students then (before they discovered the 'bourgeoisie') called the 'establishment': the nature of democracy. The students of the 1960s were the first student generation to have been completely socialized in the post-fascist era,[3] and 'democracy' had a special significance for them as the defining characteristic of their society in contrast to both its immediate predecessor, fascist Germany, and immediate enemy, communist Germany. Yet they found themselves confronted with the reality of a

2. A contemporary account of these events in English, written by sympathetic American observers, can be found in Barbara and John Ehrenreich, *Long March, Short Spring: The Student Uprising at Home and Abroad* (New York and London, 1969), pp. 23–50. For a more analytical perspective, see also Gianni Statera, *Death of a Utopia: The Development and Decline of Student Movements in Europe* (New York and Oxford, 1975).

3. German university students tend to be older, on average, than their counterparts in Britain and the USA, with many activists of the protest movement being in their mid to late twenties.

'liberal democracy' severely deformed by the intensity of the Cold
War confrontation and the unmastered legacy of the Third Reich:
1964 to 1969 brought the Auschwitz Trials and regular revelations
about the Nazi past of key politicians (including the then Federal
President Heinrich Lübke and Grand Coalition Chancellor Kurt-
Georg Kiesinger), joint government (from 1966) by the two largest
parties effectively abolishing ideological polarization and parliamentary opposition, preparations for Emergency Laws that could be
used to suspend basic democratic rights, the legal persecution of
communists and Marxists and an apparent electoral resurgence of
the far right. Beyond Germany, they were years in which the image
of the USA suffered irreparable damage through the escalation of
the Vietnam War under Presidents Johnson and Nixon, and the
explosion of the civil rights movement in America's black ghettos.
For West German students, the USA was more than just the leader
of the 'Free World': it was a direct military presence in German
cities (above all, and crucially, in the centres of the student movement, Berlin and Frankfurt) and the *spiritus rector* behind Germany's
re-education in liberal democracy. The discovery that the American-
led 'free world' included a number of unsavoury dictatorships –
from Franco's Spain and the colonels' Greece to the Shah's Iran
and Tshombe's Congo – came as a severe shock.

West German students, like the East German activists of the 1980s,
did not therefore start out in fundamental opposition to their social
and political system. Just as most members of the GDR's peace and
ecology groups would stress, in principle, their commitment to
socialism, the Federal Republic's student activists did not reject
liberal and representative democracy as such but, on the contrary,
cut their critical teeth by counterposing the principles of democracy as they had been taught to understand them with the reality
they experienced.

It was only when the gulf between ideology and reality became
unbridgeable that larger numbers of students adopted the kind of
Marxist analysis which had been developed by the SDS (*Sozialistischer
Deutscher Studentenbund*, the official student organization of the
Social-Democratic Party until its expulsion in 1961). Significantly,
this version of Marxism drew heavily on the critical theory of the
Frankfurt School (Herbert Marcuse, Theodor W. Adorno, Max
Horkheimer) with its emphasis on the ideological manipulation of
the 'administered society' and its dismissal of the revolutionary role
of the working class. More orthodox forms of Marxism – predominantly a rigid Mao-Stalinism – only found adherents towards the end

of the decade when the spontaneous mass movement began to recede after the change of government in Bonn.

The intense preoccupation with theory and organization was a characteristic feature of the West German student movement. Indeed, after the spontaneous protest actions against the Springer press following the shooting of the SDS leader Rudi Dutschke during the Easter holidays of 1968, its demonstrations assumed an increasingly ritualistic character with little of the inventiveness and militancy shown elsewhere in Europe. Instead, the far left consolidated its influence on the campuses by drawing thousands of students into Marxist seminars, discussion circles and, eventually, the 'mass organizations' of 'revolutionary parties', spawning a flourishing left-wing publishing and book-selling industry and giving rise to a plethora of rival militant organizations distinguished from one another principally by the texts from which they drew their quotes. This devotion to theory and organization certainly contributed to the continued isolation of the movement, and its eventual sectarian degeneration, but it also gave the radical milieu an extraordinary stability. After graduation, many radical students resurfaced in teaching or other public service professions, a development which prompted the notorious *Berufsverbot* of 1973, a government decree against the employment of radical left-wingers in public service.

From the APO to the Greens

Although apparently isolated from any broader social and political unrest, the extra-parliamentary student movement was also the harbinger of the break-up of the Grand Coalition and the *Machtwechsel* of 1969, with the Brandt era of *Neue Ostpolitik* and '*Mehr Demokratie wagen*'. It articulated a diffuse but nevertheless very real sense of the necessity for reform and renewal that reached deep into the ranks of the liberal centre, and is today acknowledged as having fundamentally altered the intellectual and political climate of German society.

From the early 1970s onwards, so-called *Bürgerinitiativen* (citizens' initiatives) began to disseminate a new-style politics from below that clearly owed much to the student movement. Indeed, the initiators and organizing backbone of such groups were often former student activists who now mobilized their neighbours around local issues in their new, post-university environments. By the mid-1970s, opposition to nuclear power stations became the most prominent focus for the most spectacularly successful of such citizens' initiatives, bringing about successful alliances between the militant left, local activists and previously unpoliticized local residents alarmed by the implications of such dangerous projects for their livelihoods. By the late 1970s, the resumption of the Cold War provided a national focus for an even more powerful mobilization of much the same forces in the shape of the mass peace movement against the deployment of a new generation of nuclear missiles (Cruise and Pershing II) on West German territory.

The peace movement was up against the same Cold War consensus as the APO of the 1960s, in that the three established parties SPD, CDU and FDP (*Freie Demokratische Partei*), formed a *de facto* Grand Coalition in favour of NATO rearmament. But by now the transformation of the West German political culture since the 1960s had gone too far for the mass extra-parliamentary protest movement to yield a mere reshuffle between the established parties: it now forced its way onto the party-political stage itself in the shape of the Green Party.[4]

In its early days, the Green Party saw itself very much as the parliamentary arm of an extra-parliamentary mass movement. Its internal structures were designed to prevent the emergence and consolidation of a caste of professional politicians, and its programme was characterized by a radical, leftist utopianism. Over the years, the parliamentary orientation has become more dominant at the expense of the mass movement, its leadership has become professionalized and the programme has evolved from an eco-socialist to a more eco-liberal one as the age profile of its membership and voters has risen.[5] But the hard core of the Greens remain the '1968 generation'.[6]

A cultural revolution

It is impossible to discuss 1968 in merely sociological and political terms without considering the broader cultural context in which it

4. For an English-language account of the origins and formation of the Greens, see Werner Hülsberg, *The German Greens: A Social and Political Profile* (London and New York, 1988).
5. For an illuminating study of the evolution of the Greens from the revealing perspective of their role in local politics, see Thomas Scharf, *The German Greens: Challenging the Consensus* (Oxford and Providence, 1994).
6. The best-known politician of the Greens, Joschka Fischer, is a true representative of the party in this respect, too: in the late 1960s, today's leader of the moderate, 'realo' wing was a well-known agitator of the ultra left in Frankfurt.

was set. The 1960s were the decade of the birth of the rock music and hippie cultures, of long hair and cannabis, of the expansion of educational opportunities and youth consumerism, of 'sexual revolution' and anti-authoritarianism – of the deepest and most generalized rupture between the generations since the World War. Against this background, the student movements of the 1960s are often interpreted as harbingers of 'new social movements' (ecology, feminism) and a 'new politics' resulting from a 'paradigmatic shift' from materialist, class-based paradigms to post-materialism.[7] In West Germany, the weight of the Nazi past gave this intergenerational rupture a particularly sharp edge and the isolation of the student movement and its successors in the 1970s and 1980s from organized labour was particularly pronounced. As a result, the leaders and theorists of these movements gradually reinterpreted their own significance as the influence of Marxism declined sharply.[8]

While a discussion of the validity of such interpretations would exceed the limits of this chapter, it is important to note that the phenomena that gave rise to them were not confined to the West. From the 'cultural revolution' of the 1960s to the reorientation of the critical intelligentsia towards 'post-materialist' values, developments in East Germany closely paralleled those in the Federal Republic, although perhaps in weaker form and with a certain delay.

1989

The Stalinist regime in the GDR and its methods of control were, of course, qualitatively different from what radical students in the West had perceived as the 'repressive tolerance' (Marcuse) of liberal-democratic capitalism: it was certainly repressive but there was little tolerance of dissent even if from relatively marginal social forces such as intellectuals or students. The universities, in particular, were under tight ideological supervision, with a highly selective admissions system and severe penalties for the merest hint not only of open dissent but of a lack of demonstrative commitment to the regime. Since the 1950s at least, students in the GDR had been among the most conformist sections of the population and they

---

7. Cf. Ronald Inglehart, *The Silent Revolution* (Princeton, 1977), and *Culture Shift in Advanced Industrial Society* (Princeton, 1990).

8. For a critical view of the 'new social movements' interpretation in international comparison, see Karl-Werner Brand (ed.), *Neue Soziale Bewegungen in Westeuropa und den USA: Ein internationaler Vergleich* (Frankfurt and New York, 1985).

played little or no role in the dramatic events of 1989. The real institutional base of the 1989 movement was the protestant churches, even if many church leaders and local pastors were barely more welcoming of some of the activities taking place under their roofs than West German university administrators and professors had earlier been. The church was the only social institution free from direct control by the ruling party and state, though indirect control mechanisms, behind-the-scenes pressures and intimidation were certainly present. Compared to the role of the Catholic churches in Poland, for example, the Evangelical Church of the GDR was itself a marginalized institution, relatively isolated from a population with traditionally weak religious affiliations, and struggling to attract young people into its fold. It could therefore ill afford to turn away the young activists, however much they tended to antagonize both conservative traditionalists within the church and the *Stasi* outside.

The origins of the independent East German citizens' movement can be traced back to two quite separate sources: the dissident movement of leftist intellectuals expelled from the ruling Socialist Unity Party, and the protestant-pacifist resistance to the introduction of military education into the curriculum of East German schools in 1978. The churches had attracted pacifists, religious or otherwise, ever since the introduction of conscription in 1962, since when[9] religiously motivated conscientious objection had been the sole legal means of avoiding armed service, providing the option of service in the unarmed 'construction brigades' instead. Support from one's local pastor was a prerequisite for exercising this option, and hence the churches had gradually become rallying points for pacifists and anti-militarists. Parental resistance to compulsory military education in schools was much more widespread than draft resistance, and again the church became the principal voice of protest. Where previously the church's room for manœuvre had been strictly limited, it now found a much more favourable climate for assuming a role as independent interlocutor between anti-militarist protests and the party and state authorities in the 1970s and 1980s. At this time, party and state decided to adopt a more permissive attitude towards religion, and then desired to win the church as an ally in their campaign against NATO's decision to deploy a new generation of

9. Although conscription was introduced in 1962, conscientious objection and service in the 'construction brigades' was not provided for until 1964. For a brief overview of the role of the protestant church in the birth of the peace movement, see: John Sandford, *The Sword and the Ploughshare: Autonomous Peace Initiatives in East Germany* (London, 1983).

nuclear missiles on West German soil – the close links between the East and the West German protestant churches being a crucial factor in both decisions.

This protestant pacifism was given a sharper political edge by two other influences upon it. One was the close links that existed between the anti-militarist and socialist-dissident milieux: the 'Berlin Appeal' of 1982, for example, one of the crucial milestones in the evolution of the independent peace movement, was jointly initiated by the East Berlin pastor Rainer Eppelmann – who would ironically become the GDR's last defence minister and is today a CDU politician – and the veteran communist Robert Havemann, the intellectual father figure of a leftist opposition current that included the popular singer-songwriter Wolf Biermann and their widespread network of friends and supporters. The other was the rise of the massive West German peace movement, which also enjoyed considerable support in the protestant churches and whose agitation dominated the annual church conventions of the early 1980s.

Marxist dissidents such as Havemann, Biermann and Rudolf Bahro – imprisoned in 1977 for the publication, in the West, of his influential book *The Alternative* and released into the Federal Republic in 1978 – enjoyed considerable standing in these groups. By the 1980s, however, the influence of critical Marxism had clearly begun to wane, much as it had elsewhere in Europe, above all in West Germany. The language of class struggle was being super-seded by the language of the 'new social movements' – feminism, peace, ecology – in tune with the 'paradigmatic shift' that occurred in the ideological and thematic preoccupations of youthful and intellectual radicals of the West. Yet very few of the East German activists desired anything else but a reformed and democratized socialism, and demands for unification with the FRG were virtually unknown.

The social and organizational profile of this movement just before the eruption of the open crisis that would lead to the collapse of the GDR, was as follows:

In Spring 1989 there were about 150 alternative groups in the GDR; a further 10 attempted to unify and coordinate the alternative move-ment across the republic. The majority of its members were between 25 and 40 years old; the proportion of those with college qualifica-tions was high compared to that of workers. A fair number (12%) had no regular employment, thus rejecting the official norms even in this key area. Up to 100,000 took part in the activities, 2,500 were regular activists, 600 belonged to 'leadership bodies', 60 were counted by the Stasi as the 'hard core'.[10]

In terms of age and education, the East German ecology, peace and human rights activists of early 1989 were thus not very different from those in the West German 'new social movements' and Greens.

The main reason why the Greens became the chief point of reference for the emerging East German *Basisgruppen* movement, however, was that they alone among the major West German political forces unambiguously sided with the independent groups while the established parties hobnobbed with the SED in the name of détente, and the Communist Party and much of the Marxist left denounced them as petty-bourgeois counter-revolutionaries. To the extent that the SED wanted to retain some influence in a mass West German peace movement, the solidarity of the Greens even afforded the East German activists a certain measure of protection from the worst excesses of repression. The common language of peace and disarmament, of environmentalism and non-violence, of solidarity with the Third World and grass-roots democracy, as well as the cultural affinities between West and East Germans of roughly the same generation, made for easier communication than was generally the case between citizens of the two states. Whereas the student radicals of 1968 had found the 'other Germany' a largely incomprehensible and hostile territory, the Greens of the 1980s found a ready and sympathetic audience in the GDR.

From Gorbachev to the autumn 1989 revolution

Yet in one crucial respect, the East German *Basisgruppen* were in the same predicament as the APO of 1968 had been: isolated from any broader social and political discontent. If East German workers were disaffected with the regime, it certainly did not show, at least not until the mass exodus from the GDR after the opening of the Austro-Hungarian border during the summer holiday period of 1989. There was no hint of an East German *Solidarnosc*, nor even of the culture of dissent which, in Hungary and Czechoslovakia, represented the echo of a reformist era and a deep split in the ruling elite. As has already been mentioned, even the church was nothing like the popular force it was in other East European states.

10. Sigrid Meuschel, 'Revolution in der DDR: Versuch einer sozialwissenschaftlichen Interpretation', in Hans Joas und Martin Kohli (eds), *Der Zusammenbruch der DDR* (Frankfurt, 1993), p. 107.

Despite all the inventiveness and courage of its activists, therefore, the peace and ecology groups attached to the protestant church remained a peripheral force with little apparent hope of transforming themselves into a mass movement – even as late as spring 1989.[11] Although increasingly bold in leaving the protective cover of the church, and developing a stronger infrastructure (with regularly published journals such as *Grenzfall* and *Umweltblätter*), political change seemed as far away as ever. The catalysts for the dramatic events of autumn 1989 were located outside rather than inside the GDR: in Moscow and Budapest.

Without Gorbachev's *perestroika* in Moscow, the decision made in Budapest to open its sector of the 'Iron Curtain' at the Austro-Hungarian border would have been unthinkable. Without the opening of the border, there would not have been the mass exodus (via Czechoslovakia) of summer 1989, and without the mass exodus there would not have been the atmosphere of crisis that encouraged the formation of the Social-Democratic Party of the GDR, the *Neues Forum, Demokratischer Aufbruch, Demokratie Jetzt,* the *Vereinigte Linke* and other explicitly political groups, and the largely spontaneous eruption of street demonstrations. The visit of Gorbachev to East Berlin on the occasion of the fortieth anniversary of the GDR further heightened expectations of imminent change, with intensive speculation about a reformist, pro-Gorbachev successor to the ailing Honecker.

For a brief period during the stormy months of September to December 1989, the peace and ecology activists from the small groups around the protestant churches were propelled into the vanguard of a mass movement which they had not created, did not control and, beyond the most immediate demands for free assembly and expression, did not represent. In the absence of organized opposition currents or structured mass movements beyond these groups, demonstrations tended to start from local churches, where the initial mass meetings also took place until the numbers of participants became too large for them. Spokespersons for these groups as well as the local priests[12] tended to represent the mass

11. Just how unexpected the events of autumn 1989 were is rather painfully brought home by a re-reading of the proceedings of the 22nd annual conference of Western GDR researchers held in May 1989, especially my own contribution on the East German opposition and one on the same topic by Wolfgang Templin, a leading activist of the East German peace movement then in enforced exile. See *Die DDR im Vierzigsten Jahr: Geschichte, Situation, Perspektiven* (Cologne, 1989).

12. Former churchmen still play a prominent role in the political leaderships of the major parties in the Eastern states of the united Germany today.

movement in negotiations with the authorities, and from November onwards in the local, regional and national Round Tables.[13] Their meteoric rise from marginality to political power seemed to reach its high point in January 1990, when the citizens' groups represented at the Round Tables formally joined an all-party coalition government, but by then their real influence was already declining to the extent that the West German parties had begun to build up their organizations in the East. In the elections at all levels in 1990, the candidates representing the citizens' movement fared badly, well behind not only the pro-Western parties but also the successor party of the SED, the PDS (Party of Democratic Socialism).

In terms of its own aims, the East German citizens' movement had clearly failed. Instead of bringing about a democratically reformed socialism, the GDR had been absorbed by the capitalist FRG. Appearances in autumn 1989 which suggested a revolution led by the citizens' movement had been deceptive: in reality, the mass mobilizations were not led by the citizens' movement but followed their own rhythm which was determined by events unfolding on the Austro-Hungarian border, in the West German embassies in Prague and Warsaw, and in the negotiations to resolve the crisis between Bonn, East Berlin and Moscow. The citizens' groups played a crucial part in providing the catalyst that encouraged ordinary people to take to the streets, but once the masses were truly on the move they looked to Bonn rather than to the churches for guidance.

Conclusion

The Cold War between East and West was fought by many means, but in Germany it was above all an intense ideological confrontation. The frontier between the two German states, including that between the two halves of Berlin, had been drawn arbitrarily and it was of key importance for both sides to neutralize the potentially explosive issue of German reunification by ensuring political stability in their respective client states. Purely repressive methods, although used on both sides against opposition forces that were considered to be direct agents of the 'other side' (the Communist Party and Marxism in the West; 'bourgeois forces' and 'agents of

13. The Round Tables were institutions of dialogue between the SED regime after the fall of Honecker and the citizens' movement. For a detailed account, see Walter Süß, 'Mit Unwillen zur Macht: Der Runde Tisch in der DDR der Übergangszeit', in *Deutschland Archiv* 5 (1991), pp. 470–7.

imperialism' in the East), were clearly not enough to achieve this if the social and economic needs of the population were not satisfied and, above all, if the young post-Nazi generation was not won over to the ideological values of the opposing regimes.

Such ideological mobilization would have been difficult by simple imposition from the outside. Both the West and the Soviet Union, however, could rely on local allies with strong roots in the German political culture: in the case of the former, the mainly Catholic Christian Democrats (heirs of the old Centre Party) who just happened to have their strongholds in western and southern Germany, in the case of the latter the Communists with their strong roots in eastern Germany. In a sense, the post-war division of Germany developed into a geographical consolidation of the old, civil-war-like confrontations between left and right in Wilhelmine and Weimar Germany, and there can be little doubt that these historical roots of the Cold War contributed significantly to the intensity of the ideological confrontation.

By the early 1960s, the ideological *Gleichschaltung* on both sides was so complete that there was virtually no real opposition in either state. Hostility to, and fear of, the other side was the defining element in the consciousness of even those from whom a challenge to their regimes would perhaps be most expected: the social democrats in the West and communist dissidents in the East. Loyalty to the United States and the Soviet Union was elevated to the status of state religions.

The true significance of the mass mobilization of West German students in the late 1960s was neither, as much of the 'establishment' believed, as a response to the crisis of higher education, nor, as many students themselves believed, as the beginning of a revolutionary era. It was the response of a section of the intelligentsia to the previously unchallenged grip of Cold War ideology over Germany. For the rising academic generation of the 1960s, the sharp contrast between the ideological claims of the 'Free World' and the realities of censorship, support for corrupt dictators and, above all, imperialist warfare in Vietnam belied everything that they had been socialized to believe in. The challenge to the Cold War ideology began in Berlin, where these contradictions were more acute than anywhere else, and spread rapidly across all West German universities.

The ideological constellation in East Germany was not dissimilar, as the independent groups in and around the protestant churches essentially began by turning what they understood to be the fundamental values of socialism against the reality of the SED regime. A sociologist working for the theological academy of the East German churches, writing in early 1989, described the ideological consensus in the *Basisgruppen*:

> Because the groups want to come to terms with the existing society they transcend its values. The values of 'equality and justice', in particular, are applied to many different situations. Thus they remain within a minimal consensus with the traditions and intentions of socialist visions of society. A new left has emerged in the groups and is beginning to take shape . . . Their understanding of socialism is not defined by the particular state interests of the GDR but by the philosophical horizon of its main principles.[14]

In both German states, the ideological rebellions of the marginal intellectuals against what they perceived as the official distortions of their own values assumed their most explosive form when they took on the core issues of the Cold War. In West Germany in the mid-1960s, these were the all-pervasive anti-communism and the unquestioned loyalty to the leading power of the 'Free World', the USA. In East Germany in the 1980s, this was the regime's own propaganda offensive against NATO rearmament around the theme of 'peace'. In normal times, such marginal movements confronting powerful regimes over core elements of the ruling ideology would, of course, be crushed. Significantly, neither the West German APO nor the East German citizens' movement was crushed – even if they failed to achieve their aims as they themselves had formulated them.

For perhaps their most important role was that of a seismographic indicator of the impending end of an era, of a decisive tectonic shift in the deeper structures of Germany's Cold War environment. The year 1968 certainly marked the end of the 'first' Cold War and the beginning of a normalization in intra-German relations and more general East–West détente in Europe. In fact, such détente had already been in the making between the superpowers since the end of the Cuba crisis and West Germany was in danger of international isolation if it continued its hard Cold War line. Demands for a new *Ostpolitik* were already being raised in liberal and social-democratic circles but faced what seemed an insuperable task in changing the hardened anti-communist climate enough to make such new initiatives possible. The student movement of the

---

14. Ehrhart Neubert, 'Gesellschaftliche Kommunikation im sozialen Wandel: Ausgewählte Aspekte einer Bewegung', in *Die DDR im Vierzigsten Jahr . . .* (Cologne, 1989), pp. 38–57.

1960s played a crucial part in clearing the road for the Brandt government of 1969.

There are striking parallels to this in East Germany in the 1980s. With Gorbachev's *glasnost* and *perestroika*, and above all Moscow's refusal to intervene militarily against the reform policies pursued in Poland and Hungary, the writing was on the wall for the SED leadership, which was incapable of initiating change and increasingly isolated, despite attempts to forge an anti-Gorbachev alliance with Prague and Beijing. Yet while some semblance of economic stability could be maintained, a mass uprising remained unlikely. Reformers in the party, while gradually more vocal, seemed incapable of sweeping away the obstacles to an East German *perestroika*. But, once again, a marginal intellectual protest movement applied the pressure for change, and became the catalyst, in those turbulent months of autumn 1989, for a decisive breakthrough. This time, of course, the breakthrough marked not just a new phase in the East–West confrontation but its very end.

PART FIVE

The Ongoing Battle

Student Movements in Confucian Societies: Remembrance and Remonstration in South Korea

ALAN R. KLUVER

Student protest is often seen as a product of the philosophical and political traditions of the West. In fact, in the West it is a relatively recent phenomenon, whereas in other cultures it has been a political force for hundreds of years. Probably no other nation in the world has as long a tradition of 'student demonstration, memorializing, and active participation in national politics' as the Republic of Korea.[1] In contemporary South Korea, university students are probably the strongest non-governmental political force. Students influence policy-making in issues as far-reaching as political organization and process, reunification talks, and foreign policy.[2]

This chapter argues that student protest in the Republic of Korea specifically, and in East Asia generally, reflects the values and roles inherited from centuries of Confucian political tradition. Although student protests often articulate an ideological commitment to the modern themes of nationalism, democratization, and anti-colonialism, the motivating psychological force behind student protests lies in East Asia's pre-modern, Confucian political culture. In fact, the student movement in South Korea serves as an illustration of the interaction between traditional Confucian ideals of politics and modern concepts of democracy and human rights. It is this interaction between traditional beliefs and modern ones that accounts for the dynamic and perpetual nature of student activism in Korea. In order to illustrate this interaction, recent Korean student

---

1. Gregory Henderson, *Korea: The Politics of the Vortex* (Cambridge, Mass., 1968), p. 201.

2. Myungsoon Shin, 'Political protest and government decision making: Korea, 1945–72', *American Behavioral Scientist* 26 (1983), pp. 395–416.

protest, in particular the 1980 'Kwangju Incident', will be examined, before the salient characteristics of Confucian political culture which relate to student activism are identified.

The role of students in Korean politics

During the Yi Dynasty (1392–1910), students at the Confucian universities regularly protested against official corruption and, towards the end of the dynasty, argued for modernization of the nation. After the fall of the dynasty in 1910, students turned their oppositional activities to the Japanese colonization of Korea. Since the founding of the Republic of Korea, student activism has been a part of the political landscape in every government, with the exception of the communist government in the North.

Student activism escalated during the April Revolution of 1960 which led to the overthrow of the Syngman Rhee government. On 19 April, an estimated 30,000 students took to the streets of Seoul, and thousands converged on the presidential palace. When police opened fire on the demonstrators, an estimated 200 were killed.[3] The ensuing protests and demonstrations eventually led to American withdrawal of support for Rhee. His resignation quickly followed.

After the assassination of President Park Chung-hee in 1979 and the military coup led by General Chun Doo-Hwan, the student activism accelerated. In 1980, in protest against martial law and Chun's role as head of the military, students seized control of Kwangju, capital of Cholla province. Students and civilians, expecting aid from the USA in their struggle for democracy, seized arms and took control of the city on 22 May. The USA, however, failed to intervene, and within a day or so Chun ordered troops to retake the city. In the ensuing battle between crack government troops and untrained, poorly organized students, the military retook the city. Estimates of the number of students killed range up to 2,000, although the government claimed only 189 were killed.[4]

Since the Kwangju Incident, no other protests have brought such a direct threat to the government, nor such intensity of governmental

3. Sungjoo Han, 'Student activism: a comparison between the 1960 uprising and the 1971 protest movement', in Chong Lim Kim (ed.), *Political Participation in Korea: Democracy, Mobilization, and Stability* (Santa Barbara, Calif., 1980), pp. 143–61.

4. Myung Hyun Cho, 'The new student movement in Korea: emerging patterns of ideological orientation in the 1980s', *Korea Observer* 20 (1989), p. 97. See also Donald N. Clark (ed.), *The Kwangju Uprising: Shadows over the Regime in South Korea* (Boulder, Colo., 1988).

response. The Kwangju Incident did, however, serve as an ideological watershed, driving many students into a more leftist political
agenda, and caused many of them to become disillusioned with the
United States as a model of democracy.

In the mid to late 1980s, the student movement began to take on
an increasingly radical stance in order to maintain pressure on the
government towards reunification. Radical student parties which
devoted themselves to the overthrow of the Chun government
proliferated.[5] As the ideological tension between state and students
intensified, the movement turned increasingly to the dramatic use
of violence and self-immolation. There were regular episodes of
students throwing rocks and Molotov cocktails. In 1987 and 1988,
student protests attracted even more international attention due to
the visibility South Korea gained during the 1988 Olympics in Seoul.

The increased radicalization discredited the government, leading Chun to abandon plans for another term as president, and
strengthened more moderate opposition parties. However, as democratic mechanisms have become more firmly established in Korea,
the movement itself has lost focus, and in many ways 'capsized'.[6]
Although students are still regularly involved in protests and political activism, the radical nature of the movement and the increased
democratization of Korean society have cost the movement some
popular support. As recently as 1996, student protests at Yonsei
University led to over 1,000 injuries among students and police,
5,715 detentions, and eventually 438 indictments.[7]

A typical pattern for the protests is that students at Seoul's major
universities begin a round of protest, leading eventually to larger
regional or national participation.[8] However, many protests, such as
those in 1986 against mandatory military training at Seoul National
University, do not achieve national or even regional scope, and
remain localized.[9] The student movement has relied primarily on

5. Manwoo Lee, *The Odyssey of Korean Democracy* (New York, 1990), p. 8.
6. Chung-In Moon and Kang Mun-gu, 'Democratic opening and military intervention in South Korea: comparative assessment and implications', in James Cotton
(ed.), *Politics and Policy in the New Korean State: From Roh Tai-Woo to Kim Young-sam*
(New York, 1995), p. 187.
7. 'South Korea indicts 438 students', *Chronicle of Higher Education* 43 (July 1996),
p. A49.
8. Han, 'Student activism', p. 152.
9. 'SNU students stage violent rallies against in-camp drill', *Korea Herald* (29 April
1986), p. 8. Students called the mandatory military training 'colonial, slavery education' in protest at what is often seen as US attempts to maintain an atmosphere of
hostility between North and South Korea. See 'SNU resumes classes amid sporadic
rallies by student groups', *Korea Herald* (2 May 1986), p. 8.

an ideological foundation known as *minjung* or *sammin*. The three constituent elements of this philosophy are *minjung* (the people), *minjok* (the nation), and *minju* (democracy). The *minjung* ideology articulates a fusion of Marxist, nationalistic, and traditional beliefs about the welfare of the populace.[10] Protest during the last several decades has revolved primarily around fuller democratization, Korean reunification, and anti-Americanism. Although probably only a minority of Korea's students fully endorse the *minjung* philosophy, it has provided an evaluative basis for arguing about Korea's political system. In spite of some shared commitment to *minjung*, the student movement seldom demonstrates centralized leadership. Rather, as with many student movements, the demonstrations are led by various student groupings, with diverse groups and parties rising and falling in influence.

In some ways, since the Kwangju Incident, the student movement has become somewhat more professionalized, as permanent opposition parties, sometimes associated in the popular mind with the North Korean government, have been formed. However, the majority of protesters do not share leftist sentiments, and radical leaders of movements rarely maintain long-term influence. The 'amateur' participants typically protest only during their high school and university years, and immediately upon graduation, assume responsible roles in society. These participants are not identified with radical organizations and do not advocate the overthrow of the existing system. Probably only about 5 per cent of the total student population at any given time can be identified as militant student activists. Another 5 to 10 per cent are considered strongly sympathetic to the cause, and can be counted on to join protests. This leaves approximately 85 to 90 per cent who, if they join a protest, do so spontaneously, without a strong commitment to movement ideology.[11]

This raises an interesting question: how is it that the movements generate such support when so many of the participants are not firmly committed? The answer probably lies in the fact that the protest plays an important social role prescribed by Korea's premodern past. Because student protest has such a strong tradition in the nation, students participate, not because they are firmly committed to the beliefs of movement leaders, but because society

10. Kenneth M. Wells (ed.), *South Korea's Minjung Movement: The Culture and Politics of Dissidence* (Honolulu, 1995).
11. Vincent S.R. Brandt, 'South Korean society', in Chong-Sik Lee (ed.), *Korea Briefing, 1990* (Boulder, Colo., 1991), p. 92.

preserves a role for student protest. Students see themselves at least to some extent as actors, fulfilling their role on a cosmic, historical stage.

This leads us to another key factor in Korean student protest, namely the legitimacy society ascribes to it. Although the movement has lost much in terms of popular support, there remains widespread sympathy for many causes put forth by students. The conservative nature of Korean society creates a certain amount of space for student activism because of the differentiated roles associated with Confucian society.

Because of their education and privileged positions, students in Korea find themselves as the 'conscience of the emperor', a role arising not just from Confucian doctrine, but also in their role as university students in the developing world. University education in developing nations, including Korea, is typically an avenue to privilege and prestige, both social and economic, thus giving students a sense of being a part of a political and moral elite.[12] Thus, students see themselves as the only portion of the population realistically able to take on politically activist positions. As students, they have neither jobs to lose, nor families to support, so they participate in rituals against an order which they fully expect to join one day. Their brief career as students is the only period of their lives when they will be able to concentrate on political activism. As part of the educated elite, moreover, the students believe that their privileged positions give them both the insight and the prestige to effect change, a view seemingly shared by wider Korean society.[13]

For South Korea's rulers, it is tempting to explain away student activism as naive idealism, since the students often do not remember the Korean War and have little direct experience of communism. This charge might have some merit, but it is insufficient as an explanation of the scope, the strategies, and the legitimacy of student protest. Although lack of knowledge might open students to anti-governmental perspectives, it certainly will not account for the passion which underlies student activism. Rather, passion arises from deeply held cultural values and beliefs. It is more helpful, then, to identify the underlying cultural values that motivate student protest and provide the legitimacy necessary for the maintenance of this strong tradition. With this background in recent Korean political

12. Sunhwa Lee and Mary Brinton, 'Elite education and social capital: the case of South Korea', *Sociology of Education* 69 (1996), pp. 177–92.

13. Philip G. Altbach, 'Students and politics', in Philip Altbach (ed.), *The Student Revolution: A Global Analysis* (Bombay, 1970), pp. 52–3.

protest, we turn our attention to a discussion of Confucian political doctrine to identify ways in which the traditional political culture might have salience to contemporary protests.

Confucian doctrine and political opposition

Since the teachings of Confucius were first brought to Korea, probably as early as the first century BC, Confucianism as a political force has had a tremendous impact. Confucian doctrines were reinforced by the establishment of a Confucian-style political system and by Korea's tributary relationship with China, giving Korea a reputation of being more Confucian than any other nation.[14] Although there were certainly other influences on Korean political culture, perhaps none is as far reaching and deeply rooted as Confucianism. In fact, Korea was the last of the East Asian nations to adopt Western technologies and social organization, maintaining a strict adherence to Confucianism even after China and Japan had largely abandoned Confucian orthodoxy.

Confucianism, of course, provided a great variety of visions for social and political life. A tradition formed and shaped over two millennia by countless numbers of thinkers provides for a tremendous amount of subtlety and complexity in issues of political theory, dissent, and legitimacy. One of the foundational doctrines in Confucian statecraft was that of the mandate of Heaven. This doctrine, first articulated during the Chou Dynasty in China (*c.*1050–771 BC), asserted that political legitimacy is grounded in the *tao*, or way, of Heaven. The mandate, however, unlike the Western doctrine of the divine right of kings, was not absolute and unconditional, but, rather, was predicated upon the ability of the ruler to serve the interests of the population.

The moral way of the king or emperor was to be fulfilled through political, ritualistic, and ethical duties. When the government maintained certain ethical and ritualistic standards, the citizenry in turn would be able to fulfil the duties and responsibilities assigned it. Conversely, a government neglectful of its own duties was responsible for the moral laxity of the citizenry. Since the government is the wind and the populace the grass, the direction of the government determined the moral stance of the citizenry.

14. Lucian Pye, *Asian Power and Politics: The Cultural Dimensions of Authority* (Cambridge, Mass., 1985), p. 223.

A second crucial Confucian doctrine related to political role is that of social responsibility. Harmony in a society was always based on the correct fulfilment of all duties and responsibilities implied by the 'five relationships': ruler to ruled, father to son, husband to wife, elder to younger, and friend to friend. Benevolence was expected from superiors, and loyalty and obedience from inferiors. Only when people truly lived up to their titles could society function as it should; hence, Confucius' doctrine of the rectification of names. Only when kings behaved as kings, advisers as advisers, and subjects as subjects, could social harmony prevail.

These doctrines helped to establish a highly centralized meritocracy composed of ministers, advisers, and various other bureaucrats, typically chosen from the ranks of scholars on the basis of academic achievement and imperial examinations. In Korea, China, and Vietnam, the civil examination systems provided the human personnel responsible for running governmental functions. In theory, if not always in practice, the examination system was open to commoners, as well as elites, and, to an extent, checked the abuse of power by elites. Those who performed well at exams served not only as bureaucrats and administrators, but also had a responsibility to provide wise counsel to the emperor. In fact, scholarship was a more prestigious and rewarding profession than any other.

Given their expertise in the classics, it was assumed that scholars had a more implicit understanding of good and evil, which enabled them to act as a moral compass, or the 'conscience of the emperor'. This role in the political order implied certain duties. Just as the king was obliged to fulfil certain rituals to guarantee the stability and longevity of the state, so loyal officials, drawn from the ranks of scholars, had a moral duty to guide the king in the administration of the nation.

Because of the integral role that education played in Confucian meritocracy, the role of the scholar/official was often extended to include those in preparation for ministerial or governmental service, i.e. students. Since the purpose of education in Confucian societies was to raise up civil officials, students in Korea have been given status as a *de facto* element of the government, long after the responsibilities assigned them had passed into oblivion.[15] In traditional Korea, students at the Four Colleges, Confucian academies for higher learning, would go on strike as a means of remonstration, a practice known in Korean as *kwondang*.[16]

15. Henderson, *Korea: The Politics of the Vortex*, p. 200.
16. Chung Chai-sik, 'Confucian tradition and nationalist ideology', in Wells (ed.), *South Korea's Minjung Movement*, p. 71.

For several hundred years before the fall of the Yi Dynasty in 1910, Korea's literati performed leadership roles in various ways, such as replacing Buddhism with Confucianism as the exclusive body of normative and religious values in society. It was this clearly delineated responsibility of the educated that helped to provide normative restraints on royal authority, in that the aristocratic *yangban* class used Confucian doctrines to check royal despotism.[17] In the case of an unjust ruler who refused to fulfil the obligations of the mandate, scholars were given the explicit task of confronting the authority through remonstration. By calling the ruler to account for malfeasance or injustice, scholars could actually prolong the rule of the emperor. As an example, the Duke of Chou voices the attitude of the loyal minister in the Chinese context: 'My way is simply to continue and extend the virtue of our peace-establishing king, and Heaven will not have occasion to remove the mandate received by [the] King.'[18]

Remonstration, however, typically incurred the wrath of the emperor, since scholars often called attention to practices which the rulers did not want to change. Thus, 'over the centuries thousands of officials were flogged, demoted, banished, or exiled for having complained when the emperor neglected his ritual duties, tolerated corrupt officials, tampered with the line of succession, or disregarded the popular welfare'.[19] The personal sacrifice of career, riches, and position provided moral legitimacy for the scholars.

When remonstration failed, subjects and ministers were left with two alternatives. The first was to resort to violence as a legitimate means of achieving temporal political goals. Since the ruler refused to submit to the mandate of Heaven, others were justified in seeking to replace the unjust with just rule. Violence, rather than being something which destroys the order of human relations, helped to 'reestablish new social relations through disorder'.[20] Violence directed towards immediate moral and political goals was often a justifiable response to governmental corruption.

An alternative to violence directed towards the overthrow of the emperor was the ultimate act of remonstration, suicide. Only an act of suicide on the part of a minister fully illustrated to the emperor,

17. James B. Palais, 'Political leadership in the Yi Dynasty', in Dae-sook Suh and Chae-Jin Lee (eds), *Political Leadership in Korea* (Seattle, 1976), pp. 14–15.

18. Wing-tsit Chan, *A Sourcebook in Chinese Philosophy* (Princeton, 1963), p. 7.

19. Andrew Nathan, *Chinese Democracy* (Berkeley, Calif., 1986), pp. 24–5.

20. Kil-song Ch'oe, 'The symbolic meaning of shamanic ritual in Korean folk life', *Journal of Ritual Studies* 3 (1989), p. 229.

and the populace, the depth of moral error into which the government had fallen. 'When remonstrance failed, the act of self-sacrifice affirmed the moral character of the state.... "He who restrains his prince", wrote Mencius, "loves his prince".'[21] A poet/minister of the third century BC, Chu-yuan, often wrote poems critical of the emperor of the kingdom of Tsu and warned of the state's neglect of its moral duties. Out of frustration, the emperor dismissed him, and the poet was forced into exile. When his predictions regarding the impending overthrow of the ruler came to pass, the poet threw himself into a river where he drowned. Remonstration, violence, and suicide are required on the part of scholars when the state has been betrayed by the moral laxity of its leaders.

Traditional doctrine and contemporary protest

With the development of a new nationalism, inspired both by the introduction of Western social sciences into East Asia in the nineteenth and early twentieth centuries and by the Japanese colonization of Korea, the social, political and educational institutions of Confucianism came under fierce attack. The traditional sinocentrism, the overwhelming hierarchical social order, and corruption among ministers all contributed to a perception that the Confucian doctrines were 'morally bankrupt, ceremonious, and barren'.[22] Confucianism was lambasted as a feudal, reactionary set of dogmas that prevented full modernization by the nations in which it was most firmly entrenched. Because of its emphasis on duty and responsibility, Confucianism was blamed for deficiencies in Asian political, economic, and educational systems. Even today, it remains somewhat fashionable to blame traditional cultural values for deficiencies in the political system. Thus, one Korean analyst blames the Confucian tradition for 'blind obedience to superiors, hierarchical interpersonal relationships, emphasis on conformism, and loyalty'.[23] Another argues that Confucianism has 'been more of an impediment than a contributing factor to democratization in Korea'.[24]

21. Nathan, *Chinese Democracy*, pp. 24–5.
22. Chung, 'Confucian tradition and nationalist ideology', p. 85.
23. Lee, *The Odyssey of Korean Democracy*, p. 10.
24. Sung Chul Yang, 'An analysis of South Korea's political process and party politics', in James Cotton (ed.), *Politics and Policy in the New Korean State* (New York, 1995).

Largely because Western social science seemed to be so much more progressive and scientific, Confucianism as a motif of analysis and critique fell into disfavour. However, even as Confucian terminology fell into disuse, the underlying values and presumptions continued to motivate and guide political and social life. Korea's self-strengthening movement in the early part of this century, like similar movements elsewhere in East Asia, attempted to fuse the technologies and social organization of the West with the traditional Confucian spirit of the nation. Although Korean intellectuals began to use the language of democracy, equality, and human rights, the motivating force behind many progressive movements remained a Confucian sense of propriety and justice. Korea's political processes and institutions are Western in form, but remain motivated by pre-modern values. Benevolence on the part of the rulers is expected, as is loyalty and obedience on the part of citizens. As a part of this Confucian constellation of values, the role of students and scholars to remonstrate on behalf of the citizens of the nation remains a fundamental part of the political culture.

With careful analysis, it is possible to see the underlying assumptions and values of the traditional Confucian world-view embedded within the discourse of the protests. Although the protests articulate modern ideals of democracy, nationalism, and human rights, they are best understood as protests of remonstration of the government, since the interests of the Korean people are overlooked in favour of the private gain of rulers. Students might perceive that the government has betrayed the interests of the people, usually either for personal gain or by allowing the United States or other foreign powers to dominate Korean political life.

Charges of corruption and complicity with US dominance of Korea are probably those most frequently levelled at the government. Ever since American involvement in the post-World War II partition of Korea, the unequal relationship between the USA and the Republic of Korea has perpetuated the division of Korea into two separate nations, dividing families as well as individual loyalties. When students have attacked American interests, as with the burning of the American Cultural Center during the Kwangju uprising, the government (specifically, Chun) has been perceived as acting on behalf of the Americans, rather than for the citizens of Korea. Thus, the students perceived Chun's regime as immoral, in that it failed to provide for the welfare of the citizenry. This laxity in the government's moral duty provoked the remonstration founded in a strong sense of loyalty to the Korean nation.

Not only do the students act from a perception that the government has betrayed the nation, and the mandate of Heaven, they typically see themselves as inheritors of the long legacy of scholarly critique of an unjust society. They argue from a stance of moral purity that condemns the government for overlooking the interests of the people. For example, in 1986 a student who drowned herself in a river left a note reminiscent of the death of Chu-yuan: 'I can no longer contain this feeling of guilt for the deprived and oppressed in this land.'[25] Many students believe that their status as scholars gives them insight into the true situation facing the nation, and thus perceive a moral duty to call attention to it. One student who committed self-immolation in 1986 left a note that said, 'the masses are silent and appear stupid . . . I urge my friends to shed new light on the threat from Japan.'[26]

The government, for its part, goes to great lengths to demonstrate that student protests are in fact led by small groups of North Korean instigators or extremists. To acknowledge the student protest as consonant with the tradition of remonstration would be to undermine the legitimacy of the governing structures, as well as US involvement in Korea. An editorial in the *Korea Herald* of 1 May 1986 argued that 'certainly, the extremist activists are extremely small in number, and we are sure that the absolute majority of the people will not allow them to prevail any longer'.[27] By contending that the citizens disagree with the protesters, the government attempted to undermine the students' legitimacy as loyal remonstrators.

Students not only find a motive for protest in the Confucian tradition, but also look to the tradition for the methodologies employed in their demonstrations. Chinese students in Tian'anmen Square in 1989, for example, sent representatives with a scroll of remonstration to the Great Hall of the People, where they then bowed before the government to present the petitition. This action alone provoked great conflict among the demonstrators, as students recognized the traditional reference implicit in the action. After ignoring the students for over twenty minutes, a low-ranking official finally received the list because for a higher-ranking individual to receive it would have legitimated the remonstration.

Student protest, then, is not really spontaneous, nor is it solely due to the organizational efforts of student groups. When students

---

25. Shim Jae Hoon, 'The ultimate protest: students choose death as a weapon against Chun', *Far Eastern Economic Review* (5 June 1986), p. 30.
26. Ibid.   27. 'Extremist student slogans', *Korea Herald* (1 May 1986), p. 2.

participate in the rituals of remonstration, they are playing roles in a drama over 2,000 years old. The mandate, the pattern, even the strategies and methodologies are borrowed from hundreds of protest movements spread over thousands of years.

Finally, student protest in Korea is characterized by an intensity and longevity that are sustained by the values of the pre-modern past, in that the violence and suicides typify the pattern of remonstration of old. When protest is ineffective in obtaining the interests of the people, students turn to violence, arson, and even suicide. Throughout the decades of the 1980s and 1990s, self-immolation was a regular occurrence on Korean campuses. In 1986 alone, one hospital in Seoul received 18 cases of politically motivated self-immolation. In the spring of 1991, at least seven more acts of self-immolation occurred on Korean campuses.[28] During a series of protests in 1986, police in Seoul were instructed to maintain special vigilance to guard against attempts at self-immolation, while building owners were urged to make sure that no 'radicals' were able to get on to the roofs of their buildings.[29] An article in the *Far East Economic Review* was subtitled 'Students choose death as a weapon against Chun'.[30] Chun, as President and as the General who oversaw the Kwangju Massacre, was seen as an embodiment of the specific sins of the government as a whole, and was directly responsible for the continuing immoral and humiliating relationship.

Given the clear legitimacy afforded dissident activity by the residue of state Confucianism, why is it that student protest is not more typical in East Asian nations? In fact, student/scholar protest has been a part of East Asian political culture for centuries, and remains so. China's May Fourth Movement of 1919, which probably sparked the rise of the Chinese Communist Party, was preceded two decades earlier by the Hundred Days reform and China's Self-Strengthening movement, both of which had strong student participation. Students in Hong Kong recently vowed to use their campuses to continue to uphold democracy before China's resumption of sovereignty over the former British colony, and the 1989 student demonstrators in Tian'anmen Square made explicit their understanding of their role as scholars, arguing at one point, 'Our sacred mission is to uphold the people's interests . . . Our actions

---

28. Jae Ho Suk, Chang Hwan Han, and Byeong Kil Yeon, 'Suicide by burning in Korea', *International Journal of Social Psychiatry* 37 (1991), pp. 141–5.

29. 'Police vigilance to be hiked against suicide attempts by radicals', *Korea Herald* (25 May 1986), p. 8.

30. Shim Jae Hoon, 'The ultimate protest', p. 30.

these last few days sprang from our patriotic hearts, from our pure and loyal love for our great motherland . . . Citizens, our interests are now closely bound together.'[31]

But Korea's political culture does encourage a more visible, risk-oriented protest style than in other East Asian nations. Korean culture maintains a highly developed sense of rights, whose origin probably rests with the rights bestowed upon the aristocracy, or *yangban*, during pre-modern times.[32] Traditionally, the *yangban* could demand certain prerogatives, regardless of economic status. This tendency to seek what one is owed encourages risk-taking that would be unacceptable in many Asian cultures. One scholar has remarked that 'no country in the Confucian cultural areas has shown greater tolerance for competitive politics'.[33]

And so, Korean student protests, like student protests throughout East Asia, rely on modern themes for an ideological basis, while at the same time they find their motivating force in pre-modern Confucian political culture. At times, the values of these systems come into conflict. There remains a tension between the Confucian values of loyalty, conformity, and obedience and the Western political values of independence, egalitarianism, and self-expression. The example of the Korean student protests, however, demonstrates how a pre-modern, Confucian world-view motivates political protest in a cultural context far removed from the West. Korean student protesters act upon a conviction that the government owes justice to the citizenry, based not on contractual obligations, such as are popular among Western political theorists, but instead rooted in the moral order of the universe.

31. Minzhu Han, *Cries for Democracy: Writings and Speeches from the 1989 Chinese Democracy Movement* (Princeton, 1990), p. 75.

32. Pye, *Asian Power and Politics*, pp. 216–17.

33. Peter R. Moody, Jr., *Political Opposition in Post-Confucian Society* (New York, 1988), p. 1.

CHAPTER SEVENTEEN

Between the Shah and the Imam: The Students of the Left in Iran, 1977–81

BEHROOZ GHAMARI-TABRIZI

This chapter draws attention to the significant contribution of the students of the Left in overthrowing the monarchy in Iran, and to their eventual suppression under the Islamic Republic. After some historical background, the first part examines the role of students of the Left in organizing the anti-Shah revolutionary movement. The second part discusses how the monopolization of political power by militant clerics resulted in the Islamic Republic's brutal crackdown of 1980–81. The conclusion proposes that the students of the Left were preoccupied with broad issues of social justice and fragmented by the political and theoretical infighting of the Iranian communist groups. They therefore failed to organize a student movement for tangible and attainable demands related to specific issues of student life, such as curricular reform or admission policies.

Given the fact that I was a student activist of the Iranian Left during the years 1977–79, this account of the events that led to the collapse of monarchy manifests a leftist standpoint. In a neo-Orientalist fashion, academic and journalistic works often emphasize the *Islamic* character of the Iranian revolution and sweep the role of the Left under the rug of religious revivalism.[1] In contrast, this depiction of the non-hegemonic role of the Left student movements reveals the diversity of the revolutionary movement in Iran. Tragically, the establishment of the Islamic Republic was followed by the massive suppression of the Left – tens of thousands were executed, many more were imprisoned or exiled. Consequently, documents were destroyed, either by the agents of the new regime

---

1. For a review of this literature see Yahya Sadowsky, 'The new Orientalism and the democracy debate', *Middle East Report* 183 (1993).

or by those subject to persecution (the mere possession of a leftist pamphlet could bring years of imprisonment). Inevitably, given the dearth of records pertaining to the student movements, the following explication of the role of the leftist students during the revolution relies significantly on my own recollection.

The Iranian revolution, 1977–79

Revolution is a volcanic eruption of a negation. Revolutions are defined in terms of the rejection, rather than the embrace, of a social order. As in the Iranian case of 1979, it is only in retrospect that a 'master frame', which defines revolutionary objectives affirmatively, is conceived. It is also in retrospect and for the purpose of legitimizing the victors' authority that a genealogy of the revolution's ideology is constructed, its major participants are identified, and the 'true' martyrs, after whom streets, public buildings, and parks are named, are selected. Stripped from its contingencies, a revolution appears monolithic – historically inevitable. Thus, the establishment of the Islamic Republic in Iran, through the monopolization of power by the militant clergy, remade the *Iranian* revolution into an *Islamic* one. The monopolization of power by the militant clergy transformed Islam as a revolutionary idiom into Islam as the revolutionary objective.

During the 1980s and 1990s, the Iranian revolution became the signifier of Islamic revivalism. Especially with the collapse of communism, Islamism became the ideology through which nationalist movements of Muslim societies expressed their anti-imperialist and social justice agenda. Consequently, most histories of the Iranian revolution trace its Islamist currents, and thus discount the influence of the predominantly secular Left student movement, one of the most significant political forces during the years preceding the 1979 revolution.

In 1977, when President Carter called Iran an 'island of stability',[2] the authority of the Shah was undisputed, the economy was reasonably healthy, the bust period of the booming oil prices of the mid-1970s had not yet asserted its ills, and leftist opposition was effectively suppressed. In 1975, the Shah extended his repressive authority by abolishing all official political parties and established his own *Rastakhiz* (Resurgence) party. This officially sanctioned

2. New Year's Eve speech, President Carter, Tehran, 31 December 1977, 'Weekly Compilation of Presidential Documents', 14 (1978), p. 47.

single-party system was not welcomed by the USA and the Shah's other allies.

In July 1977, the first signs of instability appeared. Over 141 lawyers announced the formation of an Association of Jurists, to protect the judiciary from the arbitrary intrusion of SAVAK (the Shah's infamous secret police) and the military courts. At the same time, the Iranian Writers Association asked for official recognition by the government. Soon thereafter, the Writers Committee for the Defence of Political Prisoners was formed. Finally, the Bazaar Guild officially protested against the policy of coerced membership in the Shah's *Rastakhiz*. On the street, this was pejoratively termed the 'PPP policy', a reference to three options available to Iranian citizens: Passport (get a passport and leave the country), Pepsi (a reference to a method of torture by the SAVAK in which male prisoners were anally raped with Pepsi bottles), or *Payvand* (joining the party).

These letter-writing campaigns soon turned into violent demonstrations. At the end of summer 1977, the Shah released a few prominent political prisoners, but this failed to cool dissent. Around the same time, economic discontent fuelled the anger of the poorer classes. Shanty towns around Tehran, swelled by the influx of informal labour, presaged an economic downturn which had yet to affect the middle and working classes. Riots occurred in response to slum clearance measures in Tehran; roads were blocked and bulldozers stoned. The police opened fire on the protesters, killing four and injuring many.[3] Although for the most part the riots were spontaneous, underground literature suggested some leftist agitation.

In October 1977, during ten days of poetry reading, commemorating the death of Jalal Al-e Ahmad, a writer and social critic, the Goethe Institute in Tehran became the meeting place of thousands of members of the intelligentsia. Not only did the crowd cram the area inside the Institute, the pavements and streets around the German Cultural Centre were jammed by masses of enthusiastic spectators. They voiced their opposition to the Shah's political oppression and experienced for the first time the possibility of an oppositional gathering without violent police intervention.

By November, a sustained protest movement was emerging. On 3 November, the unexpected death of Ayatollah Khomeini's eldest

3. For a chronology of revolutionary events, see Ervand Abrahamian, *Iran Between Two Revolutions* (Princeton, 1981); Michael Fischer, *Iran: From Religious Dispute to Revolution* (Cambridge, Mass., 1980); Shaul Bakhash, *The Reign of the Ayatollahs, Iran and the Islamic Revolution* (New York, 1986); Ali Rahnema and Farhad Nomani, *The Secular Miracle: Religion, Politics, and Economic Policy in Iran* (London, 1990).

son in Iraq brought the exiled Ayatollah back to public consciousness. Ayatollah Khomeini, exiled after leading the protest movement against the Shah's White Revolution of 1964, had remained
a vocal force, especially after the formation of the *Rastakhiz*. The
death of his son, which prompted memorial ceremonies all over
the country, provided a public context within which his call for
ousting the Shah could be heard by a large audience. Police raided
many of these gatherings, and many mourners were killed or injured.

When the Shah visited Washington in November, Iranian student organizations in the USA organized a major demonstration
in front of the White House. Members of the Iranian armed forces
(who were being trained in the USA) and a large entourage of
Iranian secret service agents clashed with the demonstrators. Meanwhile, in Tehran, the police blocked the entrance to Aryamehr
University, where Said Soltanpour was to recite his poetry. Many
students were arrested. More than ten thousand students staged
a sit-in at the University's gymnasium, demanding the immediate
release of those arrested. The next day, joined by thousands of
bystanders, students marched quietly towards Tehran University.
Fearing that others might join the demonstration, the police reacted violently. Shouts of 'Down with the Fascist Regime' echoed
through the streets.

Protests entered a new phase in January 1978. An editorial in the
daily newspaper *Ettela'at* vilified and ridiculed Ayatollah Khomeini.
Qom Seminary students, enraged by this attack, took to the streets.
The police opened fire, killing and injuring many students. Vigils
were held in cities throughout the country to honour the Qom
martyrs, which in turn provoked a violent police response and
a cycle of martyrdom and commemorations. The demonstrations
rapidly spread. By the end of summer 1978, protesters were openly
demanding the abolition of the monarchy.

At the end of Ramadan, on 7 September, millions joined in
demonstrations throughout the country. On the same day, government troops, responding to the Shah's declaration of martial law,
fired upon demonstrators. Thousands were slain by military forces in
what later became known as Black Friday. Tanks appeared on the
streets of Tehran and nine other cities. By this time, the opposition
movement, which hitherto had been heavily dependent on elite
groups of intellectuals, clerics, and bazaaries, began to embrace
large numbers of ordinary urban dwellers. The key to mass participation in the revolutionary movement was the emergence of a
'safe space', a context within which the masses could justify their

involvement culturally and politically.[4] Islam was the ideological idiom through which this safe space was constructed. Millions stood on rooftops, and in the alleys and streets, shouting *Allah-o Akbar* (God is Great). *Allah-o Akbar* became the sound of political defiance even for those whose devotion to Islam was not deep.

The oil workers' strike in the south in October 1978 sealed the fate of the regime. On 29 October, the workers announced their explicitly political demands in solidarity with their fellow Iranians, including an end to martial law, the unconditional release of all political prisoners, the dissolution of SAVAK, and punishment of corrupt government officials and ministers.[5] The strike rapidly spread through the public sector and government agencies. The Shah's policy of the iron fist proved ineffective. On 29 December 1978, the military government resigned and the Shah appointed Shahpour Bakhtiar, a social democrat opposition leader, to form a new government. Bakhtiar initiated negotiations with strikers and ordered the troops not to provoke clashes on the streets. He encouraged the Shah to leave the country for a long vacation, believing that he could sacrifice the Shah to save the monarchy. But the nationwide strikes continued and, after fifteen years of exile, Khomeini returned to Iran. In a three-day street battle in February 1979 all the military bases, the radio and television stations, and the Shah's palace fell into the hands of the people, thus closing the book on monarchy in Iran.

The role of students

Unlike the students' movements of the 1960s and 1970s in Europe and the United States, which were associated with New Left counterculture, the Iranian student movements, both internally and abroad, were culturally conservative and politically militant. They were primarily organized around issues of social justice, and anti-imperialist politics, advocating economic and political independence, and eradication of cultural dependence or *gharbzadegi* ('westoxication').[6]

4. The notion of safe space is not meant to suggest that revolutionary participation occurs only if it is risk-free, since risk-free revolutionism is inherently contradictory. Rather, the aim is to emphasize the significance of cultural resources in the *formative* stages of a mass movement.
5. See the account of an anonymous oil worker in Terisa Turner and Petter Nore (eds), *Oil and Class Struggle* (London, 1980).
6. *Gharbzadegi* was the title of a monograph published in 1962 by Jalal Al-e Ahmad, an Iranian social critic. Al-e Ahmad argued that Western technology was polluting

In the three decades prior to the 1979 revolution, two definitive moments mark the student movement inside Iran. The first was the demonstration at Tehran University on 7 December 1953, against Vice-President Nixon's official visit and the university's bestowal of an honorary degree upon him. This took place just a few months after the CIA-designed *coup d'état*, after which the leaders of the pro-Moscow Tudeh Party were executed, imprisoned, or fled the country. Demonstrations spread throughout the campus. Troops sent in to quell the dispute opened fire on the protesters, killing three. The day, sixteenth of *Azar* in the Iranian calendar, was thereafter commemorated as Students' Day. This first definitive moment established the students' profound discontent with the American role in reinstalling the Shah. At the same time, however, it marked the end of an era of massive student participation in Iranian politics. After the 1953 coup, protest was no longer tolerated.

The second definitive moment came in 1970 and inaugurated a new wave of student protest. In March 1970, thousands of students took to the Tehran streets to protest against the hardships an increase in bus fares would inflict on the poor. What started as an objection to the fare increase turned into an indictment of the regime. The whole city of Tehran became the battleground between the riot police and students. Buses were stopped, and ticket kiosks set afire. Chants of 'Unity, Struggle, Victory' and 'Down with the Fascist Regime' haunted the streets. Five students were killed, more than five hundred injured, and many more jailed.

Many of those involved in the bus riots subsequently abandoned the reformist and non-violent politics favoured by the Tudeh Party and the National Front. Inspired by the Cuban Revolution, and the Algerian and Vietnamese liberation movements, in the mid-1960s small cells of student activists began preparing for urban guerrilla warfare. In February 1971, the Iranian army attacked a guerrilla training base in northern Iran and killed thirteen of the newly established *Cherikha-ye Fadaeiy-e Khalq-e Iran* (The Guerrilla Devotees of Iranian People). Nine of the thirteen were students of universities in Tehran. During the same period, an Islamist militant group with strong socialist tendencies was formed. This group, *Sazman-e*

Iranian cultural authenticity and political sovereignty, hence the notion of 'westoxication'. This Heideggerian notion was appropriated by the Iranian Left. For a discussion on the notion of *gharbzadegi*, Brad Hanson, 'The "westoxication" of Iran: depictions and reactions of Behrangi, Al-e Ahmad, and Shari'ati', *International Journal of Middle Eastern Studies* 15 (1983).

Mojahedin-e Khalq-e Iran (The Organization of the Holy Warriors of Iranian People) was originally founded in 1965 by nine Tehran University students. Although the organization's founders had strong religious convictions, the source of their political militancy was the national liberation movements of the 1960s. During the years preceding the 1979 revolution, a total of 341 guerrillas were killed of whom 147 were students, 36 were recently graduated engineers, six were physicians, and 27 were teachers.[7]

After the 1953 coup, many of the members of the Tudeh Party's youth organization and of Mohammad Mossaddeq's National Front left the country. They formed small student associations for cultural and political activities in Germany, France, and England. In 1961, in a joint convention in Paris, the American-based Iranian Students Association and the European-based Confederation of Iranian Students announced the establishment of the Confederation of Iranian Students (National Union).[8] The visibility of Iranian students in the European political scene of the early 1960s and their militancy against the Shah's dictatorship remained a major source of embarrassment for the Iranian monarch.

By the mid-1970s, this external students' movement had grown significantly, due in part to the sharp increase in oil prices which allowed thousands of middle-class families to send their children to study abroad. By the end of 1978, more than 45,000 Iranians were enrolled at American colleges and universities.[9] Consequently, membership in oppositional student organizations swelled.

Students and the revolutionary movement of 1977–79

Contrary to their own expectations, the leftist guerrilla organizations were not crucially important to the revolutionary process set in motion after 1977. In fact, the revolutionary mass movement began at the moment when both *Fadaeiyan* and *Mojahedin* organizations had been decimated by SAVAK. Most of the *Fadaeiyan*'s founding

7. Ervand Abrahamian, 'The guerrilla movement in Iran, 1963–1977', *MERIP Reports* 86 (1980), p. 4.
8. For an extensive account of the formation of the Confederation of Iranian Students in Farsi, see Hamid Showkat and Mehdi Khanbaba-Tehrani, *The Iranian Left: A Look from Within* (Paris, 1990), pp. 311–50. For a brief review in English, see Valentine Moghadam, 'Socialism or anti-imperialism? The Left and revolution in Iran', *New Left Review* 166 (1987).
9. *The Chronicle of Higher Education*, 19 September 1997, p. A51.

members were killed and their key cadres imprisoned. The *Mojahedin*, battered by SAVAK assaults, was also paralysed by internal conflicts. In contrast, the students of the Left played a significant role in the early stages of the movement. However, soon after millions of people marched on the streets in the major cities and nationwide strikes crippled the political and economic apparatus of the regime, they had to redefine their role. Events quickly overtook them; demonstrations on university campuses could no longer sway the course of the revolution.

On 7 September 1978, the day before Black Friday, students sought to assert their influence upon mass demonstrations. They prepared hundreds of banners with distinctively leftist slogans such as 'Workers of the World Unite!' or 'Long Live the Democratic Republic under the Leadership of the Working Class!' and distributed them among the crowd. Their goal was to radicalize the protest by shifting the crowds' demands from mere democratic reforms to wholesale abolition of the monarchy. The police had allowed the demonstration only after the liberal Islamic Liberation Movement of Iran had agreed that no slogans against the Shah and monarchy would be chanted. Yet before long the estimated crowd of two million was chanting 'Down with the Shah', partly due to the students' influence. When Prime Minister Sharif Emami subsequently pleaded for the declaration of martial law, he showed pictures of the students' radical banners and warned of widespread communist infiltration.

The period after Black Friday and the declaration of martial law was a crucial conjuncture for the students to determine their future role in the revolutionary movement. The indisputable influence of the guerrilla organizations over the student movement was challenged by a new political tendency. The guerrilla movement had so far proven unsuccessful; it was the poetry readings, the open letters in defence of human rights, sermons by junior clerics, and Ayatollah Khomeini's taped messages which had brought the masses out on the streets.[10] The new Left political tendency, known as the 'Third Line', was broadly based upon: (1) a negation of Soviet socialism and of the Tudeh Party's satellite relation with Moscow; (2) disillusionment with guerrilla warfare and its intrinsic elitism; and (3) the belief that the urgent responsibility of the students was to organize

10. For a discussion on how the revolutionary movement was successfully organized through small media, see Annabelle Sreberny-Mohammadi and Ali Sreberny-Mohammadi, *Small Media, Big Revolution: Communication, Culture, and the Iranian Revolution* (Minneapolis, Minn., 1994).

the revolutionary masses, especially the working class. The last concern acquired more importance after the institution of martial law. In order to ensure that the Black Friday massacre was indeed the point of no return for the Shah, street demonstrations had to continue. Long pauses between demonstrations could have been interpreted as a demonstration of the regime's power.

By autumn 1978, active members of the Confederation of Iranian Students had already begun repatriating to take part in the revolution. They brought with them rigidly defined boundaries between different factions of the Left. Inside the country, the lack of access to Marxist literature prevented the development of doctrinal distinctions between Marxist, Leninist, Maoist, or Trotskyist groups. Students' exposure to the ideas of the Old and New Left and to the ideas of the 'Third Line' contributed to the emergence of new currents in the student movement. With small home-made mimeograph machines, activists produced thousands of flyers for distribution in working-class neighbourhoods. At the same time, in order to create confusion among troops in the streets, they formed committees to organize high school students throughout the city to foment continuous disturbances. Although many students lost their lives during these demonstrations, the action revealed the vulnerability of the martial law.

By January 1979, Tehran University had become a revolutionary information clearing house. Thousands of people gathered on campus and the nearby streets to exchange news and plan further strategic action. Flyers and newsletters were distributed freely and 'white-cover books' – illegal Marxist literature – were sold on campus. However, the departure of the Shah shattered the precarious unity of the revolutionary movement.

A mysterious mob group called *Hezbollahis*, 'the partisans of Allah', began an organized attack on the activities of the Left and other secular opposition groups. They assaulted the street vendors who were selling the 'white-cover books', tore up leftist flyers, and threatened female demonstrators who defied Islamic dress codes. *Hezbollahis* marched on the university campuses and chanted 'Death to Communism'. Although Khomeini officially continued his policy of *vahdat-e kalameh*, 'the unity of the word', and assured Marxists that they were 'free to voice their demands', he remained silent about the atrocities of the *Hezbollahis*.[11]

---

11. *Kayhan*, 16 January 1979, in Rahnema and Nomani, *The Secular Miracle*, p. 171.

The Militant Student Organization (MSO)

After the Shah's departure, the *Hezbollah,* known pejoratively as the party of club-wielders, established the foundation for the assertion of political hegemony by militant Muslim clerics. The student-based Left was ill-equipped to pose any major threat to their desire for a monopoly of power.[12] Although communists were instrumental in organizing the workers of the major industries and engaging them in the revolution from its inception, masses of workers from small industries were still unaffected by the revolution. They became involved only after they were directly affected by the crippling consequences of the nationwide strikes.

In late December 1978, a group of workers from Tehran's largest cement factory introduced a grievance at a Tehran University rally. They had not been paid for more than two months, and asked students to join their demand for back pay. The next day, several hundred students joined the few hundred workers at the plant. The students showered the workers with thousands of leftist flyers. But the demands of the workers were forgotten amidst the pamphlets that littered the factory yard.

After the fiasco at the Tehran Cement Factory, a group of 'Third Line' students, along with some activist workers, held a meeting at Tehran Polytechnique University. A strategic plan for systematic actions at factories where workers had not been paid was formulated. At the second meeting, at the School of Economics at Tehran University, *Sazman-e Daneshjouyan-e Mobarez,* or Militant Student Organization (MSO), was established. Following the general outline of the Third Line position, the MSO's immediate agenda was to organize small industrial workers in Tehran, connect their economic demands to the anti-Shah revolutionary movement, and expand the social base of the Left.

Seventeen factories in the Tehran vicinity were initially targeted. Activist workers in each plant were contacted and a date for a sit-in at the factory arranged. Large numbers of workers attended these rallies and listened to propaganda about the ills of capitalism. The MSO was occasionally successful in mediating between workers and management. Consequently, more and more workers contacted MSO

---

12. Ashtiani argued that despite its significant contributions to the revolutionary movement, the Left remained marginal in Iranian politics because its social base was limited to students. See Ali Ashtiani, 'A balance sheet of the Left', *Kankash* 1 (1987).

members and invited them into their plants. In just a few weeks, membership rapidly grew from just a handful of students on each campus to four to five hundred. These actions provided an opportunity for the students of the Left to step out of their university enclave, at a time when the campuses were dominated by the club-wielding thugs of the *Hezbollah*.

The MSO's most successful action, which drew nationwide attention, was the sit-in at the General Electric plant twenty kilometres west of Tehran. GE's 4,000 workers, who had not been paid for two months, had begun selling factory products to compensate for their back pay. The sit-in lasted for eight days, during which the oil workers in the south and other oil refineries in Tehran sent messages of solidarity. The Organization of Militant Clergy (*Rohaniyyat-e Mobarez*) and other leaders of non-leftist organizations sent messages of support, food, and blankets. Small groups of students and workers patrolled the plant to protect it from surprise attack by the military or mobs of *Hezbollahis*. During the day, student groups performed plays, sang folk and revolutionary songs, and showed films.

On 9 February 1979, the situation intensified with news from Tehran of a mutiny in the air force. Aided by armed guerrillas, masses of people broke into the military bases in Tehran. They armed themselves with machine guns and stormed the prisons, SAVAK installations, radio and television stations, royal palaces, and other government buildings. Workers at the GE plant, still preoccupied with their own demands, seemed uninterested. The MSO students were divided: some wanted to continue the action on the factory floor while others insisted on joining the riots in Tehran. At the end, after nine days, most students left the factory to take part in striking the final blow against the monarchy.

Immediately after the revolution, students of different political tendencies established official chapters in all the universities in the country. Five major student organizations emerged: *Sazman-e Daneshjouyan-e Pieshgam* (The Organization of Vanguard Students, OVS), which represented the *Fadaeiyan* line; *Anjoman-e Daneshjouyan Mosalman* (The Association of Muslim Students), which consisted of the followers of the Muslim *Mojahedin* organization; the MSO; the Tudeh Party's *Anjoman-e Democratik-e Daneshjouyan* (The Democratic Students' Association); and *Anjoman-e Eslami-ye Daneshjouyan* (The Islamic Students' Association, ISA), comprised of the followers of Khomeini and the newly established Islamic regime. Though strong in the country, within the universities the Islamists remained weak. On some campuses, the ISA was unable to send a single representative to the university councils.[13]

The Third Line was more explicit in its discontent with the establishment of an Islamic Republic than other leftist groups, for instance the *Fadaeiyan* and the Tudeh Party. However, it was divided between those who were oriented towards the liberals and the provisional government, and those who sympathized with the clergy's anti-imperialist rhetoric. These different tendencies, in addition to strong sectarian tendencies of the Left, eventually led to the fragmentation of the MSO.

The Islamic cultural revolution

Four months after the revolution, 105 newspapers and magazines were published in Tehran, the majority of non-Islamic orientation.[14] Hundreds of book-vendors sold Marxist literature and communist pamphlets and journals on the pavements bordering the Tehran University campus. While the newly established Committees of Islamic Revolution (IRC), an armed militia organization, in cooperation with the *Hezbollah,* took control of law and order in other parts of the city, the area around the university remained a liberated zone. It operated as a distribution post for opposition media. Large anti-government demonstrations were held on the campuses, and prominent leaders of the opposition voiced their dissent in lecture halls. Despite arson attacks on bookstores and the brutalization of street vendors by *Hezbollahis,* the universities permitted a continuous flow of information and freedom of expression.

The Islamic Republic had yet to consolidate its power. The regime was already engaged in a bloody war with Kurdish rebels; workers were still unsatisfied with the post-revolution arrangements of workers' councils; and internal conflicts delayed the final monopolization of power by the militant clergy. The state-owned media chastised universities as the breeding ground for communism. They considered leftist student activism to be one of the main obstacles to the establishment of law and order.

13. The university councils were established after the revolution as a democratically elected institution which represented the student body, faculty, and staff. See Sohrab Behdad, 'The Islamic Republic's Cultural Revolution', *Kankash* 7 (1996).

14. *Tehran Mosavar* 22 (1980). See Rahnema and Nomani, *The Secular Miracle,* pp. 176–82, and Bakhash, *The Reign of the Ayatollahs,* pp. 117–24.

More than a year after the revolution, students and professors affiliated with the Islamic Republic Party (IRP), the dominant state party, were still in the minority on campus. The regime decided that the problem of the universities could not be resolved from within the campus. In a conversation with ISA leaders, Hassan Ayat, an ideologue of the IRP, revealed a plan to unleash a decisive attack on the universities. A tape-recording of Ayat's conversation was leaked to the press. 'The universities in their present state', he remarked, 'should be closed down . . . but the Imam [Khomeini] has to be informed before we put our plan into action.'[15] The call from Ayatollah Khomeini finally came on 21 March 1980:

> All universities in Iran should be subjected to a proper revolution and all those professors who are connected with the West or East should be purged . . . Our dear students should not follow the misleading footsteps of faithless university intellectuals.[16]

In April 1980, the ruling clerics' attack on the universities reached a climax. In Friday sermons in all the major cities, neutralization of the universities' influence was formulated as the next immediate step towards the realization of the Islamic revolution. On 18 April, a warning was issued by President Bani Sadr's office that the student groups should evacuate their offices immediately. Meanwhile, scores of *Hezbollahis,* militias of the IRC, and ordinary people surrounded Tehran University and other campuses. Student groups of the Tudeh Party and the *Mojahedin* evacuated their offices. The OVS (followers of the *Fadaeiyan* organization) and the students of the Third Line refused to abandon their facilities. Thus, the week-long battle over the occupation of the universities began.

The focal point of resistance was the Tehran University campus. Students inside the campus made an appeal to the people to help them save the last sanctuary of democracy. The armed Islamic militia prevented supporters from approaching the campus. On the second day of the seizure of the campus, shots were fired by the Revolutionary Committee militias. Wounded students were smuggled out to hospitals, but many, along with doctors who treated them, were arrested. From the roofs of several colleges, members of a radical *Fadaeiyan* faction fired back at the Muslim militia. Students decided to leave the campus before a bloodbath resulted.

Similar attacks occurred in the cities of Mashad, Tabriz, Isfahan, and Shiraz, with the bloodiest in Rasht and Ahvaz. The government

15. Cited in Rahnema and Nomani, *The Secular Miracle,* p. 225.
16. Ibid., p. 227.

announced that twenty-four counter-revolutionaries were killed during the clashes, with opposition claims much higher.[17] On 22 April 1980, President Bani Sadr led a large crowd of more than fifty thousand into the 'liberated' Tehran University. While workers on one side of the campus washed blood from the walls, in the stadium Bani Sadr announced the beginning of the Cultural Revolution to Islamize institutions of higher education.

The majority of professors were either purged or voluntarily left the country. On 21 April 1981, the first anniversary of the massacre of the students, more than a thousand students rallied in front of the Tehran University campus. They demanded the immediate reopening of the universities and reinstitution of students' political rights. *Hezbollahis* attacked the students and threw hand grenades into the crowd. *Paykar,* the largest Third Line organization, which organized the event, subsequently claimed that two students were killed and fifty were seriously wounded.[18] The universities remained closed for two years. According to one estimate, between the years 1981 and 1984, more than 12,000 members of opposition groups, most of whom were university and high school students, were executed and more than 140,000 were imprisoned.[19] *Paykar* had 380 of its members arrested, of whom 246 were executed.[20] *Payam-e Enqelab,* the official organ of the Guardians of the Islamic Revolution, admitted that more than 75 per cent of all the members of leftist groups who had been arrested since the summer of 1981 were executed. When the universities were reopened, the students of the Left were conspicuously absent.[21]

Conclusion

The majority of the leaders of the movement were executed after the 1981 crackdown on the opposition parties. Their stories remain

17. The government also alleged that armed students opened fire on the revolutionary militia, though a photograph distributed by the OVS showing armed *Hezbollahis* firing at the students in Rasht contradicted the government's claim. Pamphlet published by *Sazman-e Daneshjouyan-e Pieshgam (Rasht)*, 26 April 1980, James Hitselberger papers, Box No. 4, Hoover Institute, Stanford University.

18. *Paykar* political pamphlet, 24 April 1981, Hitselberger papers, Box No. 2.

19. In a well-documented appendix to *Mojahed* 261 (1985), the journal of the Organization of People's Mojahedin, names and dates of executions of 12,028 were published.

20. The official number announced by the government in *Ettela'at,* 5 May 1984.

21. In an interview, Abdolkarim Soroush, the spokesperson for the Cultural Revolution Council, explained the details of the university admission policies without

largely untold. Nevertheless, the contribution of the students of
the Left to the Iranian revolution is indisputable. Their role in
radicalization of the movement and sustaining the revolutionary
zeal after the massacre of Black Friday of 1978 should not be
ignored. They remained a potent voice of dissent until they were
violently obliterated by the Islamic Republic in 1981.

Despite its crucial role in the revolution, the student movement
lacked distinct objectives of its own, and therefore never established
a separate, viable identity. The Left reduced the student movement
to an appendix to its general struggle against imperialism and for
socialism. For instance, at the beginning of the 1979–80 academic
year, a typical leftist position placed the student movement within
the following context:

> [1] the Kurdish people is under the brutal attack of the reactionary
> regime . . . [2] progressive papers are closed down . . . [3] inflation
> and unemployment is ravaging the lives of our workers . . . [4] with a
> new mask, reactionary agents of imperialism are deceiving our masses
> and suppressing their resistance.[22]

Accordingly, 'revolutionary students' were asked to concentrate their
efforts on these issues.

In Leninist fashion, the Left advocated a state-centred politics in
which any movement that neglected the centrality of the assumption of political power was regarded as mere bourgeois reformism.
The Left was either suspicious of reformist democratic actions, such
as the women's movement against the Islamic dress code,[23] or had
an instrumentalist relationship with it. The Left manipulated struggles on university campuses for the recognition of organizations for
students' extracurricular activities – such as mountaineering clubs,
film and photography associations – as a means for recruiting new
cadres for underground activities.

Consequently, the students were divided by the political and
theoretical infighting of a Left which proved ineffective in configur-
ing a non-sectarian democratic politics. Since leftist students were

---

a single reference to the political agenda which originally motivated the cultural
revolution. See *Iranshahr* 2 (1980).

22. *Razmandegan-e azadi-ye tabaqe-ye kargar* [The Warriors for the Liberation of the
Working Class], message to revolutionary students, September 1979. Hitselberger
papers, Box No. 2, Hoover Institute, Stanford University.

23. None of the major leftist groups supported the women's anti-*hijab* (Islamic
dress code) movement. They regarded it as a bourgeois diversion from the 'real
issues' of the revolution. Mahnaz Matin, 'The Iranian Left and women's movement',
Noqteh 3 (1997).

primarily engaged in the general struggle for social justice, matters relating to students' lives and to education were never properly addressed in their agenda. The Left's failure to take the specific issues of the student movement seriously made their physical elimination from the university campuses more feasible for the Islamic Republic. During the days when the universities were rampaged by the *Hezbollahis*, the student body remained disengaged and perceived the whole event as merely another episode in the ongoing war between the Left and the newly established regime.

In recent years, a new generation of student activists has emerged in Iran. Though these students have no recollection of the revolutionary years, they are nevertheless wiser in situating themselves at the centre of the quest for academic freedom, educational reform, and a democratic participatory politics. Although the *Hezbollahis* are still active in suppressing dissent, this time they are facing an activist tendency initiated by a generation born and raised under the Islamic Republic.

CHAPTER EIGHTEEN

The 1989 Chinese People's Movement in Beijing

FRANK N. PIEKE

The death of Hu Yaobang

In the summer of 1988, price liberalization led to high inflation and panic buying in China, particularly in urban areas. Conservative leaders, such as Premier Li Peng, responded with a policy of economic stabilization and partial restoration of central control. The prospect of at least two years of government-inspired austerity was highly unpopular with the majority of the urban population, dependent upon fixed state sector wages.

On 15 April 1989, Hu Yaobang, the former party secretary stripped of his post in 1987 because he had been too soft on the 1986 student demonstrations, died of a heart attack. To progressive students at Beijing universities this presented an unexpected opportunity to carry out long-planned demonstrations.[1] Two strategic problems evident in past waves of student activism (1980, 1985, 1986 and 1988) seemed germane. The first was to avoid an immediate government crackdown, since it would take time to win popular support. Criticizing the political system and the Communist Party might cause the party leadership to unite against the students, label their movement counter-revolutionary, and crush it before it could gather momentum. Even more seriously, such criticism might also alienate the majority still loyal to the party and the political system.

Students also had to rise above factional struggles within the party and, specifically, avoid identification with the radical, reformist

This article is mainly based on ethnographic research conducted in Beijing during the People's Movement in 1989. For a fuller report, see Frank Pieke, *The Ordinary and the Extraordinary: An Anthropological Study of Chinese Reform and the 1989 People's Movement in Beijing* (London, 1996).

1. Christophe Nick, 'De Chinese Cohn-Bendits', *Haagse Post*, 4 November 1989, p. 60; Shen Tong, *Almost a Revolution* (New York, 1991), chs 6 and 7.

faction led by party secretary Zhao Ziyang. If student activists were openly connected with Zhao, conservative leaders might perceive them as a threat, and immediately crush the movement to prevent Zhao from using the students to his advantage. Identification with the reformers would also destroy the students' most important long-term political capital, namely their traditional role as the nation's conscience. They had to remain selfless petitioners, willing to risk their positions and maybe their lives for the common good. If they came to be identified with the reformers, they would never be able to speak on behalf of 'the people'. In short, they had to exploit party divisions without becoming embroiled in them.

The second strategic problem involved the need to mobilize the urban population so as to maximize pressure on the authorities. The students knew the ground was fertile, given mounting dissatisfaction with urban reforms, economic hardship and the resultant moral crisis which threatened the legitimacy of the political system.[2] The students' most powerful discursive resource was China's tradition of protest, particularly the May Fourth Movement of 1919 and the April Fifth Movement of 1976. To invoke this tradition, students had carefully to play the role of independent, altruistic representatives of 'the people'. They had to avoid the mistakes of earlier student demonstrations in the 1980s, which had demanded material improvements in student life. Other concrete complaints like inflation or the threat of redundancy, though shared with the majority of the urban population, would smack of self-interest, of little legitimacy in the Chinese tradition of protest. On the other hand, slogans about democracy and freedom, although non-partisan and representing the common good, by themselves mean little to most Chinese, and would not arouse their enthusiasm.

Mass mobilization was especially problematic because of the dominant role which the 'work unit' (*gongzuo danwei*), and through it the party, played in urban China. There was no alternative organizational focus beyond the work unit which could organize political activities, including demonstrations, outside party supervision. Since its victory in 1949, the party had taken great pains to prevent the emergence of organizations which would threaten its bureaucratic dominance.

Students could therefore not expect the active participation of the people during the initial phases of protest. The challenge was to create avenues for people to express sympathy without becoming

---

2. Pieke, *The Ordinary and the Extraordinary*, ch. 4.

tainted politically. Students immediately understood that Hu's death provided such an avenue. During the April Fifth Movement, the death of Premier Zhou Enlai had provided a similar rallying point for demonstrations.[3] That movement, moreover, had symbolically significant overtones since it had pitted Deng Xiaoping, a moderate and follower of Zhou, against the Maoist faction (some of whom were later branded the 'Gang of Four'), and had become enshrined in official party history as a 'completely revolutionary movement' after Deng's final victory over the remnants of Maoism in 1978. Comparison with the April Fifth Movement thus triggered a powerful legacy of righteous struggle.

The combination of mourning and protest, and the legacy of 1976, provided the student movement with temporary legitimacy. It proved an effective means by which to counter quick government suppression, buying precious time with which to coordinate organizations and develop strategy. At the same time, mourning Hu gave the people of Beijing the opportunity to observe the students, and see for themselves that they were not selfish youngsters or, worse, political fanatics bent on a second cultural revolution. The students proved themselves disciplined patriots in the tradition of the April Fifth and May Fourth Movements,[4] who expressed the people's sadness about Hu's death, and only desired an open dialogue with the government about the ills of Chinese society.

The students' strategy was to develop independent organizations to provide leadership and continuity for a prolonged movement, gradually gaining concessions from the authorities toward a more open political system. This necessitated forcing the authorities into a dialogue which recognized the students as patriotic and loyal to the party. Students had therefore to cultivate their image of selflessness, moderation, and discipline, and to avoid violence. Public relations became a priority. Pamphlets, wall-posters, and unofficial periodicals were produced in great quantity. But students also recognized that accurate reporting in the domestic and foreign media would provide an audience much larger than could be reached by demonstrations, petitions, and pamphlets alone. Freedom of the press was considered profoundly important, as evidenced by the insistence that negotiations with government representatives be

3. Anne Thurston, *Enemies of the People: The Ordeal of the Intellectuals in China's Great Cultural Revolution* (Cambridge, Mass., 1987), ch. 1.

4. The May Fourth Movement of 1919 is conventionally taken as a defining moment in the formation of China as a modern nation, with the Communist Party the direct heir to its legacy.

broadcast on television live and uncensored. Throughout, the foreign media – above all the Chinese bulletins of the BBC World Service and Voice of America – helped spread news of the demonstrations all over Beijing and China.

Propaganda and media reporting had further importance. First, the media mobilized international public opinion. During the final weeks Beijing was flooded with journalists and China specialists, making the People's Movement an international media event of immense magnitude. Chinese leaders knew that their reaction was closely monitored by millions around the world. Excessively harsh action could (and eventually did) damage China's international reputation. Second, propaganda and reporting created an immediate historical record. Students and other participants were keenly aware that the movement's real impact would only be felt after it had subsided. It had to be incorporated into the Chinese tradition of protest to be exploited by future movements. Nearly everyone, therefore, busily recorded speeches, demonstrations, slogans, poems, pamphlets and wall-posters by every available means.

While students maintained the semblance of mourning, Deng and other conservative leaders became increasingly alarmed by events. On 22 April, during the official memorial for Hu held at the Great Hall of the People, thousands of students assembled at Tian'anmen Square for their own memorial rally. Going down on their knees in traditional fashion, three students presented a petition to the leaders assembled in the hall. This effectively destroyed the pretence that the students were only mourning Hu.

The authorities felt pushed into a corner. On 26 April, an editorial published in the *People's Daily*, the official newspaper of the Chinese Communist Party, declared the establishment of autonomous student unions an illegal act, and that 'a very small number' of people were trying to create chaos, using as a cover their fellowstudents' grief over Hu's death. This, the editorial argued, amounted to a premeditated conspiracy to undermine the leading role of the Communist Party and socialism.[5]

Conservative leaders probably carefully timed the editorial to coincide with Zhao's official visit to North Korea on 23 April. The editorial was a watershed, effectively ruling out negotiations with students at the very moment when their movement had lost much

5. 'Bixu qizhi xianmingde fandui dongluan' ('It is necessary to take a clear-cut stand against disturbances'), *Renmin Ribao*, 26 April 1989. Translated in Michel Oksenburg *et al.* (eds), *Beijing Spring, 1989: Confrontation and Conflict: The Basic Documents* (Armonk, NY, 1990), pp. 206–8.

of its initial impetus. The theme of mourning Hu's death had lost its force, and students were uncertain what to agitate for next. They were desperate to maintain the struggle until the 70th anniversary of the May Fourth Movement. The 26 April editorial proved that the students had solved the second strategic problem: staying clear of intra-party factional struggle. But it also paved the way toward a solution to the first problem: forging an active link with the dissatisfied masses in Beijing.

The role of bystanders

On 27 April, students marched in protest over the editorial.[6] The demonstration was unprecedented not only in its size but, more importantly, in the way bystanders along the route clearly expressed support, by giving money, ice lollies, food, and drink. By their support, bystanders made clear their disagreement with the *People's Daily's* editorial. This support gave the demonstrations a political impact which the students could never have achieved on their own. Just as importantly, the anonymity and outward passivity of the bystanders provided a way of circumventing the Chinese system of political control, which focuses on people as members of work units, not as individual citizens. Through this control system, the party achieved a degree of supervision which made it unnecessary to develop instruments to monitor outside political activities. This system was ironically beaten exactly because of its unprecedented dominance of organized Chinese society. Since bystanders are not part of the bureaucratized social structure, they cannot be controlled by it.

Consequently, the continuing demonstrations most importantly revealed the movement's success at popular mobilization. Specific demands and slogans were less important. Demonstrations, watched by tens of thousands, expressed and renewed the students' mandate to speak on behalf of the people. The actions of bystanders in turn emancipated the concept of 'the people' (*renmin, laobaixing*) from official discourse. Instead of an empty propaganda slogan, 'the people' became a real and autonomous political actor.

Yet this new political actor had a limited vocabulary at its disposal. Support, applause, and donations expressed a range of often contradictory complaints about current problems. The same held

6. See Ji Shi, 'Beijing: 4.27 xuesheng youxing mujiji' (An eye-witness account of the student demonstration in Beijing, 27 April), *Xin Guancha* 10 (1989), pp. 20–30; and Shen, *Almost a Revolution*, pp. 202–6.

true for the students, whose demands had to be supported by the people. Demands were either so general as to be virtually devoid of meaning, such as for 'democracy' and 'freedom', or very specific, such as for the downfall of corrupt officials (*dadao guandao*). These demands, heard all through the movement, provided the necessary continuity during lulls in development. They also provided a framework to which concrete demands could be attached.

Because student demands had no direct relation to the concrete interests of the population, identifying with the movement was easy. Every individual, acting as an anonymous member of 'the people', could give the students the mandate to represent his or her specific, but unstated, political frustrations. For instance, a bicycle repairman volunteered the following opinion:

> My business has been contracted out (*chengbao*) to me for a while now, or actually it has been only partially contracted out. Now it is me who is running the financial risks, but the decisions are still made by the cadres of the organization to which my business belongs. They aren't doing a thing, but nevertheless hang on to their positions, *and that is the reason the people are demonstrating now.*[7]

Thus, at this stage, the People's Movement conformed to the pattern of traditional Chinese petitioning movements, in which concrete sectional or individual interests were not allowed to play a role.

Large-scale demonstrations supported by the people made it possible to sustain the movement to the symbolic date of 4 May. But the demonstration organized for that day lacked a new theme, being only a re-enactment of the 27 April demonstration. The students were confronted with the same problems faced before 27 April: What is the next symbolic date to exploit? How can we keep the movement alive and retain the initiative? Meanwhile, two related but independent developments caught up with the students. These, while solving the above problems, also radically altered the nature of the movement.

Journalists

While students were refining the art of demonstrating, progressive intellectuals and journalists tested the limits of the new political situation by campaigning for greater press freedom. At issue was the closure of the semi-independent Shanghai-based *World Economic*

7. Fieldnotes, May 1989.

Herald (Shijie Jingji Daobao) by the local party secretary, Jiang Zemin (later Zhao's successor as national party secretary), because of a controversial article about Hu published on 24 April.[8]

On 4 May, a group of Beijing journalists joined the student demonstration, an act hardly noticed at the time. For the first time during the People's Movement, an interest group had grasped the opportunity to start demonstrating for its own set of demands: passive bystanders had become active participants. The journalists, acutely aware of the problematic character of their move, were quick to contextualize their demand for general press freedom by calling for the right to report truthfully about the movement. On 9 May over 1,000 journalists and editors demonstrated, and presented a petition demanding greater press freedom. The following day, the students organized demonstrations in support of the journalists. They demanded press freedom and mocked the media's dependence on the party through slogans like 'The *People's Daily*: bullshit!' (*Renmin Ribao: hu shuo ba dao!*).

During these demonstrations, students for the first time wore headbands and sashes emblazoned with slogans or the name of their university. Copied from Korean and Japanese student demonstrations, they would eventually become the most important symbols of activist status. New, too, was the frequent use of slogans written in English. Earlier, flashing a 'V' for victory with one's fingers, apparently copied from the 1986 movement in the Philippines, had been introduced. These developments demonstrate the importance assigned to an international audience.

The second development which permanently changed the nature of the movement was Zhao's return from Korea on 1 May. Before his departure, Zhao had avoided stating his opinion on the movement, but on 3 and 4 May he presented an assessment clearly at odds with the *People's Daily* editorial. According to Zhao, students were not conspiring against the state; he advocated meeting their reasonable demands through legal, democratic channels. Thus, an irreparable rift had occurred within the leadership, which could only end with the defeat of one faction. From then on, Zhao's fate and that of the movement were interlinked. This meant that he had to find ways to control the movement. However, for the students, the problem of becoming coopted into the factional struggle had suddenly become acute.

8. Seth Faison, 'The changing role of the Chinese media', in Tony Saich (ed.), *The Chinese People's Movement: Perspectives on Spring 1989* (Armonk, NY, 1990), pp. 151–5; Kate Wright, 'The political fortunes of Shanghai's "World Economic Herald"', *Australian Journal of Chinese Affairs* 23 (1990), pp. 121–32.

Zhao's relationship with the students did not develop smoothly, despite the latter's establishment of a Dialogue Delegation (*Duihua Daibiaotuan*), composed largely of older, more moderate students.[9] Closed meetings between the Dialogue Delegation and members of Zhao's faction, mediated by prominent intellectuals, yielded no compromise about a public dialogue.[10] Meanwhile, developments at Tian'anmen Square overtook these negotiations.

The hunger-strike

The participation of journalists provided the impetus to sustain the movement until Mikhail Gorbachev's state visit to Beijing on 15 May – the next target date. But, before that occurred, some 2,000 students, gathered at Tian'anmen Square, began a hunger-strike on 13 May. The participants were mainly students who had felt marginalized during earlier phases of the movement. Secret negotiations between their leaders and Zhao's faction left them restless and alienated. This provided the context for a new group to bid for power. Their undisputed leader was Chai Ling, a Beijing Normal University student who, speaking at the Beijing University campus on 11 May, addressed student impatience, galvanizing them into action.[11] Her speech, recorded and quickly distributed all over Beijing, had such immense impact that many established leaders, such as Wang Dan and Wu'er Kaixi, had no choice but to join the hunger-strike in order to preserve their credibility. The hunger-strikers acquired great moral authority, giving them absolute say over the movement. Consequently, a new group of leaders emerged, the movement's populism was rejuvenated and its strategy radicalized.[12]

The hunger-strikers seemed at first eminently reasonable, demanding an equal dialogue with the authorities, and recognition that the movement was both patriotic and democratic.[13] But their political message lay not in their demands, but in the uncompromising nature of the strike itself. If the authorities agreed to negotiations at this stage, it could only be interpreted as a defeat,

9. Luo Qiping *et al.*, 'The 1989 pro-democracy movement: student organizations and strategies', *China Information* 5, no. 2 (1990), p. 35; Shen, *Almost a Revolution*, pp. 215–19.

10. Nick, 'De Chinese Cohn-Bendits', pp. 64–5; Shen, *Almost a Revolution*, pp. 249–51.

11. Li Lu, *Moving the Mountain: My Life in China: From the Cultural Revolution to Tiananmen Square* (London, 1990), pp. 131–3; Shen, *Almost a Revolution*, p. 237.

12. Shen, *Almost a Revolution*, pp. 243, 272, 275–6.

13. See Oksenburg *et al.* (eds), *Beijing Spring*, pp. 258–9; Han Minzhu and Hua Sheng (eds), *Cries for Democracy: Writings and Speeches from the 1989 Chinese Democracy Movement* (Princeton, 1990), pp. 199–202.

an unthinkable loss of face. The only course left was to attack, with the aim of a decisive victory. Thus, the hunger-strike sealed the fate of Zhao's attempts to forge a dialogue and to use the movement for his own purposes. Since a dialogue had not materialized, his final defeat was inevitable. His only hope was to strengthen the movement prior to its suppression by the conservatives.

The hunger-strike attracted student delegations from all over the country. Connections between students throughout China were established early in the movement when representatives from Beijing visited other university towns.[14] This practice of despatching delegations to and from the centre of a movement, also evident during the Cultural Revolution, was a vital element in China's repertoire of protest, because it served as a countermeasure against official attempts to contain social unrest. On a more cognitive level it expressed the national, as opposed to local, significance of protest movements. Travel and liaison allow the acting out of China's unified polity, and reproduce nationalism among its future elite. This, and the support students received in transit, were important in constructing the People's Movement as a national event, not only geographically, but also in terms of its social support base.

But by far the most significant aspect of the hunger-strike was that it gave the people of Beijing a de-politicized vehicle for action. It became possible to demonstrate simply to support hunger-strikers (*shengyuan xuesheng*). It was both the spark and the excuse to express a long-felt sympathy for the students, born out of a dissatisfaction with the regime which remained unexpressed. The overt message was that leaders who let the hunger-strikers die by refusing to negotiate were inhumane and unfit to govern. This rendered it difficult for the government to label demonstrations counter-revolutionary and crack down on them. Even party members of some importance could demonstrate for the resignation of individual leaders, without casting doubt upon their loyalty to the party or socialism.

The first to realize the hunger-strike's potential were reform-oriented intellectuals, whose first demonstration occurred (not by coincidence) on the day of Gorbachev's arrival in Beijing. The visit, an event of historic importance to China and ostensibly the final display of Deng's statesmanship, was inevitably disrupted. The welcoming ceremony had to be shifted to the airport, because hunger-strikers refused to vacate Tian'anmen Square. Coverage by

---

14. Li, *Moving the Mountain*, p. 114; Shen, *Almost a Revolution*, p. 183.

the domestic and foreign press caused severe loss of face for the Chinese government. The whole world could see that Chinese authorities had lost control of their capital.

Zhao quickly exploited the government's dilemma. On the day of Gorbachev's arrival, he praised the domestic media's accurate reporting of events, thus drawing attention to government mishandling of the crisis. Zhao also pointedly informed Gorbachev that Deng still had ultimate authority over important policy matters, thus implying that Deng was behind the authorities' uncompromising response to the movement.

Zhao's open criticism of Deng, when combined with the hunger-strike and the intellectuals' participation, inspired mass demonstrations by work unit delegations on 17 and 18 May, demonstrations so large that they amounted to a general strike in the Beijing area. Though the scale of the demonstration was impressive, more important were its moral and cognitive aspects. The new demonstrators consciously styled themselves as two actors crucial to Marxist theory – namely 'the people' and 'the workers' – by carrying banners with slogans such as 'big brother [i.e. the workers] has come' (*dage lai le*) or 'the people of the city support the students' (*shimin shengyuan xuesheng*). Marxist dogma was remoulded to its original form: a theory for revolutionary action.

Given the increased scale of the demonstrations, maintaining order became acute. Students assumed new roles as policemen. Some wore fake police uniforms, but for most the familiar headbands were sufficient indication of activist status. This new role was also symbolically important since it implied that the government no longer controlled Beijing, and that the students were now the legitimate authority. The fact that demonstrators and bystanders behaved in an orderly fashion, voluntarily complying with instructions from student-policemen, reinforced this image. In fact, many people noted, with undisguised pride, that Beijing was safer and more orderly than ever before.

The most striking aspect of this new phase was the role of the work unit. People demonstrated not as individuals, but as members of work unit delegations (literally 'demonstration troops', *youxing duiwu*). Delegations were strictly separated from each other and especially from bystanders along the route, first by a ring of demonstrators walking hand in hand at the boundaries of the delegation (*shoulashou jiuchadui*), later by strings used to delineate the delegation. The spatial organization reflected the social organization of society as it was understood by movement participants. The same was true of the student delegations at the square. From the start of the hunger-strike until the army forced them to leave on 4 June, students kept the square permanently occupied. Thus, because they were the initiators and leading force of the movement, and (at least momentarily) of the whole nation, they occupied the symbolic political centre of the nation: Tian'anmen Square. Student leaders in turn occupied the platform around the Monument of Revolutionary Heroes at the epicentre of the square. Moreover, their organization and activities were all oriented northwards in the direction of the Tian'an Gate of the imperial Forbidden City, the symbolic location of the movement's opponents. Supportive demonstrations by 'the people' made their way to the square and, on arrival, walked around the square one or more times, before returning to their work unit. This resulted in a continuous revolution of the people around the pivot of the nation, the students.

Around the Monument of Revolutionary Heroes, headquarters of delegations from participating universities were established. Each sealed off a section of the square using strings tied to bamboo poles or potted plants. A 'gate' at the front was formed with a single piece of string, with a delegation member often standing guard to monitor those entering the 'compound'. Within the fenced-off territory a makeshift shelter was constructed using plastic foil, bamboo poles, cloth and rope, thus copying in miniature a Chinese work unit compound.

At first, people were allowed to walk freely between the fenced-off compounds but, on 19 May, students sealed off the square, forcing outsiders to watch from a distance. Only officially recognized students or journalists were allowed entry, with an impromptu office issuing IDs. The official reason given was that, due to hygiene problems, an epidemic was feared. A more likely reason was that on 19 May it became known that Zhao had lost his struggle with conservative opponents, thus finally ruling out a compromise. This motivated more radical students to complete their seizure of power from moderate leaders. The new, radical leadership abandoned the hunger-strike and prepared for violent confrontation. The occupation of the square had become a military operation, and preventing infiltration became important. Only after several days were people admitted again, by which time the square resembled a semi-permanent settlement. Delegation territories were relocated to provide clearly recognizable alleys and streets. Gone were the strings stretched between poles. Most delegations had real tents, mainly sent by sympathizers from Hong Kong. Only the *sanctum sanctorum*, the platform around the monument, remained out of bounds and sealed off by strings. Here the students' headquarters and subordinate organizations, such as the Propaganda Department, could be found.

The division of social space at the square reflected the strict separation between demonstrating delegations and bystanders established early in the protest. According to the explanation given, separation was necessary to ensure order. If riotous elements could enter and create trouble, this would give the authorities justification for suppressing the demonstrations and occupying the square. Whether rightly or not, the demonstrators saw the unpredictable mass of bystanders as the most immediate threat to their movement. Although the bystander role was the most important political invention of the movement and its greatest source of strength, it still provoked a distinctly Chinese fear of the unknown outsider with no identifiable ties to familiar social groups.

Martial law

Martial law was proclaimed on 20 May. Afterwards, it became impossible for work units to allow demonstrations to continue. Demonstrating became illegal, an open challenge to the authorities. Leaders of work units, following the dictates of the 26 April *People's Daily* editorial, began a campaign aimed at ferreting out activists who had organized the demonstrations. The old system of political control reasserted itself.

Although demonstrations by work units could be curtailed, informal demonstrations composed of bystanders were beyond the reach of the work unit control system. After martial law, the threat of an army invasion changed the passive, mandate-giving role of bystanders into an active one: protector of students at the square. Citizens of Beijing, frustrated at being forced to go to work and keep quiet while at the work unit, stood guard after work at street-corners, waiting for the army's inevitable arrival. In this way the students at the square were protected by millions of people prepared to sacrifice their lives.

During the first two days after the declaration of martial law, it seemed as if the impossible might happen. Throughout the city makeshift barricades blocked the main thoroughfares leading to the square. Army units of the Beijing regional command entered the city from the west and south-west, but were stopped about five kilometres from the square by the population, led by student propaganda teams. Hardly any violence erupted. The student propaganda teams presented martial law as proof that some party leaders had lost touch with the people. The army was presented as an innocent instrument of incompetent leaders. At barricades appeals were made to 'the soldiers who are our sons and younger brothers' (*zi-di bing*) not to raise their weapons against their own people. Food and drink were offered to soldiers to express the bond between the people and the army. Since many of the soldiers and commanders came from Beijing or had long been stationed there, they were sensitive to this appeal. According to one rumour, the commander-in-chief of Beijing's regional command refused to order his troops to use violence.

The party leadership quickly concluded that using local troops was futile. An almost surreal period ensued, during which nothing seemed to happen. Although student numbers gradually decreased, they continued to occupy the square, while the population continued to protect them. All were convinced that very soon the army would come again, but nobody knew when or how.

The initiative no longer rested with the students or their allies. All they could do was maintain the appearance of full control of the city. At the square, they erected the now-famous replica of the Statue of Liberty, the 'Goddess of Democracy' (*Minzhu nüshen*), which gave foreign media something pleasing to report to audiences back home. Though it succeeded in further aggravating the authorities, it could not conceal the fact that political machinations within the party leadership were now the only decisive factor.

It is still unclear what happened within the select circle of leaders during the days before the 4 June massacre. Certainly there must have been strong opposition to the use of violence. An especially prominent role in the subsequent military suppression was played by Yang Shangkun, President of the People's Republic and Vice-Chairman of the party's Military Commission.[15] On 24 May, after the initial attempts to capture Beijing had failed, he made a speech at a special meeting of the Military Commission designed to secure support for the crackdown among leading military figures. This paved the way for new preparations to capture Beijing. Large-scale troop-movements were carried out around the capital, with troops from all over China arriving.

15. The Military Commission is the party's most important formal instrument of control over the army. Its chairman at the time was Deng Xiaoping.

The crackdown

Although everyone realized that violence was inevitable, the students and people of Beijing refused to strike the first blow. Only after the army opened fire on the evening of 3 June did they resort to violent, often gruesome behaviour. Even so, their violence was patterned by a moral and cognitive frame, just as earlier non-violent behaviour had been. Violence arose not from a simple life-and-death struggle, but as an expression of moral outrage. Soldiers were not just disarmed and taken prisoner, they were pulled out of their tanks and stoned or beaten to death. Some were hanged from trees or light-poles. Moreover, violence and resistance continued for days after Beijing had been taken by the army, long after the cause was lost. Again and again, people blocked roads or set fire to abandoned army trucks, actions which at this stage made little rational strategic sense. The violence was therefore simultaneously excessive and irrational, and patterned and significant. It was patterned on a new moral and cognitive order of retribution. At the same time, it was excessive, the result of moral outrage, rather than calculated to achieve specific goals.

The nature of the people's violence can best be understood in ethnomethodological terms.[16] The army's violence constituted an illegitimate breach with the earlier, non-violent moral order established by the People's Movement. The authorities and the movement participants no longer acted according to the same moral and cognitive frame, and they therefore no longer considered each other as legitimate social actors, i.e. as human beings. Since the army had also ignored appeals to refrain from violence, the people of Beijing concluded that the soldiers, too, were less than human.

The pattern of violence served important political goals. Both to the authorities and to the movement participants, the 'facts and truth' (*shishi zhenxiang*) about the massacre were not so much concerned with immediate events, but were designed to serve as the moral basis of future actions. To movement participants, the death of so many innocent people confirmed the wickedness of the authorities and the legitimacy of future protest. The dead were pointedly displayed in front of photographers and cameramen. Moreover, narrating to each other what had happened or recollections one had heard ensured that the massacre would not be forgotten. In

16. Harold Garfinkel, *Studies in Ethnomethodology* (Cambridge, 1984); John Heritage, *Garfinkel and Ethnomethodology* (Cambridge, 1984).

other words, the recording of the massacre's history had already begun, aided by a plethora of written or audiotaped eyewitness accounts. The most famous such account was by Chai Ling, leader of the hunger-strikers, which was taped and smuggled out of China. In this way, what almost immediately came to be called 'six-four' (*liu-si*), i.e. the crackdown on June Fourth, was constructed, placing the movement firmly within the tradition of protest of the earlier 'five-four' (May Fourth 1919) and 'four-five' (April Fifth 1976) movements.

The authorities were also determined to record its history, but for opposite purposes. The crackdown had to be portrayed in such a way that the People's Movement could not be enshrined in China's tradition of protest. Thus, official propaganda blamed the violence after 4 June not on the students or the population, but on a handful of counter-revolutionary 'bad' and 'violent elements' (*daitu* and *baotu*), who left the army no option but to respond with measured violence. Within this context, soldiers who had died became heroes who sacrificed their lives to protect socialism from counter-revolutionary turmoil.

Official propaganda took great pains to establish the validity of this account. But too many people had seen what had actually happened. To regain the monopoly of truth about the crackdown, the propaganda had to enter into an indirect debate with its adversaries: fugitive student activists, intellectual dissidents, and anonymous rumour. A central theme in the propaganda war was whether any deaths had occurred at the square itself. After the massacre, rumours spread of hundreds, maybe thousands of fatalities, when tanks rolled over the tents. Official propaganda, however, denied any deaths in the square.

After several days, reports by foreign journalists and other eyewitnesses confirmed that the official propaganda was probably right.[17] The government had taken great pains to engineer this outcome. A massacre at the square would have been sacrilege, and, since the square had been the students' stronghold, it would have been impossible to maintain that only *baotu* and *daitu* had been killed. Moreover, the propaganda suggested that if all the dramatic stories about a massacre at the square turned out to be unfounded, were not other stories of bloodshed elsewhere also lies?

17. For reliable reconstructions of the capture of Beijing, see Amnesty International, China, *The Massacre of June 1989 and Its Aftermath* (London, 1990); Donald Morrison (ed.), *Massacre in Beijing: China's Struggle for Democracy* (New York, 1990); Robin Munro, 'Who died in Beijing: and why', *The Nation*, 11 June 1990, pp. 811–22.

Yet by resorting to (excessive) violence the army committed an illegitimate breach with the moral order of the People's Movement. For this the authorities paid a heavy price. Army and party leaders had not only placed themselves outside the actional framework of the movement, but disqualified themselves as responsible, accountable human beings. In this way, they also destroyed any common moral ground for future dialogue with their citizens. The suppression destroyed faith in the credibility of the party and its ideology. Because of this, the People's Movement's moral order has the potential to become a viable alternative to this ideology, rather than just serving to correct and rejuvenate it. This breach with the official ideology, and the resulting emancipation of the tradition of protest, are the most important lasting results of the movement. It will give the movement a historic significance far greater than that of its predecessors, which have always remained trapped in traditional Chinese assumptions about the remonstrative nature of protest.

Many scenarios of future political movements are possible, but it seems unlikely that students will ever play such a prominent role. The authorities have learned important lessons from their inability to contain the movement. Campuses are monitored as never before, and potentially disruptive student activities are strictly proscribed. The secret police, crowd control units and legislation have all been improved to reduce reliance on the old methods of control centred on the work unit. During the People's Movement, progressive intellectuals played a vital role in coordinating and advising student activities. These intellectuals were, in general, frightened by the radicalization that took place during the later phases and have become reluctant again to rely on hot-headed, 'irresponsible' youngsters. Chinese society as a whole has changed greatly since 1989, with social inequality much more pronounced. In recent years, massive lay-offs in the state sector and heavy illegal taxation in the countryside has sparked waves of peasant protests and strikes. The initiative for future political movements in China seems to lie with the leaders of these peasant and worker protests, while Chinese dissidents at home and abroad prepare for a facilitating and coordinating role. Although future movements will undoubtedly invoke the memories of 1989, students will probably be allowed no more than an auxiliary and symbolic role.

CHAPTER NINETEEN

'With a Little Help from Our Friends': Student Activism and the 1992 Crisis at San Diego State University

JAMES L. WOOD

The title of this essay is ironic like the song which served as its inspiration is ironic: the faculty at San Diego State University received *tremendous* help from many politically active students in 1992. This allowed the university to survive what the American Association of University Professors (AAUP) described as one of America's worst academic crises. SDSU became the most politically active campus in the country, resembling a campus of the 1960s instead of the more conventional 1990s. Student political activists focused national attention on SDSU, and ultimately aided a return to normality.

This chapter describes and analyses the students' response to San Diego State's difficulties, the nature of those difficulties, and the unique long-term commitment of these students. The emphasis will be on the students' non-institutionalized political activities, analysing these according to existing social movement theories. It will be argued that by uniting around the common threat to their education and careers, and their shared commitment to the university, the students benefited themselves, the faculty, the university, and the American academy.

Background to the 1992 crisis

In the early 1990s the state of California faced a daunting financial recession, the worst since the Great Depression.[1] This led to the first round of budget cuts for California public higher education in

---

1. B. Kantrowitz and P. King, 'Failing economics', *Newsweek*, 28 Sept. 1992, pp. 32–3.

1991, which eliminated thousands of class sections and part-time faculty. It was not realized by most, but well understood by the SDSU president Thomas B. Day, that the cuts in 1991 cleared the way for lay-offs of tenured faculty during the 1992 crisis.[2] The 1992 cuts seemed even more drastic because the Day administration insisted on a 'deep and narrow' approach which concentrated upon a small number of departments which were to be entirely eliminated or deeply cut. The customary practice, as in 1991, was to make 'across-the-board' cuts or to let departments work out their own solutions through temporary leaves of absence without pay, salary cuts, use of grant money, and other responses, to avoid laying off tenured faculty. Alternative approaches were summarily rejected by the administration, which was bent upon culling tenured faculty.[3]

SDSU was particularly vulnerable to budget cuts in the early 1990s because of the ramifications of Proposition 98. The measure, passed in 1987, guaranteed approximately 40 per cent of California's General Fund Budget to grades Kindergarten through High School and Community College (K–14). The California State University (CSU) system (which includes SDSU) and the University of California (UC) system were not provided for in this amendment, leaving them without budgetary protection. CSU and UC were instead dependent upon the discretionary funds available, which make up only around 15 per cent of California's budget. Thus the two systems are easy targets for budget cuts.[4]

The highly regarded Master Plan for California Public Higher Education, created by Clark Kerr in 1960, has *no* constitutionally or legally protected funding mechanism. In 1993, Kerr called for a 'Resource Master Plan'[5] providing predictable financial support for public higher education, but his demand fell on deaf ears, leaving higher education prey to budget cuts in bad years but also in good years, as nearly happened in 1997. Cuts are a constant threat because other priorities, such as prisons, have successfully competed with higher education in recent years. Thus, even though money

2. The 1991 cuts inspired 'The Wall', an imaginative series of protest murals painted by students on a temporary construction barrier. This received nationwide media attention, and many of the students active in this protest then participated in the 1992 campaign.

3. *San Diego Union-Tribune*, 2 February 1995; *Los Angeles Times*, 13 August 1992; 'San Diego State University: an administration's response to fiscal stress', *Academe*, March/April 1993, pp. 94–118.

4. See James L. Wood and Lorena T. Valenzuela, 'The crisis in higher education', in Charles F. Hohm (ed.), *California's Social Problems* (New York, 1997), pp. 81–98.

5. Clark Kerr, 'Preserving the master plan', testimony before California Higher Education Summit, 1993.

may be available, the lack of budgetary protection means that universities will not necessarily receive it.[6]

In 1992, virtually all of the approximately 30 universities in the CSU and UC systems were scheduled for cuts. But SDSU was unique in the way the budget crisis was used in an attempt to eliminate many academic departments and effectively rescind tenure. SDSU, according to the AAUP, suffered the 'worst case' of attempted lay-offs of tenured faculty in US history, totalling 111 tenured and 35 tenure-track faculty, coupled with a simultaneous attempt to eliminate nine academic departments and deeply cut six others. One quarter of SDSU's approximately 60 departments was affected.

The fact that 83 per cent of all tenured lay-offs in the 20-campus system were to occur at SDSU seemed curious.[7] Evidence suggests that SDSU was singled out because the Day administration sought to end the tenure system, in order better to control the faculty. Without tenure, effective control of the university would pass to the administration, with considerably diminished faculty, student, and staff input. The administration had tried to implement versions of this strategy *three other times,* twice at SDSU in 1979 and 1980, and once earlier at another university.

The student response

The campus was plunged into crisis on 13 May 1992, when the cuts were announced. Among those who reacted were a determined group of students who peacefully challenged administration policy. They became known as the 'Vigil', after their principal method of protest. The students responded much faster than the rest of the university, including the stunned and temporarily immobilized faculty. On 15 May, a huge rally which drew thousands of students, faculty and staff was staged outside the Administration Building, the largest demonstration at SDSU since the Vietnam War protests over twenty years earlier. The rally began with a student attached to a cross, Christ-like, symbolizing the sacrifice the campus was about to endure, which startled the tense crowd. This dramatic demonstration riveted the crowd's attention to the developing calamity.

Many students spoke about how their lives, education, and careers had been completely disrupted within the space of two days,

6. Wood and Valenzuela, 'The crisis in higher education', pp. 86–7; and Stephen J. Carroll *et al.,* 'California's worsening budget crisis', RAND Institute, 1994.
7. *Academe,* ff.

and how they refused to accept the administration's draconian measures. None was more outspoken or eloquent than Deborah Katz, a sociology undergraduate, one of the rally organizers. Her commitment and passion made her seem, to those disturbed by the crisis, like a modern-day Joan of Arc. She began her talk by listing several well-known faculty who were to be laid off, discussing their contributions to the university, the importance of higher education to her generation, and the great damage which would result from the proposed cuts. The spirit of her speech was reminiscent of the charismatic Mario Savio, leader of the UC Berkeley Free Speech Movement (FSM), whose speeches electrified students in autumn 1964.[8] Echoing the FSM, Katz immediately established a peaceful, constructive tone to the protest.

As 1992 was a critical election year, several sympathetic politicians also spoke at the rally. Congressman Bob Filner, former SDSU history professor (he had recently decided to retire – in part due to the budget crisis), pledged to do what he could to restore the campus to normality, a pledge echoed by other politicians. These were not idle promises: several legislators, such as now-State Senator Dede Alpert and then-Assemblyman Mike Gotch, would play an important role in solving the crisis. Thus the rally of 15 May, organized by students, immediately established an alliance with influential politicians, which remained strong until the crisis abated the following autumn.

The Vigil

One entirely unexpected development on 15 May was the formation of the now-famous student Vigil. Echoing Lysistrata, who occupied the Acropolis in pursuit of peace in Ancient Greece, SDSU students staged a round-the-clock protest outside the Administration Building and Library. There are few similar events in history where the protesters – over a lengthy period – *live* at the site where they protest. Perhaps the most notable recent example was when feminists protested against the deployment of Cruise missiles at Greenham Common Air Force Base in the United Kingdom.[9] Even

8. Seymour Martin Lipset and Sheldon S. Wolin (eds.), *The Berkeley Student Revolt* (Garden City, NY, 1965); and the documentary *Berkeley in the Sixties*.
9. See Alice Cook and Gwyn Kirk, *Greenham Women Everywhere* (London, 1984); James L. Wood and Patricia A. Wood, 'Dilemmas and opportunities of international collective behavior/social movements research: a case study', *International Journal of Mass Emergencies and Disasters* 4 (1986), pp. 193–210; and Wood, Wood, and Robert

FSM activists went home to eat and sleep before returning to campus for the next day of protest.

The Vigil formed without plan. In her speech, Katz suddenly announced that the day's rally was just the beginning, that the professors to be laid off were given 120 days' notice, and that she was going to stay outside the Administration Building 120 days, around the clock, in protest against the cuts. The crowd was startled and, though recognizing the symbolic importance of her plan, naturally wondered whether she would persist. Immediately after the rally, she went home to get a sleeping-bag for the night to begin the Vigil. Several students then said that they would join her. Despite administration attempts to eject the Vigil from campus, it eventually stayed not just 120 days, but for nearly six months, until Election Day in November 1992, a date later selected as strategically significant.

Vigil participants

Vigil participants came from a variety of academic departments, including Art, Film, English, Child Development, Psychology, Biology, Engineering, Physics, and Sociology, with the latter two disproportionately represented. This informal alliance between sociologists and physicists was also evident among faculty members active in the protest. In terms of gender, men and women participated in similar numbers. The majority of Vigil members were white, with some Asian, Indian, and Chicano representatives. As regards financial status, no notable trend was evident: some had financial help from their family, while others were self-supporting.

Some students from departments that were not immediately affected, or only moderately affected, by the proposed cuts were still active Vigil participants. All feared the consequences for SDSU and objected to the lack of input from the two groups most affected: students and faculty. Thus, even those not personally affected saw the exercise of arbitrary authority as incompatible with higher education as they understood it. They felt that if the fifteen departments under threat could be so easily dismantled, their own department, even if temporarily safe, could easily be endangered.

Mitchell, 'Sur la ferme a Maggie: les camps pour la paix en Grande-Bretagne', *Revue Internationale d'Action Communautaire/International Review of Community Development* 12 (1984), pp. 137–47.

Indeed, a study revealed that, since the Day administration arrived on campus in 1978, over 40 per cent of the departments had been threatened with deep cuts or elimination at least once.[10]

About 25 students slept outside at one time or another, with a core group of a dozen. Several others were loosely connected to Vigil activities, and hundreds more took part in large demonstrations with which the Vigil was centrally involved. This commitment is all the more significant since the protest extended into the summer when most students leave for home and summer jobs. Over 11,000 students signed a petition supporting Vigil objectives. The Vigil was supported by many SDSU faculty, especially the politically active, with whom a uniquely close alliance was formed. The 'historical accident' of the Vigil site being located right below the California Faculty Association (the faculty union) office undoubtedly strengthened this alliance.

Three major motives for participation stand out. By participating in the Vigil, the students were (1) supporting their departments, professors, and future careers; (2) opposing steep student fee increases; and (3) opposing arbitrary administrative authority. While these three motives are distinct, they are also related. In order to continue their education and prepare themselves for their careers, the students needed viable departments and professors, and fees they could afford. The administration's arbitrary actions in eliminating departments and terminating faculty threatened all that. As a result, Vigil students wound up assisting themselves, their departments and professors, the campus as a whole, and the American academy, which watched the events at SDSU with great interest since their outcome would influence the way other universities addressed financial difficulties and threats to tenure.[11]

Goals of the Vigil

Five central goals motivated the Vigil. The first two were to persuade the administration to rescind the faculty lay-offs, and to restore the departments to be eliminated. The Vigil eventually decided that, in order to attain these goals, a third had to be set: President Day would have to go. In response to the overall financial situation

10. James L. Wood, unpublished report to the San Diego State University community on the proportion of departments to be eliminated or deeply cut 1979–1992, 1992.

11. *Academe*, March/April 1993; Stanley Aronowitz and William DiFazio, *The Jobless Future: Sci-Tech and the Dogma of Work* (Minneapolis, Minn., 1994), pp. 223, 263; and Aronowitz and Henry Giroux, *Education Still Under Siege* (Westport, Conn., 1993).

in California, the Vigil set two additional goals: to secure a better and more secure share of the state budget for higher education; and to prevent further student fee increases or, preferably, reduce existing fees.

Whereas there is an implied sequence to these goals, they were interconnected. The 13 May announcement by the administration forced protesters to concentrate on the proposed faculty lay-offs and departmental eliminations. If the campus was ever to return to 'normal', these proposals would have to be rescinded, a *sine qua non* of SDSU's recovery. However, since the lay-offs and departmental eliminations were central to the administration's plans, to the exclusion of any other alternatives, it followed that the administration would mobilize its considerable resources to combat the Vigil. Thus, a dialectical relationship between the administration and Vigil emerged: each needed to neutralize the other in order to achieve success.

The Vigil did not, however, immediately adopt an inflexible stance toward the administration. It was at first felt that Day might be open to reason. It soon became clear, however, especially after Katz met Day in televised debates, that the president could not be steered toward a less apocalyptic approach. When confronted with the 11,000-signature petition, Day indicated in no uncertain terms that he intended to ignore it. This prompted an indignant response (in *The Daily Aztec* campus newspaper) from one of the students involved in gathering the signatures, who resented the fact that Day could so easily ignore such an overwhelming expression of opinion. These events convinced Vigil members that, in order for the campus to be restored, the president had to depart. 'Day Must Go' buttons became ubiquitous.

While Vigil students confronted the university president, they simultaneously accumulated considerable knowledge about California's budget, functioning as an information clearing-house which distributed data and analyses to interested parties. The Vigil discovered that for several years, partly as a result of Proposition 98, there had been a shrinking proportion of the state's General Fund allocated to higher education, especially to the CSU and UC. Responding to this situation, Vigil students made several trips to Sacramento to meet state legislators about higher education funding. This led to the Vigil's close involvement with various local legislators. Vigil members also launched a major student voter-registration at SDSU and on other campuses throughout California, eventually obtaining over 8,000 registrants. This effort may have influenced some of the closer elections involving pro-higher education legislators such as Dede Alpert in San Diego.

One immediate consequence of the budget cuts (and which probably helped in the voter registration drive) was the rise in student fees for all branches of California public higher education in the 1990s. In some cases, fees more than doubled.[12] Students were faced with a grim choice: pay the additional fees out of existing finances, go into financial debt, or drop out of school.[13] This inspired the Vigil goal of preventing further student fee increases, and possibly reducing these fees. Yet a dilemma became apparent: without additional student fees during the recession, universities such as SDSU would have been in even worse financial shape.

Kerr's Master Plan for California Higher Education called for affordable, accessible, quality higher education for all.[14] The Vigil argued that fee rises essentially implied abandoning the Master Plan, since the increases made education less accessible, a fact demonstrated by the 206,000 students who dropped out of California colleges and universities in the early 1990s.[15] With much less money, the quality of education, as well as the quantity of course offerings, would be seriously reduced. Thus, the students faced a major contradiction: they were being asked to pay more for a higher education that was becoming less accessible. Many students and faculty therefore decided to campaign for the passage of Assembly Constitutional Amendment 25 (ACA 25), which would have included CSU and UC in Proposition 98 provisions, guaranteeing funding for all of higher education. Since ACA 25 did not pass, budgetary threats continue, and pressure will remain to increase student fees during economic recessions.[16]

Vigil tactics

The Vigil mounted some of the most imaginative student activist tactics seen in over twenty years, reminiscent of the colourful 1960s activist, Abbie Hoffman, unofficial leader of the anti-establishment Yippies.[17] Vigil tactics included giant mannequins of 'Dummy Day'

12. *Union-Tribune*, 14, 17 July 1997. See also James L. Wood and Lorena T. Valenzuela, 'The crisis of American higher education', *Thought & Action: The NEA Higher Education Journal* 12 (1996), pp. 59–71.

13. *Sacramento Bee*, 22 May 1994.

14. See Clark Kerr, *The Great Transformation in Higher Education: 1960–1980* (New York, 1991).

15. See Wood and Valenzuela, 'The crisis in higher education' and 'The crisis of American higher education'.

16. *Union-Tribune*, 14 July 1997.

17. See Abbie Hoffman, *Woodstock Nation* (New York, 1969); and *Soon To Be A Major Motion Picture* (New York, 1980). Hoffman refused to stand in court upon the

(an intentionally unsubtle ridicule of the president), a satirical song entitled 'Knocking on Tommy's Door', a clock which 'had the right time, but the wrong Day', and tabloid-like newspapers such as the *SDSU Star, Special Edition*, which sardonically described political events on campus.

The Vigil was a constant reminder of the university's problems and the need for solutions. Vigil members sought to inform visitors to the campus, and the outside world, about the situation. This task was immeasuably aided by the keen interest taken by television journalists. Coverage totalling over four hours (most in 30-second pieces) accumulated during the period up to the election, making SDSU the most televised campus in the world at that time. Similarly, *Newsweek, Los Angeles Times, San Diego Union-Tribune*, and *The Daily Aztec*, among other print media, reported on the Vigil and the unfolding drama at SDSU.

The Vigil was instrumental in inspiring the faculty to oppose the cuts. At one faculty meeting open to the public, a Vigil student argued that, given present conditions, no one's job was secure. His comments had a disturbing effect upon the audience, undoubtedly influencing a subsequent faculty vote of no confidence in the administration. At another meeting, a Vigil student attacked the president's 'Restructuring Document', which justified the 'deep and narrow' approach, by presenting a 'Destructuring Document', which pointedly rebutted the administration's arguments. This presentation effectively de-legitimized the Restructuring Document, which was later vetoed by the SDSU Senate, after the Chair of Physics urged colleagues to 'drive a stake through the heart of the Restructuring Document'.

The Vigil and social movement theory

General and middle range social movement concepts and theories can shed further light on the Vigil.[18] Neil Smelser's theory of collective behaviour is especially helpful for general social movement

---

arrival of Judge Julius Hoffman at the Chicago Seven trial; burned money on Wall Street calling attention to the idolization of money in American society; and threatened to 'levitate' the Pentagon during a guerrilla theatre ceremony, among many other media-attracting tactics. See also David Dellinger, *More Power Than We Know* (Garden City, NY, 1975).

18. James L. Wood and Maurice Jackson, *Social Movements: Development, Participation, and Dynamics* (Belmont, Calif., 1982).

theory; while status strain and resource mobilization theories are particularly helpful for middle range social movement theories. General social movement theories are characterized by the inter-relationship between multiple variables that explain social movement phenomena. Middle range social movement theories are character-ized by one or a few variables that also explain social movement phenomena.

There is abundant evidence of all six conditions which Smelser stipulates constitute necessary (required), and, when combined, suf-ficient (fully predictive) conditions for the development of a social movement. There is similarly abundant evidence of these six condi-tions occurring within the same time period at SDSU at high levels of intensity, as implied by the theory.[19]

The collapsing state of California's economy in 1991–92 was *struc-turally conducive to* – that is, *encouraging of* – the rise of many protest movements. With California's unemployment rate well over the national average, several groups in society experienced 'downsizing' occupationally, accompanied by great financial stress and con-sequent family and personal problems. California had a $14 billion budget deficit beginning in 1991, which led to large budget cuts in the unprotected parts of higher education, namely CSU and UC. The potential for student – and faculty – protests was therefore clearly apparent.

Structural strains – problems widely experienced in a community – were ubiquitous at SDSU in 1992. When the administration attempted to eliminate nine departments and deeply cut six others, thousands of students realistically wondered if the courses they wished to study would still be offered, and if graduating from college was still a possibility. Indeed, students from immediately affected depart-ments, *as well as* those from departments not immediately affected, felt a particular kind of strain, known as *status strain*.

Status strain theory focuses on the increased likelihood of social movement participation among those who have actually experienced a loss of social or economic status, or who perceive they will experi-ence such a loss. For students in the fifteen affected departments – especially in the nine slated to be eliminated – the experience implied actual loss of their majors and career opportunities. For those in the remaining 45 unaffected departments, the experience was perception of potential loss of educational and career oppor-tunities, if cuts continued. As one professor in an unaffected

19. Ibid.

department publicly stated: 'if there is another round of budget cuts, my department is a goner'. This sentiment was shared by students and faculty in otherwise unaffected departments. Thus, *status strain theory* is a useful middle range social movement theory that helps to understand why students from affected and unaffected departments alike joined the Vigil. The existence of widespread status strains on campus in 1992 is evidence of *structural strains*, the second of Smelser's six conditions of social movement development.

The third, *Growth and spread of generalized beliefs*, occurred on campus very rapidly. Rumours immediately spread as to who was responsible for the crisis. Was it the university president? The chancellor? The board of trustees? The governor? A combination of culprits? Or someone else? Generalized beliefs are ideas that identify the source of social difficulties and spell out reform or radical solutions. After much discussion and investigation, the president of the university emerged as the focus of student (and faculty) indignation, especially since his campus was to bear 83 per cent of the tenured lay-offs and was the only one where entire departments faced elimination. The students felt that Day was acting in a significantly more damaging fashion than other CSU presidents, thus making his removal a necessity. Technically, this could be seen as a reform since the students hoped the university would return to something like normality after Day departed. From the president's standpoint, it seemed a radical, even revolutionary, action – essentially a 'coup'. Reform or radical, norm-oriented or value-oriented, the generalized beliefs on campus pointed to the necessity of the president leaving before a restored campus could be effected. 'Day Must Go' became a powerful rallying cry.

The *precipitating factor* (Smelser's fourth condition) which began the Vigil movement, and campus protests generally, was the announcement on 13 May of the widespread lay-offs and departmental eliminations. Precipitating factors are specific events which crystallize the strains and can provide 'evidence for' – or at least illustrations of – the generalized beliefs. As noted, the faculty was initially stunned; but the students began organizing. On 15 May the rally was organized to respond to the major precipitant of two days before.

Mobilization of participants for action (the fifth condition) began on 13 May, continued through the 15 May rally, and quickly evolved into the Vigil. *Mobilization* refers to the organization of potential protesters into actual protesters, with leadership often crucial. The details of Vigil formation are discussed above, including the crucial role of leadership in this formation. What needs clarification is how the Vigil mobilized resources to ultimately achieve its goals. *Resource mobilization theory* is a useful middle range social movement approach to help understand these dynamics.

A casual observer would have initially estimated that the administration had the two resources essential to victory: money and access (to the media, politicians, alumni, and the larger community). Indeed, the odds were overwhelming that the administration would accomplish its goals, as it confidently expected to do. Yet the students, while lacking the same resources, nevertheless established their own avenues of access to the media, politicians, alumni, and larger community.

While the media increasingly focused on the students' perspective of the crisis, the community and politicians were especially receptive to the students' argument because both had an interest in avoiding the collapse of a major higher educational institution in the area, or having it become a national academic pariah. Maintaining its stature in the larger American academy was essential to SDSU for recruiting outstanding faculty. Similarly, positive university stature attracts grants and socially useful research to universities which enjoy this stature, but not to those without it. When the American academy learned of SDSU's problems (a prominent academic commented that 'bad news travels fast'), grants were threatened, potential colleagues lost interest in joining the faculty, and employers indicated less interest in hiring the students, ramifications which were discussed quite publicly in an ABC television interview on campus in 1992. Indeed, as recently as 1997, long after the crisis was resolved and President Day had departed, new faculty recruits still asked about the viability of the university (which by 1997 was quite viable). Both the community and the politicians felt that damage to the university had to be corrected as quickly as possible, which mobilized their participation.

In addition, several professional organizations of sociologists, along with the AAUP, ACLU, and other such bodies, were mobilized by faculty and students.[20] There were many different ways these organizations used their resources to assist SDSU, including establishing a legal defence fund, supporting students' free speech rights, publicizing the campus problems in newsletters, and publishing a highly critical report circulated among thousands of academics

20. James L. Wood, 'Professional organizations to the rescue: ASA, CSA, PSA, AAUP and the San Diego State University crisis', Paper presented to the 92nd Annual Meeting of the American Sociological Association, 12 August 1997, Toronto, Canada.

nationally. These and many other instances of mobilization of participants for actions against the lay-offs and departmental eliminations eventually helped to get the administration proposals revoked.

Ineffectiveness of social control, namely the weakness of agents of social restraint, is the last of Smelser's six conditions. This was evident at the onset of the crisis, and was typical of American college campuses. Social control on this campus (as with others) consists of a relatively small number of campus police to prevent problems of theft, assault, and rowdiness. The campus police were too small to prevent the first large rally of 15 May, and did not try to do so. Thus, with social control powerless to stop a large gathering outside the Administration Building, all of Smelser's six conditions clearly existed on 15 May, igniting the protest.

So, too, the Vigil originated out of the simultaneous occurrence of these six conditions, which included the conditions of the middle range theories discussed. However, the administration immediately saw that the Vigil would keep alive the issue of departmental eliminations and faculty lay-offs. As a result, social control increased via the harassment of the Vigil, which lasted the duration. Protesters were woken up at all hours, threatened with prosecution under vagrancy laws, issued with citations and arrested (though charges were later dropped). Materials were confiscated, as were the 'Dummy Day' effigies. University authorities invoked a law against sleeping outside on campus, forcing Vigil members to exhaust themselves in an effort to stay awake. Yet to no avail. The Vigil, with help from outside bodies like the ACLU and support from the faculty, persisted (as it had planned) to Election Day in November 1992.

Indeed, a dual circumstance of *weakness and harshness of social control* developed, a condition which Smelser argues aggravates and intensifies conflicts. The Vigil movement benefited from initially weak social control, and coped with the much stronger attempts at control which then followed. By resisting prolonged attempts at control, the Vigil increased its resolve and evolved into the unique movement at SDSU, a significant force with which the administration had to contend. It also earned the respect of the campus community and the outside world.

Abatement, summary and reflections

In late summer 1992, California passed its budget, including funding for higher education, albeit at a reduced level. The CSU Chancellor,

Barry Munitz, and the CSU Board of Trustees then rescinded the faculty lay-offs and departmental eliminations. Though the campus breathed a collective sigh of relief, a crisis atmosphere persisted, which the Chancellor felt must end. Yet, from the standpoint of many faculty and students, especially Vigil members, the crisis could not end if the Day administration remained. There was widespread fear that, given future budget cuts, the same scenario would be repeated, a view supported by administration memoranda and legislative testimony even after the budget was passed. Day's eventual departure therefore brought a sense of closure and signalled a complete victory for the Vigil.

Both practically and symbolically, the Vigil was instrumental in rescuing SDSU from the planned cuts and in getting the Day administration replaced. Day was asked to resign in 1995. He was replaced by Stephen Weber, a widely respected figure. Similarly, fee increases were avoided for three consecutive years, and legislation has been passed by the California legislature to reduce student fees for two years (Assembly Bill 1318). In addition, a bill expressing legislative intent to stabilize funding for California public higher education (Assembly Bill 1966) is pending. Thus, the Vigil essentially achieved all of its five goals.[21]

At Berkeley in 1964, Free Speech Movement (FSM) activists protested against an administration attack on the right of political expression and thus preserved this vital element of university life for that campus and others in the United States. SDSU students acted in a similar way to preserve their departments, professors, courses, and, in consequence, their own educational and career opportunities. Without their efforts, not only SDSU, but the American academy, would have been far more susceptible to the exercise of arbitrary authority.

Public response to the Vigil was much more positive than to the FSM. The community and the politicians have a significant interest in maintaining the integrity of the university. In contrast, the public had little initial understanding of the FSM. Protesters were considered an alien force and their cause seemed suspect.[22] Though over 80 per cent of the UC Berkeley faculty supported the students (thereby ensuring an FSM victory), appreciation of the FSM effort

21. *Union-Tribune*, 2 February 1995; *Daily Aztec*, 15 May, 2 September 1997; California Faculty Association e-mail, 15 September 1997; and personal e-mail archive, 1997.

22. Seymour M. Lipset and E.C. Ladd, Jr., 'College generations from the 1930s to the 1960s', *The Public Interest* 25 (1971), pp. 99–113.

outside the campus did not come until long after the fact.[23] Vietnam War protests had a similar, if more complex, reception by the public, with only about 20 per cent initially supporting the protesters from 1965 to 1968, with support improving somewhat after middle America turned against the war.[24] But the escalation of violence at the end of the decade caused support for the right of students to protest (even peacefully) to decline steadily, to less than 40 per cent in 1969.[25] A Gallup Poll in March 1969 found 82 per cent of Californians in favour of expelling militant students and 84 per cent in favour of withdrawing their federal student loans.[26] This trend occurred at the same time as a steady and rapid decline in the public's support for the Vietnam War; therefore sympathy with the students' main cause was not translated into sympathy for students. In contrast, the Vigil enjoyed solid public support.

Both the FSM and the anti-war movements of the 1960s organized large-scale demonstrations, as did the Vigil.[27] But the Vigil rejected the standard sixties tactic of occupying the administration building. Evidence suggests that while this tactic created an impressive spectacle, it achieved little, and antagonized many. In this sense, the Vigil was closer to the women at Greenham Common, who focused public attention on nuclear missiles by remaining outside the base perimeter and left large-scale demonstrations to the Campaign for Nuclear Disarmament.[28]

In sum, the Vigil differed from sixties movements by remaining outdoors for its round-the-clock protest, receiving initial public and political support, relying less on large-scale demonstrations, and focusing on the retention of educational and career opportunities in a close alliance with the faculty. It acted to protect the university rather than to challenge it. Yet it shared with sixties movements a determined but peaceful approach to its goals and utilized colourful

23. Witness the television mini-series *Loose Change* (1977).

24. Lipset, *Rebellion in the University* (Boston, Mass., 1972); *San Francisco Chronicle*, 20 July 1971; Howard Schuman, 'Two sources of antiwar sentiment in America', *American Journal of Sociology* 78 (1972), pp. 513–36; Jerome Skolnick, *The Politics of Protest* (New York, 1969).

25. Republican Research Report, 7 Feb. 1968. Reagan MSS, Hoover Institution Library, Stanford University. See also *The Sacramento Bee*, 31 March 1969. Evidence suggests that the protesters seldom actually caused the violence. See Rodney Stark, *Police Riots* (Belmont, Calif., 1972).

26. *San Diego Union*, 13 March 1969.

27. Todd Gitlin, *The Sixties: Years of Hope, Days of Rage* (New York, 1987); Max Heirich, *The Spiral of Conflict: Berkeley, 1964* (New York, 1971).

28. Nigel Young, *An Infantile Disorder? The Crisis and Decline of the New Left* (Boulder, Colo., 1977); *The Observer*, 3 April 1983.

tactics reminiscent of the sixties. Thus, although differences existed, the Vigil at least in part duplicated the student protests of the sixties and, like them, significantly influenced public sentiment and public policy.

It is perhaps more appropriate to look to the 1930s for historical parallels to the Vigil. Student protesters during that decade often sought to defend state provisions like education from budget cuts. They tried to conserve the status quo, instead of attempting to challenge authority and extend freedoms, as in the 1960s. The most striking parallel to the Vigil is also the most ironic. In 1928, Ronald Reagan was a ringleader in a student protest at Eureka College. As he described it:

> In the dark days of the depression in this little college . . . the endowment was virtually wiped out by the crash . . . we had one man, a president of the University, whose solution was going to be to change the curriculum so drastically, discharge professors and so forth that students . . . would be unable to complete their majors.

During his 1966 campaign for Governor of California, journalists reminded Reagan of this incident, challenging him to admit that his experiences were similar to those of Berkeley student activists. Reagan replied that to compare the 'beatnik picketing' of today with the students of his generation who were desperate to get a good education was 'like comparing Castro's take-over of Cuba with the American Revolution'.[29] It is ironic that, when history repeated itself at SDSU in 1992, the Vigil students protested against inadequate state funding of higher education, itself a legacy of Reagan's period as Governor of California.

29. ABC 'Issues and Answers', Brown/Reagan Interview, n.d., transcript in Reagan MSS.

Notes on the Contributors

INGO CORNILS (Ph.D., Hamburg) is a Senior Teaching Fellow in the Department of German at the University of Leeds. He has published on German current affairs, the student movement and science fiction in Germany. He is currently working on a book on the Utopian and the Fantastic.

GERARD J. DEGROOT is Senior Lecturer in Modern History at the University of St Andrews. He is the author of numerous books and articles, including *Blighty: British Society in the Era of the Great War* (1996). His work on student protest has been published in the *Pacific Historical Review, History Today* and *History*. He is currently writing a history of the Vietnam War and a monograph on women in the military.

SYLVIA ELLIS is a Senior Lecturer in American History at the University of Sunderland. She specializes on the effect of the Vietnam War on Anglo-American relations, a subject on which she has published a number of articles and reviews. Her Ph.D. dissertation, through the Department of History at the University of Newcastle upon Tyne, is nearing completion.

SANDRA HOLLIN FLOWERS is an Associate Professor of English at Mercer University in Macon, Georgia. She is an African American Studies scholar, a novelist, dramatist and non-fiction writer. Her article arises from research begun originally for her book *African American Nationalist Literature of the 1960s: Pens of Fire* (1995) and in support of her novel in progress, *I Heard a Crazy Woman Speak*.

BEHROOZ GHAMARI-TABRIZI is a Mellon Post Doctoral Fellow at the Center for the Humanities at Wesleyan University, Middletown, Connecticut. He has published a number of articles on postmodernity and the emergence of Islamist movements, and has also delivered a number of conference papers on the politics and society in the Islamic world and on the Muslim diaspora. He has been awarded grants and fellowships from the Mellon Foundation, the United States Institute of Peace and the Social Science Research Council.

BERTRAM GORDON is Frederick A. Rice Professor of History at Mills College (Oakland, California). He is the author of *Collaborationism in France during the Second World War* (Cornell University Press, 1980), the editor of *The Historical Dictionary of World War II France: The Occupation, Vichy and the Resistance, 1938–1946* (1998), serves on the editorial board of *French Historical Studies*, the international advisory board of *Modern and Contemporary France*, and co-edits the electronic newsletter H-France.

J. ANGUS JOHNSTON is a doctoral student in history at the City University of New York. He has presented a number of papers on aspects of student activism and the civil rights struggle, and his dissertation will address the role of the National Student Association in American student organizing.

ALAN R. KLUVER (Ph.D., University of Southern California) is Associate Professor of Speech and Rhetoric and director of the interdisciplinary Asian Studies programme at Oklahoma City University. His research interests are in Asian politics and political communication, and he is the author of *Legitimating the Chinese Economic Reforms: A Rhetoric of Myth and Orthodoxy*.

DONALD MABRY, Professor of History, is the author of *Mexico's Accion Nacional* and *The Mexican University and the State*, co-author of *Neighbors, Mexico and the United States*, and editor of *The Latin American Narcotics Trade and US National Security*. He has been on the faculty of Mississippi State University since 1970.

GÜNTER MINNERUP teaches politics and history in the Department of German Studies, University of Birmingham. He is the co-editor of *Debatte: Review of Contemporary German Affairs* and the author of books and articles on East and West German politics. He was an active participant in the West German student movement of the 1960s and 1970s and is currently completing a book on the German Question in the twentieth century.

A.D. MOSES has studied in Australia, Scotland, and Germany, and is currently a graduate student in the Department of History, University of California, Berkeley. He is writing a dissertation on the student movement and intellectuals in the Federal Republic of Germany.

FRANK N. PIEKE is University Lecturer in the Modern Politics and Society of China at the University of Oxford and a Fellow of St Cross College. His books include *The Ordinary and the Extraordinary* (1996), which combines an anthropological study of daily life in China with an ethnographic account of the 1989 protest movement in Beijing. Dr Pieke's current work is on Chinese migration and transnational Chinese communities in Europe and on local elites at the nexus of village communities, the market and the state in rural China.

JULIE A. REUBEN is writing a book on the impact of the 1960s protest movements on American higher education. She is the author of *The Making of the Modern University: Intellectual Transformation and the Marginalization of Morality* (1996), and an associate professor at the Harvard University Graduate School of Education.

BARBARA L. TISCHLER teaches cultural history at Columbia University in New York City. She is the author of *An American Music* (1986) and editor of *Sights on the Sixties* (1992), part of the *Perspectives on the Sixties* series that she edited. Tischler has written on civil rights, sixties music, anti-war activity in the military during the Vietnam War, and women in civilian and military movements.

NELLA VAN DYKE is a doctoral candidate in sociology at the University of Arizona. She is also a fellow of the Mellon Foundation Contentious Politics research group at the Center for Advanced Study in the Behavioral Sciences. Her research interests include the study of protest cultures and the dynamics of protest cycles, as well as topics in race, gender and sexuality.

CLARE WHITE is a third-year Ph.D. student at the University of St Andrews, and formerly a graduate fellow at Harvard University. She is currently working on a dissertation entitled 'Robert F. Kennedy and Civil Rights in America, 1960–1968', arising from her research at the Kennedy Library.

JAMES L. WOOD is Chair of Sociology at San Diego State University. Since 1992 he has been actively involved in supporting higher education against the attacks discussed in his chapter, work for which he has received many honours. His publications include *The Sources of American Student Activism, Sociology: Traditional and Radical Perspectives,* and *Social Movements: Development, Participation and Dynamics* (nominated for the C. Wright Mills Award and the American Sociological Association's Award for Distinguished Contribution to Scholarship).

ERIC ZOLOV is Assistant Professor of Latin American History at Franklin and Marshall College. He previously taught at Georgetown, the University of Puget Sound, and UC Davis. He earned his Ph.D. in History from the University of Chicago (1995), from which he also holds Masters degrees in International Relations and Latin American Studies. In addition to his forthcoming book, *Refried Elvis: The Rise of the Mexican Counterculture* (1998), he is co-editing a collection of essays on popular culture in post-Revolutionary Mexico as well as a documentary history of US–Latin American relations.

Index

Adams, Walter 59, 60, 61
Adelstein, David 59
Adorno, Theodor W. 204
Africa 174–5
African American Studies 28, 154,
   157–61
   see also Black Americans
Ahvaz 244
al-Ahmad, Jalal 234
Alameda park (Mexico) 135
Albertz, Heinrich 104
Algerian War 39, 43
Ali, Tariq 55, 62, 63, 65
Alpert, Dede 267, 270
Alternative, The 209
'America First' 21
American Association of University
   Professors (AAUP) 264, 266, 275
American Civil War 12, 14, 171
American Council on Education (ACE)
   28–9, 122
American Cultural Centre 228
American Revolution 28, 88, 279
American Student Union (ASU) 19,
   20–1, 22, 23, 32
American Universities and Colleges 32
Angeloff, Sam 92
Anjoman-e Democratik-e Daneshjouyan
   (The Democratic Students'
   Association) 242
Anjoman-e Daneshjouyan Mosalman (The
   Association of Muslim Students)
   242
Anjoman-e Eslami-ye Daneshjouyan (The
   Islamic Students' Assocaition, ISA)
   242, 243, 244
anti-interventionism 19–20
anti-segregation 24
anti-Semitism 43

anti-war 18–19, 35, 85–99, 186–7, 189,
   191, 192, 195, 197, 202
   see also conscientious objection,
   pacifism
apartheid 58
apathy 10, 103
April Fifth Movement 249, 250, 262
army see military
Arnoni, M.S. 89
Aryamehr University 235
Asia 5, 54, 123
   see also Vietnam War
Assembly Amendment 25 (ACA 25)
   271
Association of Jurists 234
Association of Socialist Students (SDS)
   9, 100–7, 109, 110
Aston University 66
Außerparlamentarische Opposition
   (Extra-Parliamentary Opposition,
   APO) 142, 143, 202, 205, 210, 214
authoritarianism 8, 70, 72, 76, 100, 102,
   103, 105, 153, 269
Autonomous Metropolitan University
   (Mexico) 137
Ayat, Hassan 244

Baader, Andreas 144, 148
Baader Meinhof see Red Army Faction
Baby Boom 24, 117
Baden Baden, Germany 41
Bahro, Rudolf 209
Baker, Ella 173
Bakhtiar, Shahpour 236
Ballabeni, Roberto 39, 50
baotu 262
Barker, Paul 64
Barros Sierra, Javier 73, 135
Basisgruppen 210, 214

285